ADVANCED CRIMINAL LITIGATION

IN PRACTICE

ADVANCED CRIMINAL LITIGATION IN PRACTICE

Inns of Court School of Law

BLACKSTONE
PRESS LIMITED

First edition published in Great Britain 1997 by Blackstone Press Limited,
Aldine Place, London W12 8AA. Telephone (020) 8740 2277
www.blackstonepress.com

© Inns of Court School of Law, 1997

First edition 1997
Second edition 1998
Third edition 1999
Fourth edition 2000

ISBN: 1 84174 004 7

British Library Cataloguing in Publication Data
A CIP catalogue record for this book is available from the British Library.

Typeset by Style Photosetting Ltd, Mayfield, East Sussex
Printed by Ashford Colour Press, Gosport, Hampshire

FOREWORD

These manuals are designed primarily to support training on the Bar Vocational Course, though they are also intended to provide a useful resource for legal practitioners and for anyone undertaking training in legal skills.

The Bar Vocational Course was designed by staff at the Inns of Court School of Law, where it was introduced in 1989. This course is intended to equip students with the practical skills and the procedural and evidential knowledge that they will need to start their legal professional careers. These manuals are written by staff at the Inns of Court School of Law who have helped to develop the course, and by a range of legal practitioners and others involved in legal skills training. The authors of the manuals are very well aware of the practical and professional approach that is central to the Bar Vocational Course.

The range and coverage of the manuals have grown steadily. All the practice manuals are updated every two years, and regular reviews and revisions of the manuals are carried out to ensure that developments in legal skills training and the experience of our staff are fully reflected in them.

This updating and revision is a constant process, and we very much value the comments of practitioners, staff and students. Legal vocational training is advancing rapidly, and it is important that all those concerned work together to achieve and maintain high standards. Please address any comments to the Bar Vocational Course Director at the Inns of Court School of Law.

With the validation of other providers for the Bar Vocational Course it is very much our intention that these manuals will be of equal value to all students wherever they take the course, and we would value comments from tutors and students at other validated institutions.

The enthusiasm of the staff at Blackstone Press Ltd and their efficiency in arranging the production and publication of these manuals is much appreciated.

The Hon. Mr Justice Elias
Chairman of the Board of Governors
Inns of Court School of Law
December 1999

CONTENTS

CONTENTS

TABLE OF CASES

TABLE OF STATUTES

PART I
EVIDENCE AND PROCEDURE

ONE

INTRODUCTION

A significant number of barristers practise exclusively in the field of criminal law. An even greater number have a general common law practice which contains an element of criminal work. As far as those in pupillage and the early stages of practice are concerned, criminal defence work is (subject to temporary fluctuations) the most common type of work, even for those who regard themselves as civil lawyers. Further, among those who decide after pupillage to become employed barristers, the most popular destination is the Crown Prosecution Service.

Accordingly, this criminal law option is aimed at two groups of students:

(a) those intending in due course to go into specialist criminal practice; and

(b) those destined for a general common law practice with a significant element of crime.

Like other subjects offered as options on the Vocational Course, this option may seem similar to one of the core subjects which students must have taken before embarking upon the Vocational Course. But this option will differ radically from criminal law studied as a core subject.

First, the topics which this course covers are those which are not dealt with in any detail in the core study of criminal law, but which are of particular value in the early years of practice, such as public order offences, road traffic law and the law relating to the misuse of dangerous drugs.

Second, in line with the spirit of the Vocational Course generally, the methods employed on this option aim to provide a taste of criminal practice. We will be dealing with a series of practical training exercises, which will provide opportunities for the use of skills in the context of criminal law, and act as a vehicle for the acquisition of knowledge. Further, a number of questions of practice, procedure and tactics will be canvassed in the course.

The chapters which follow deal with a selection of topics which represent the areas of substantive law and practice upon which the course will concentrate. They build both upon your knowledge of core law, and upon what you have already learned on the Vocational Course, particularly in criminal litigation, evidence, and sentencing.

Part I of this Manual deals with certain areas of evidence and procedure which are of crucial practical importance to the criminal practitioner. In **Chapter 2**, the new scheme of disclosure introduced by the Criminal Procedure and Investigations Act 1996 is described. This is an important area of practice, and one which is currently undergoing radical revision. The treatment is complementary to that contained in the *Criminal Litigation and Sentencing Manual*, and includes the most relevant sections of the statute, with a commentary. **Chapter 3** deals with the issues relating to search and seizure. It looks at the question of powers to search for and seize evidence, and the consequences at trial if those powers are exceeded. **Chapter 4** is concerned with the often complicated provisions relating to the trial of multiple defendants, particularly where a 'cut-throat' defence is run. Identification evidence — an area which arises with great frequency in the criminal trial — is covered in **Chapter 5**. **Chapter 6** covers the European Convention on Human Rights. The Convention is being utilised with ever greater frequency by criminal practitioners, and this chapter attempts to summarise its relevant provisions, give an idea of the procedure which it adopts, and deal with some of the cases where the United Kingdom has appeared in the Strasbourg Court.

Part II covers chosen areas of substantive law. **Chapter 7** is devoted to the offences connected with dangerous drugs, **Chapter 8** deals with a variety of offences against public order and **Chapter 9** covers offensive weapons. Road traffic is an area which is particularly required for the barrister in the first few years of practice, and it is covered in **Chapters 10**, **11** and **12** which deal with some of the most common offences and the penalty system for driving offences. **Chapter 13** is devoted to regulatory law, using the legislation relating to food safety and hygiene as an example.

Part III gives you an opportunity to practice some of the skills utilised by the criminal practitioner on a realistic set of papers for a trial in prospect. You are instructed for the defence in a Crown Court trial, the indictment containing counts of grievous bodily harm with intent, violent disorder, attempted robbery and driving while unfit through drink or drugs. The papers contain a number of the documents with which the criminal practitioner is constantly dealing, e.g., the custody record, the plea and directions questionnaire. **Chapter 14** describes the way in which the papers might be used. To start with, they form the instructions to write an Advice on Evidence. Thereafter, they can form the basis for preparing a conference with the client. Finally, they can be used in order to plan the advocacy tasks necessary for a trial. The papers themselves appear in **Chapter 15**. In **Chapter 16**, there is a sample Advice on Evidence prepared in response to the instructions in the brief.

Inevitably, given the restricted space which can be devoted here to the substantive law, topics are dealt with in an abbreviated form, and you will need to supplement what is in these pages with additional reading and research.

There are statutes dealing with virtually all the topics which we cover, and you will need to refer to these from time to time, together with any statutory instruments in point. Of particular relevance to the topic of 'Search and Seizure,' for example, is Code B issued under the Police and Criminal Evidence Act 1984.

In addition to the general law reports, the criminal practitioner relies extensively upon the Criminal Appeal Reports. For road traffic offences, there are the specialist Road Traffic Reports. In addition, the *Criminal Law Review*, in its case notes section, provides short summaries of recent cases, with a commentary.

Several practitioners' works cover the field, and it is crucial to become familiar with all of the following:

Archbold, *Criminal Pleading and Practice* (Sweet & Maxwell, annual).
Blackstone's Criminal Practice (Blackstone Press, annual)
Stone's Justices' Manual (Butterworths, annual).
Wilkinsons' Road Traffic Offences (FT Law & Tax, 1996, updated).

There are also books which cover specialist topics in detail, For example:

Stone, R., *Entry, Search and Seizure* (Sweet & Maxwell, 1996).
Fortson, R., *The Law on the Misuse of Drugs and Drug Trafficking Offences* (Sweet & Maxwell, 1996).

For commentary on the disclosure provisions dealt with in **Chapter 2**, you can refer to:

Leng, R., and Taylor, R., *Blackstone's Guide to the Criminal Procedure and Investigations Act 1996* (Blackstone Press, 1996).

TWO

DISCLOSURE

In the criminal trial, there are two ways in which the issue of disclosure may be said to arise. First, the prosecution must notify the defence of the evidence on which it intends to rely, e.g., by the revelation of evidence to the defence at committal to the Crown Court for trial. Any further evidence which the prosecution later decides that it will adduce as part of its case at trial must then be brought to the defence's attention by way of a notice of additional evidence. For further details of this aspect of the prosecution's obligations, see the *Criminal Litigation and Sentencing Manual*, **Chapters 6** and **10**.

In this chapter, however, we deal, not with the evidence on which the prosecution intends to rely, but with that on which it does *not* intend to rely. To what extent must such 'unused material' be revealed to the defence?

We are also concerned with the extent to which the *defence* has to reveal its case to the prosecution.

These two issues together are now covered by a statutory scheme of disclosure, which is contained within the Criminal Procedure and Investigations Act 1996 (CPIA 1996). That scheme is dealt with in outline in the *Criminal Litigation and Sentencing Manual*, **Chapter 10**. The current chapter seeks to deal with some further aspects of the scheme, with the relevant statutory provisions, and to look at the law relating to public interest immunity (which is a basis for the prosecution to seek exemption from any duty to disclose unused material).

2.1 Primary Prosecution Disclosure

The primary duty of disclosure for the prosecution is to disclose to the defence any prosecution material which has not previously been disclosed, and which, in the opinion of the prosecutor, might undermine the case for the prosecution. This primary duty is governed by s. 3 of the CPIA 1996:

3.—*(1) The prosecutor must—*
(a) disclose to the accused any prosecution material which has not previously been disclosed to the accused and which in the prosecutor's opinion might undermine the case for the prosecution against the accused, or
(b) give to the accused a written statement that there is no material of a description mentioned in paragraph (a).
(2) For the purposes of this section prosecution material is material—
(a) which is in the prosecutor's possession, and came into his possession in connection with the case for the prosecution against the accused, or
(b) which, in pursuance of a code operative under Part II, he has inspected in connection with the case for the prosecution against the accused.
(3) Where material consists of information which has been recorded in any form the prosecutor discloses it for the purposes of this section—
(a) by securing that a copy is made of it and that the copy is given to the accused, or

(b) if in the prosecutor's opinion that is not practicable or not desirable, by allowing the accused to inspect it at a reasonable time and a reasonable place or by taking steps to secure that he is allowed to do so;
and a copy may be in such form as the prosecutor thinks fit and need not be in the same form as that in which the information has already been recorded.

(4) Where material consists of information which has not been recorded the prosecutor discloses it for the purposes of this section by securing that it is recorded in such form as he thinks fit and—

(a) by securing that a copy is made of it and that the copy is given to the accused, or

(b) if in the prosecutor's opinion that is not practicable or not desirable, by allowing the accused to inspect it at a reasonable time and a reasonable place or by taking steps to secure that he is allowed to do so.

(5) Where material does not consist of information the prosecutor discloses it for the purposes of this section by allowing the accused to inspect it at a reasonable time and a reasonable place or by taking steps to secure that he is allowed to do so.

(6) Material must not be disclosed under this section to the extent that the court, on an application by the prosecutor, concludes it is not in the public interest to disclose it and orders accordingly.

(7) Material must not be disclosed under this section to the extent that—

(a) it has been intercepted in obedience to a warrant issued under section 2 of the Interception of Communications Act 1985, or

(b) it indicates that such a warrant has been issued or that material has been intercepted in obedience to such a warrant.

(8) The prosecutor must act under this section during the period which, by virtue of section 12, is the relevant period for this section.

It will be noted from s. 3(2) that the duty to disclose relates to prosecution material, which comprises material which:

(a) came into the prosecutor's possession in connection with the case against the accused; or

(b) the prosecutor has inspected under the Code of Practice.

The Code of Practice was published under Part II of the CPIA 1996, and is reproduced as an **Appendix** to this Manual.

By s. 3(6), material is exempted from the duty of disclosure if the court decides that it is not in the public interest to disclose it (see **2.5** for further details).

The mechanics of disclosure (by copy, or by allowing inspection) are dealt with in s. 3(3), (4) and (5).

2.2 Defence Disclosure

In cases to be tried in the Crown Court, once the defendant has been given the necessary documents, and the primary prosecution disclosure has taken place, the defendant has to comply with the duty of disclosure. As far as the defence is concerned, the obligation is set out in s. 5 of the CPIA 1996:

5.—(1) Subject to subsections (2) to (4), this section applies where—
(a) this Part applies by virtue of section 1(2), and
(b) the prosecutor complies with section 3 or purports to comply with it.

(2) Where this Part applies by virtue of section 1(2)(b), this section does not apply unless—
(a) a copy of the notice of transfer, and
(b) copies of the documents containing the evidence,
have been given to the accused under regulations made under section 5(9) of the Criminal Justice Act 1987.

(3)   Where this Part applies by virtue of section 1(2)(c), this section does not apply unless—

　　(a)   a copy of the notice of transfer, and

　　(b)   copies of the documents containing the evidence,

have been given to the accused under regulations made under paragraph 4 of Schedule 6 to the Criminal Justice Act 1991.

(4)   Where this Part applies by virtue of section 1(2)(e), this section does not apply unless the prosecutor has served on the accused a copy of the indictment and a copy of the set of documents containing the evidence which is the basis of the charge.

(5)   Where this section applies, the accused must give a defence statement to the court and the prosecutor.

(6)   For the purposes of this section a defence statement is a written statement—

　　(a)   setting out in general terms the nature of the accused's defence,

　　(b)   indicating the matters on which he takes issue with the prosecution, and

　　(c)   setting out, in the case of each such matter, the reason why he takes issue with the prosecution.

(7)   If the defence statement discloses an alibi the accused must give particulars of the alibi in the statement, including—

　　(a)   the name and address of any witness the accused believes is able to give evidence in support of the alibi, if the name and address are known to the accused when the statement is given;

　　(b)   any information in the accused's possession which might be of material assistance in finding any such witness, if his name or address is not known to the accused when the statement is given.

(8)   For the purposes of this section evidence in support of an alibi is evidence tending to show that by reason of the presence of the accused at a particular place or in a particular area at a particular time he was not, or was unlikely to have been, at the place where the offence is alleged to have been committed at the time of its alleged commission.

(9)   The accused must give a defence statement under this section during the period which, by virtue of section 12, is the relevant period for this section.

It should be emphasised that the duty relates only to the case which the defence is putting forward. There is no duty imposed on the defence to disclose material which it does *not* intend to use at trial (contrast this with the prosecution's obligations).

2.3　Secondary Prosecution Disclosure

Once the defendant has made disclosure, the prosecution has a duty to carry out secondary disclosure. This is set out in s. 7 of the CPIA 1996:

7.—*(1)   This section applies where the accused gives a defence statement under section 5 or 6.*

(2)   The prosecutor must—

　　(a)   disclose to the accused any prosecution material which has not previously been disclosed to the accused and which might be reasonably expected to assist the accused's defence as disclosed by the defence statement given under section 5 or 6, or

　　(b)   give to the accused a written statement that there is no material of a description mentioned in paragraph (a).

(3)   For the purposes of this section prosecution material is material—

　　(a)   which is in the prosecutor's possession and came into his possession in connection with the case for the prosecution against the accused, or

　　(b)   which, in pursuance of a code operative under Part II, he has inspected in connection with the case for the prosecution against the accused.

(4)   Subsections (3) to (5) of section 3 (method by which prosecutor discloses) apply for the purposes of this section as they apply for the purposes of that.

(5)   Material must not be disclosed under this section to the extent that the court, on an application by the prosecutor, concludes it is not in the public interest to disclose it and orders accordingly.

(6)   Material must not be disclosed under this section to the extent that—

(a) it has been intercepted in obedience to a warrant issued under section 2 of the Interception of Communications Act 1985, or

(b) it indicates that such a warrant has been issued or that material has been intercepted in obedience to such a warrant.

(7) The prosecutor must act under this section during the period which, by virtue of section 12, is the relevant period for this section.

2.4 Applications to the Court

The defendant can apply, under the CPIA 1996, for an order that the prosecutor should disclose material which might be reasonably expected to assist the accused's defence, as set out in the defence statement. This application can only be made after secondary disclosure has (or should have been) made. It applies only to material which might assist the disclosed defence. The provisions of s. 8 apply to such applications to court:

8.—*(1) This section applies where the accused gives a defence statement under section 5 or 6 and the prosecutor complies with section 7 or purports to comply with it or fails to comply with it.*

(2) If the accused has at any time reasonable cause to believe that—

(a) there is prosecution material which might be reasonably expected to assist the accused's defence as disclosed by the defence statement given under section 5 or 6, and

(b) the material has not been disclosed to the accused,

the accused may apply to the court for an order requiring the prosecutor to disclose such material to the accused.

(3) For the purposes of this section prosecution material is material—

(a) which is in the prosecutor's possession and came into his possession in connection with the case for the prosecution against the accused,

(b) which, in pursuance of a code operative under Part II, he has inspected in connection with the case for the prosecution against the accused, or

(c) which falls within subsection (4).

(4) Material falls within this subsection if in pursuance of a code operative under Part II the prosecutor must, if he asks for the material, be given a copy of it or be allowed to inspect it in connection with the case for the prosecution against the accused.

(5) Material must not be disclosed under this section to the extent that the court, on an application by the prosecutor, concludes it is not in the public interest to disclose it and orders accordingly.

(6) Material must not be disclosed under this section to the extent that—

(a) it has been intercepted in obedience to a warrant issued under section 2 of the Interception of Communications Act 1985, or

(b) it indicates that such a warrant has been issued or that material has been intercepted in obedience to such a warrant.

Crucially, to succeed in an application, the defendant must have reasonable cause to believe that the prosecution material requested might reasonably be expected to assist the defence, as disclosed by the defence statement.

2.5 Public Interest Immunity

The CPIA 1996 expressly preserves the existing law with regard to public interest immunity. This exemption to the normal disclosure regime applies where the prosecution takes the view, for example, that it would be contrary to the public interest to disclose particular material. The classic case is where the material discloses the identity of an informer (*Marks v Beyfus* (1890) 25 QBD 294). The obvious reason for the rule is to prevent retaliation against informers, and the fear that revelation of their identity would lead to the drying up of sources of information for the police. This was the rationale stated in *Hennessey* (1978) 68 Cr App R 419. In both *Hennessey* and *Marks v Beyfus*, however, it is made clear that the rule should be departed from if the judge is of the opinion that the informer's name should be disclosed in order to show the defendant's innocence.

In *Turner* [1995] 1 WLR 264, the Court of Appeal commented on an increased tendency for defendants to seek disclosure of informants' names and other details, alleging them to be essential to a defence of being set up, or of duress. Their Lordships warned judges to be alert to the need to scrutinise with great care applications for disclosure of such detail about informants. They would need to see that assertions of the need to know such details were justified because they were essential to running the defence. If they were not justified then the judge would need to adopt a robust approach in declining to order disclosure. On the facts of *Turner*, it appeared that the informant had participated in the events surrounding the crime, and the defence case was that the defendant had been set up. The judge's decision to refuse disclosure could therefore not be justified, and the convictions were quashed.

In *Reilly* [1994] Crim LR 279, R was charged with importing a large quantity of cannabis resin from Spain. His defence was that he believed he was being asked to assist in importing antiques, some of which were 'dodgy'. The prosecution case was in effect that R had been entrapped by an undercover officer, A, into taking part in the importation of drugs. The defence submitted that they were entitled to have the details of another participant in the enterprise, P — his name, address, status (informer/undercover police officer/ordinary civilian) and previous convictions if any. The trial judge ruled that the defence could have no details, other than that P had no convictions for serious crime. Any other details would not help R's defence, and, if the defence had access to P, it was most unlikely that they would wish to call him. R was convicted and appealed, submitting that the judge was wrong so to rule. The appeal was allowed. There was an important distinction between a person who could not give relevant evidence and a person who might well not help the defence. The court should not assume that P would not help the defence. The need to protect informers (if there was an informer in the case, which the court did not know) had to give way to the need to allow the defence to present a tenable case in its best light.

The ambit of the rule is not confined to those who provide information for the police. It has been extended to those who make available observation posts used by the police (*Rankine* (1986) 83 Cr App R 18). The reasoning is that those members of the public who make premises available for the police to observe suspected criminals might be subject to retaliation in the same way that informers are. In *Blake* v *Director of Public Prosecutions* (1993) 97 Cr App R 169, it was stated that the threat of violence was not necessary before protection could be offered to the occupier of the observation post. It is sufficient for the occupier to be in fear of harassment.

In *Brown* (1987) 87 Cr App R 52, it was made clear that the aim of the rule in *Rankine* is to protect the occupier of the premises used, rather than the premises themselves. In that case, police officers saw an offence while carrying out a surveillance operation from an unmarked police vehicle. The Court of Appeal held that the prosecution should not have been allowed to withhold information relating to the surveillance operation, and the details of the vehicle used (colour, make, model, etc.).

Where the prosecution apply to the judge to exclude from disclosure evidence tending to identify an observation post, they must lay a proper evidential basis for such an application. The requirements were laid down by Watkins LJ in *Johnson* [1988] 1 WLR 1377:

(a) The police officer in charge of the observations to be conducted, no one of lower rank than a sergeant should usually be acceptable for this purpose, must be able to testify that beforehand he visited all observation places to be used and ascertained the attitude of occupiers of premises, not only to the use to be made of them, but to the possible disclosure thereafter of the use made and facts which could lead to the identification of the premises thereafter and of the occupiers. He may of course in addition inform the court of difficulties, if any, usually encountered in the particular locality of obtaining assistance from the public.

(b) A police officer of no lower rank than a chief inspector must be able to testify that immediately prior to the trial he visited the places used for observations, the results of which it is proposed to give in evidence, and ascertained whether the occupiers are the same as when the observations took place and whether they are or are not, what the attitude of those occupiers is to the possible disclosure of the use previously made of the premises and of facts which could lead at the trial to identification of premises and occupiers.

Such evidence will of course be given in the absence of the jury when the application to exclude the material evidence is made. The judge should explain to the jury, as this judge did, when summing up or at some appropriate time before that, the effect of his ruling to exclude, if he so rules.

2.6 Procedure where Public Interest Immunity is Claimed

Even if the Crown believes that the unused material should be immune from disclosure, that does not end the matter. The case of *Ward* [1993] 1 WLR 619 makes it clear that it is for the court, and not the prosecution, to make the final decision as to whether immunity from disclosure should be granted. Judith Ward had been convicted of multiple murder and explosives offences. The prosecution failed to disclose material relevant to her alleged confessions and certain scientific evidence. The Court of Appeal held that, if the prosecution claimed that they were entitled to withhold material documents on the basis of public interest immunity, the court must be asked to rule on the legitimacy of their claim. If the prosecution was not prepared to have the issue determined by a court, they would have to abandon the case.

In *Davis* [1993] 1 WLR 613 the Court of Appeal set out further guidance as to the procedure which should be adopted where the prosecution claim immunity from disclosure. For details, you should refer to the *Criminal Litigation and Sentencing Manual*, 10.2.6.

2.7 Summary Trial

So far, this chapter has been dealing with trial on indictment. As far as summary trial is concerned, however, the concept of voluntary defence disclosure applies. Whatever the category of case, if a not guilty plea is entered, then the prosecution must make primary disclosure. If the case is to be tried summarily, however, the accused may opt to make defence disclosure under s. 1(1) as read with s. 6 of the CPIA 1996:

1.—(1) This Part applies where—
(a) a person is charged with a summary offence in respect of which a court proceeds to summary trial and in respect of which he pleads not guilty,
(b) a person who has attained the age of 18 is charged with an offence which is triable either way, in respect of which a court proceeds to summary trial and in respect of which he pleads not guilty, or
(c) a person under the age of 18 is charged with an indictable offence in respect of which a court proceeds to summary trial and in respect of which he pleads not guilty.

6.—(1) This section applies where—
(a) this Part applies by virtue of section 1(1), and
(b) the prosecutor complies with section 3 or purports to comply with it.
(2) The accused—
(a) may give a defence statement to the prosecutor, and
(b) if he does so, must also give such a statement to the court.
(3) Subsections (6) to (8) of section 5 apply for the purposes of this section as they apply for the purposes of that.
(4) If the accused gives a defence statement under this section he must give it during the period which, by virtue of section 12, is the relevant period for this section.

As appears from s. 1(1), this voluntary form of disclosure applies to all cases tried summarily, whether the offences concerned are summary, triable either-way, or even (in the case of juveniles) indictable only.

2.8 Inferences Against the Defendant

The accused risks a number of inferences for failing in some way to comply with the disclosure scheme. These are set out in s. 11 of the CPIA 1996:

11.—(1) This section applies where section 5 applies and the accused—
(a) fails to give a defence statement under that section,
(b) gives a defence statement under that section but does so after the end of the period which, by virtue of section 12, is the relevant period for section 5,
(c) sets out inconsistent defences in a defence statement given under section 5,
(d) at his trial puts forward a defence which is different from any defence set out in a defence statement given under section 5,
(e) at his trial adduces evidence in support of an alibi without having given particulars of the alibi in a defence statement given under section 5, or
(f) at his trial calls a witness to give evidence in support of an alibi without having complied with subsection (7)(a) or (b) of section 5 as regards the witness in giving a defence statement under that section.
(2) This section also applies where section 6 applies, the accused gives a defence statement under that section, and the accused—
(a) gives the statement after the end of the period which, by virtue of section 12, is the relevant period for section 6,
(b) sets out inconsistent defences in the statement,
(c) at his trial puts forward a defence which is different from any defence set out in the statement,
(d) at his trial adduces evidence in support of an alibi without having given particulars of the alibi in the statement, or
(e) at his trial calls a witness to give evidence in support of an alibi without having complied with subsection (7)(a) or (b) of section 5 (as applied by section 6) as regards the witness in giving the statement.
(3) Where this section applies—
(a) the court or, with the leave of the court, any other party may make such comment as appears appropriate;
(b) the court or jury may draw such inferences as appear proper in deciding whether the accused is guilty of the offence concerned.
(4) Where the accused puts forward a defence which is different from any defence set out in a defence statement given under section 5 or 6, in doing anything under subsection (3) or in deciding whether to do anything under it the court shall have regard—
(a) to the extent of the difference in the defences, and
(b) to whether there is any justification for it.
(5) A person shall not be convicted of an offence solely on an inference drawn under subsection (3).
(6) Any reference in this section to evidence in support of an alibi shall be construed in accordance with section 5.

2.9 Further Reading

Leng, R., and Taylor, R., *Blackstone's Guide to the Criminal Procedure and Investigations Act 1996* (Blackstone Press, 1996).

Sprack, J., 'The Criminal Procedure and Investigations Act 1996: (1) The Duty of Disclosure' [1997] Crim LR 308.

THREE

SEARCH AND SEIZURE

3.1 General Introduction

This chapter is concerned with the legal powers:

(a) to enter premises for the purpose of searching for persons or things (search); and

(b) to seize such persons or things if found (seizure).

The powers range from the general to the very specific and emphasis will here be placed upon the main powers. By far the most important statutory provisions are to be found in PACE 1984 backed up by PACE Code of Practice B.

This chapter is not concerned with situations where one person enters and remains on another's premises with that other's consent (but see the PACE Code of Practice B, para. 4), nor with the powers of the police to stop and search an individual or vehicle without entering premises (for important examples of such powers see PACE 1984, ss. 1–3 and s. 32(1) and (2)(a), Misuse of Drugs Act 1971, s. 23(2) — see generally PACE Code of Practice A).

Perhaps the main distinction to be drawn when considering the powers to enter premises is between:

(a) powers which can be exercised without a warrant; and

(b) those which can only be exercised with a warrant.

In this context the warrant referred to is an express authorisation given by 'the court' to enter premises. Such warrants are often called search warrants and are to be distinguished from arrest warrants. Further details about search warrants are given below at **3.4**.

For the evidential consequences of a failure to comply with the rules on search and seizure described in this chapter, see **3.6** below.

3.2 Powers of Search Exercisable Without a Warrant

3.2.1 POLICE AND CRIMINAL EVIDENCE ACT 1984, s. 17

A constable may enter and search premises without a warrant for the purpose of:

(a) executing a warrant of arrest issued in connection with or arising out of criminal proceedings;

(b) arresting a person for an arrestable offence;

(c)   arresting a person for an offence under the Public Order Act 1936, s. 1, the Public Order Act 1986, s. 4, the Criminal Law Act 1977, ss. 6, 7, 8 or 10;

(d)   recapturing a person who is unlawfully at large and whom he is pursuing;

(e)   saving life or limb or preventing serious damage to property.

Except for the purpose specified in (e) these powers are exercisable only if the constable has reasonable grounds for believing that the person whom he is seeking is on the premises. Also, the power of entry to arrest for the offences under the Criminal Law Act 1977 mentioned in (c) above, is exercisable only by a constable in uniform.

Section 17(5) provides that, subject to s. 17(6), all the common-law rules under which a constable has power to enter premises without a warrant are abolished. Section 17(6) preserves the common-law power of entry to deal with or prevent a breach of the peace. The scope of this common-law power was considered in *Thomas* v *Sawkins* [1935] 2 KB 249. Although it seems to be a wide power the police do not in practice appear to rely on it heavily. This may be due partly to the narrowness of the definition of 'breach of the peace' used by the Court of Appeal in *Howell* [1982] QB 416, *viz* 'an act done or threatened to be done which either actually harms a person or, in his presence, his property, or is likely to cause such harm, or which puts someone in fear of such harm'.

3.2.2   POLICE AND CRIMINAL EVIDENCE ACT 1984, s. 18

A constable may (subject to s. 18(3)–(8)) enter and search any premises occupied or controlled by a person who is under arrest for an arrestable offence, if he has reasonable grounds for suspecting that there is on the premises evidence other than items subject to legal privilege (see below at **3.4.2**) that relates to that offence or to some other arrestable offence which is connected with or similar to that offence. The constable may seize and retain anything for which he may search (s. 18(2)).

Section 18(3)–(8) provide that:

(a)   the extent of the search is limited to that which is reasonably required for the purpose of discovering the type of evidence specified;

(b)   the power is exercisable only if an officer of the rank of inspector or above has authorised it in writing (see *Badham* [1987] Crim LR 202), *unless* it is exercised before the arrested person is taken to a police station and that person's presence at a place other than a police station is necessary for the effective investigation of the offence (in such an exceptional case the constable in question must inform an officer of the rank of inspector or above that he has made the search as soon as practicable after he has made it). Note here the effect of s. 107(2), permitting a sergeant to assume the powers of an inspector if he has been authorised by an officer of at least the rank of chief superintendent;

(c)   the officer who authorises the search must keep a written record of the grounds for the search and the nature of the evidence sought.

3.2.3   POLICE AND CRIMINAL EVIDENCE ACT 1984, s. 32

By s. 32(2)(b) (subject to s. 32(3)–(7)), in any case where a person has been arrested at a place other than a police station, a constable shall have the power to enter and search any premises, in which the arrested person was when arrested or immediately before he was arrested (whether or not he was the occupier or controller of such premises, *cf* s. 18 above) *for evidence relating to the offence for which he was arrested.*

Section 32(3)–(7) provide that:

(a)   the extent of the search is limited to that which is reasonably required for the purpose of discovering the type of evidence specified;

(b) a constable may not undertake a s. 32(2)(b) search unless he has reasonable grounds for believing that there is evidence for which such search is permitted;

(c) insofar as the s. 32(2)(b) search relates to premises consisting of two or more separate dwellings, it is limited to a search of the dwelling in which the arrest took place or in which the person arrested was immediately before his arrest and any parts of the premises which the occupier of such dwelling uses in common with the occupiers of any other dwellings comprised in the premises.

3.2.4 MISUSE OF DRUGS ACT 1971, s. 23

By s. 23(1), a constable (or other person authorised by a general or special order of the Secretary of State) shall, for the purposes of the execution of this Act, have power to enter the premises of a person carrying on business as a producer or supplier of any controlled drugs and to demand the production of, and to inspect, any books or documents relating to dealings in any such drugs and to inspect any stocks of any such drugs. Section 23(2) further provides that a constable who has reasonable grounds to suspect that a person is in possession of a controlled drug in contravention of the Act may seize and detain anything which appears to him to be evidence of an offence under the Act. Section 23(4) creates a range of offences relating to the obstruction of a person exercising the powers contained in s. 23(1).

3.2.5 OTHER STATUTORY POWERS

The main powers of entry without a warrant have now been dealt with. However, there are several specific statutory powers which, in very limited circumstances, permit a search of premises to be authorised by a senior police officer (usually a superintendent). See, for example, the Prevention of Terrorism (Temporary Provisions) Act 1984, the Explosives Act 1875, the Official Secrets Act 1911.

3.3 Powers of Search with a Warrant

3.3.1 POLICE AND CRIMINAL EVIDENCE ACT 1984, s. 8

By s. 8(1), on an application made by a constable, a justice of the peace may issue a warrant authorising a constable to enter and search premises specified in the application if satisfied that there are reasonable grounds for believing:

(a) that a serious arrestable offence has been committed; *and*

(b) that there is material on such premises which is likely to be of substantial value (whether by itself or together with other material) to the investigation of the offence; *and*

(c) that the material is likely to be relevant evidence; *and*

(d) that it does not consist of or include items subject to legal privilege, excluded material or special procedure material; *and*

(e) that it is not practicable to communicate with any person entitled to grant entry to the premises, or although it is practicable to communicate with such person it is not practicable to communicate with any person entitled to grant access to the evidence, or that entry to the premises will not be granted unless a warrant is produced, or that the purpose of a search may be frustrated or seriously prejudiced unless a constable arriving at the premises can secure immediate entry to them.

(For the definition of 'excluded material' and 'special procedure material' and the special procedures relating to such material, see **3.4.2** below.)

By s. 8(2), a constable may seize and retain anything for which a search has been authorised under s. 8(1). By s. 8(4), relevant evidence (referred to in s. 8(1)(c)) means anything that would be admissible in evidence at a trial for the offence.

The most significant point about s. 8 is that it is not limited to any particular type of offence (unlike all previous statutory provisions allowing the issue of search warrants). However, under s. 8 the offence (whatever its particular type) must be a serious arrestable offence. It thus may sometimes be necessary to have regard to the *specific* statutory powers to issue search warrants which are still in force.

3.3.2 MISUSE OF DRUGS ACT 1971, s. 23(3)

If a justice of the peace is satisfied by information on oath that there is reasonable ground for suspecting:

(a) that any controlled drugs are, in contravention of this Act, in the possession of a person on any premises; or

(b) that a document relating to a transaction or dealing which was (or would if carried out be) an offence under this Act is in the possession of a person on any premises,

he may grant a warrant authorising any constable acting for the police area in which the premises are situated to enter, if need be by force, the premises named in the warrant and to search the premises and any persons found therein, and if there is reasonable ground for suspecting that an offence under this Act has been committed in relation to any drugs or document found, to seize and detain those drugs or that document. See also ss. 27 and 28 of the Drug Trafficking Offences Act 1986.

3.3.3 THEFT ACT 1968, s. 26

If it is made to appear by information or order before a justice of the peace that there is reasonable cause to believe that any person has in his custody or possession or on his premises any stolen goods, the justice may grant a warrant to search for and seize the same. The warrant must be addressed to a constable (unless a particular enactment expressly provides otherwise).

3.3.4 CRIMINAL DAMAGE ACT 1971, s. 6

If it is made to appear by information on oath before a justice of the peace that there is reasonable cause to believe that a person has in his custody, his control or on his premises something which there is reasonable cause to believe has been used or is intended for use without lawful excuse, to destroy or damage either property belonging to another or his own property (if damage to it would endanger the life of another), the justice may grant a warrant to search for and seize the same.

3.3.5 OTHER STATUTORY POWERS

The powers of entry with a warrant which are of most general application have now been dealt with. However, there are numerous specific statutory powers of entry with a warrant. For important examples see the Offences Against the Person Act 1861, ss. 5 and 65, the Obscene Publications Act 1959 s. 3, the Forgery and Counterfeiting Act 1981, ss. 7 and 24, the Criminal Justice Act 1987, s. 2, the Copyright, Designs and Patents Act 1988, s. 109, the Public Order Act 1986, s. 24.

3.4 Search Warrants — General Rules and Restrictions

3.4.1 PROCEDURE

Although PACE 1984 left intact many specific statutory powers to search *with a warrant*, the Act, in ss. 15 and 16, laid down rules and restrictions of general application to search warrants issued to a constable under *any enactment* (the rules and restrictions also apply to Customs and Excise Officers and Environmental Protection Officers).

Since these sections contain relatively straightforward procedural rules they are set out in full below. The procedure is augmented by Code of Practice B, para. 2.

15.—*(1) This section and section 16 below have effect in relation to the issue to constables under any enactment, including an enactment contained in an Act passed after this Act, of warrants to enter and search premises, and an entry on or search of premises under a warrant is unlawful unless it complies with this section and section 16 below.*

    (2) Where a constable applies for any such warrant, it shall be his duty—
      (a) to state
        (i) the ground on which he makes the application; and
        (ii) the enactment under which the warrant would be issued,
      (b) to specify the premises which it is desired to enter and search; and
      (c) to identify, so far as is practicable, the articles or persons to be sought.
    (3) An application for such a warrant shall be made ex parte and supported by an information in writing.
    (4) The constable shall answer on oath any question that the justice of the peace or judge hearing the application asks him.
    (5) A warrant shall authorise an entry on one occasion only.
    (6) A warrant—
      (a) shall specify—
        (i) the name of the person who applies for it;
        (ii) the date on which it is issued;
        (iii) the enactment under which it is issued, and
        (iv) the premises to be searched, and
      (b) shall identify, so far as is practicable, the articles or persons to be sought.
    (7) Two copies shall be made of a warrant.
    (8) The copies shall be clearly certified as copies.

16.—*(1) A warrant to enter and search premises may be executed by any constable.*
    (2) Such a warrant may authorise persons to accompany any constable who is executing it.
    (3) Entry and search under a warrant must be within one month from the date of its issue.
    (4) Entry and search under a warrant must be at a reasonable hour unless it appears to the constable executing it that the purpose of a search may be frustrated on an entry at a reasonable hour.
    (5) Where the occupier of premises which are to be entered and searched is present at the time when a constable seeks to execute a warrant to enter and search them, the constable—
      (a) shall identify himself to the occupier and, if not in uniform, shall produce to him documentary evidence that he is a constable,
      (b) shall produce the warrant to him, and
      (c) shall supply him with a copy of it.
    (6) Where—
      (a) the occupier of such premises is not present at the time when a constable seeks to execute such a warrant; but
      (b) some other person who appears to the constable to be in charge of the premises is present, subsection (5) above shall have effect as if any reference to the occupier were a reference to that other person.
    (7) If there is no person present who appears to the constable to be in charge of the premises, he shall leave a copy of the warrant in a prominent place on the premises.
    (8) A search under a warrant may only be a search to the extent required for the purpose for which the warrant was issued.
    (9) A constable executing a warrant shall make an endorsement on it stating—
      (a) whether the articles or persons sought were found, and

(b)   whether any articles were seized, other than articles which were sought.
(10) A warrant which—
(a)   has been executed, or
(b)   has not been executed within the time authorised for its execution, shall be returned—
(i)   if it was issued by a justice of the peace, to the clerk to the justices for the petty sessions area for which he acts; and
(ii)   if it was issued by a judge, to the appropriate officer of the court from which he issued it.
(11) A warrant which is returned under subsection (10) above shall be retained for 12 months from its return—
(a)   by the clerk to the justices, if it was returned under paragraph (i) of that subsection; and
(b)   by the appropriate officer, if it was returned under paragraph (ii).
(12) If during the period for which a warrant is to be retained the occupier of the premises to which it relates asks to inspect it, he shall be allowed to do so.

3.4.2   PROTECTED MATERIAL: SPECIAL PROCEDURES

Although PACE 1984 creates a general power to issue search warrants in cases where there has been a serious arrestable offence (see **3.3.1**), three categories of material are to a greater or lesser extent protected from being the object of search. These categories are:

(a)   items subject to legal privilege;

(b)   excluded material; and

(c)   special procedure material.

3.4.2.1   Items subject to legal privilege

This category should require no introduction — see *Evidence Manual* at **14.2.2**. Since:

(a)   PACE 1984 provides no power to search for legally privileged items; and

(b)   the Act states, in s. 9(2), that any Act preceding PACE 1984 shall cease to have effect in so far as it authorises a search for *any* of the three protected categories; and

(c)   no subsequent Act provides a power to grant a warrant to search for legally privileged items,

they may be treated as being fully protected (at least until a subsequent Act alters the position).

3.4.2.2   Excluded material

Excluded material consists of:

(a)   personal records acquired or created in the course of any trade, business, profession or office and held in confidence;

(b)   human tissue or tissue fluid taken for the purposes of diagnosis or medical treatment and held in confidence;

(c)   journalistic material held in confidence (s. 11).

Personal records include medical records and spiritual and welfare counselling records about an individual (whether living or dead) who can be identified from them (s. 12). A special warrant to search for such material may be obtained by leave of a circuit judge (for the procedure see **3.4.2.4**).

3.4.2.3 Special procedure material

Special procedure material consists of any material which a person acquired in the course of his trade, business, profession or employment and which he holds subject to an express or implied undertaking to keep it confidential, and journalistic material (even if not held in confidence) (s. 12). A special warrant to search for such material may be obtained by leave of a circuit judge (for the procedure see **3.4.2.4**).

3.4.2.4 Special warrants

As noted above (at **3.3.1**) an ordinary search warrant (made under s. 8 of PACE 1984) cannot be made in relation to items subject to legal privilege, excluded material or special procedure material. However, as regards excluded or special procedure material, if the procedure laid down in sch. 1 of PACE 1984 is followed (see below), a circuit judge may order that such material should be produced or that access to it should be given. If the person to whom the order is addressed fails to comply with the order the judge may then issue a special warrant (pursuant to sch. 1, para. 12).

Schedule 1 of PACE 1984 states:

1. If on an application made by a constable a circuit judge is satisfied that one or other of the sets of access conditions is fulfilled, he may make an order under paragraph 4 below.

2. The first set of access conditions is fulfilled if—

(a) there are reasonable grounds for believing—

(i) that a serious arrestable offence has been committed;

(ii) that there is material which consists of special procedure material or includes special procedure material and does not also include excluded material on premises specified in the application;

(iii) that the material is likely to be of substantial value (whether by itself or together with other material) to the investigation in connection with which the application is made; and

(iv) that the material is likely to be relevant evidence;

(b) other methods of obtaining the material—

(i) have been tried without success; or

(ii) have not been tried because it appeared that they were bound to fail; and

(c) it is in the public interest, having regard—

(i) to the benefit likely to accrue to the investigation if the material is obtained; and

(ii) to the circumstances under which the person in possession of the material holds it,

that the material should be produced or that access to it should be given.

3. The second set of access conditions is fulfilled if—

(a) there are reasonable grounds for believing that there is material which consists of or includes excluded material or special procedure material on premises specified in the application;

(b) but for section 9(2) above a search of the premises for that material could have been authorised by the issue of a warrant to a constable under an enactment other than this Schedule; and

(c) the issue of such a warrant would have been appropriate.

4. An order under this paragraph is an order that the person who appears to the circuit judge to be in possession of the material to which the application relates shall—

(a) produce it to a constable for him to take away; or

(b) give a constable access to it,

not later than the end of the period of seven days from the date of the order or the end of such longer period as the order may specify.

. . .

12. If on an application made by a constable a circuit judge—

(a) is satisfied—

(i) that either set of access conditions is fulfilled; and

(ii) that any of the further conditions set out in paragraph 14 below is also fulfilled; or

> (b) is satisfied—
> (i) that the second set of access conditions is fulfilled; and
> (ii) that an order under paragraph 4 above relating to the material has not been complied with,
> he may issue a warrant authorising a constable to enter and search the premises.

It is permissible for the police to seek voluntary disclosure even if there would be no chance of an application under sch. 1 succeeding (see *Singleton* [1995] 1 Cr App R 431).

Note: There is a distinction between (i) cases where protected material is sought in an investigation into whether a criminal offence has been committed and (ii) cases where such material is sought for the purposes of an investigation (as part of confiscation proceedings) into whether any person has benefited from any criminal conduct. In the latter situation, an order may be granted under the less stringent rules laid down by s. 93H of the Criminal Justice Act 1988 (these are not dealt with here as confiscation is a specialist area). The fact that an incidental effect of confiscation proceedings (and orders under s. 93H) might be to reveal the commission of an offence will not be a bar to the making of such an order (see *Crown Court at Southwark, ex parte Bowles* [1998] 2 All ER 193).

3.5 Seizure

Section 19 of PACE 1984 made general provisions with regard to the seizure of things in circumstances where a constable is lawfully on any premises. The constable may seize anything which is on the premises if he has reasonable grounds for believing:

(a) that it has been obtained in consequence of the commission of an offence; and that it is necessary to seize it in order to prevent it being concealed, lost, damaged, altered or destroyed; or

(b) that it is evidence in relation to an offence which he is investigating or any other offence; and that it is necessary to seize it in order to prevent the evidence being concealed, lost, altered or destroyed.

The constable may require any information which is contained in a computer and is accessible from the premises to be produced in a form in which it can be taken away and in which it is visible and legible *if* he has reasonable ground for believing:

(a) that—

(i) it is evidence in relation to an offence which he is investigating or any other offence; or

(ii) it has been obtained in consequence of the commission of an offence; and

(b) that it is necessary to do so in order to prevent it being concealed, lost, tampered with or destroyed.

It will be noted that these are very wide powers; however, s. 5(6) provides that no power of seizure conferred on a constable under *any* enactment (including an Act passed after this Act) is to be taken to authorise the seizure of an item which the constable exercising the power has reasonable grounds for believing to be subject to legal privilege.

Under s. 21 the officer in charge of an investigation is required to allow access to or provide copies or photographs of things seized unless allowing such access would prejudice the investigation in which the thing was seized (or related investigations) (s. 21(8)). However, things seized may be retained by the police for as long as is necessary in all the circumstances (s. 22(1)). Retention will, for example, be necessary if retention of a photograph or copy is insufficient for police purposes, or because the thing is stolen/or might be used to cause damage or injury.

3.6 Evidential Consequences of Breach of Rules on Search and Seizure

It is now relatively clear that a court may exclude evidence obtained by illegal search or seizure by virtue of the discretion under s. 78 of PACE 1984 even though the quality of the evidence is not affected.

FOUR

MULTIPLE DEFENDANTS: EVIDENTIAL POINTS

Evidential considerations very occasionally affect the court's decision whether two or more accused should be tried together (see *O'Boyle* (1991) 92 Cr App R 202). However, this chapter is based primarily on the assumption that the accused are being tried together, i.e., the decision for joint trial has been made. There are three main areas of difficulty: the competence and compellability of the accused and their spouses; the character of the accused; and confessions by the accused.

4.1 Competence and Compellability of the Accused and Their Spouses

4.1.1 AN ACCUSED'S LACK OF COMPETENCE FOR THE PROSECUTION

At common law an accused is not competent for the prosecution (accordingly the question of compellability does not arise). This has been enacted in statutory form by the Youth Justice and Criminal Evidence Act 1999, s. 53(4). It follows that, where there are co-accused, the prosecution *cannot* call one to give evidence against the other(s). This rule (which also applies where the co-accused are spouses — see PACE, s. 80(4)) may cause the prosecution considerable difficulty. If the prosecution wish to call one accused, X, as a witness against another, Y, they must ensure that, before the prosecution case against Y has been completed, X has ceased to be a co-accused (see the Youth Justice and Criminal Evidence 1999, s. 53(5)). This may arise in a variety of ways. As soon as a co-accused pleads guilty or a verdict of not guilty is recorded against him or her (including a directed verdict), he or she ceases to be a co-accused and becomes competent and compellable for the prosecution. This could be achieved by, for example, offering no evidence against X and accepting a plea of guilty to a lesser offence. When this occurs the trial judge would usually warn the jury to exercise caution in assessing X's evidence (see *Makanjuola* [1995] 1 WLR 1348).

The prosecution will not necessarily be able to call X as a witness by deliberately refraining from seeking joint trial (in respect of X and Y). For example, if Y's trial precedes X's trial, X can seek an undertaking from the prosecution to discontinue the proceedings (which are pending against him or her) before giving evidence for the prosecution in Y's trial (see *Pipe* (1966) 51 Cr App R 17).

4.1.2 THE ACCUSED'S COMPETENCE BUT NON-COMPELLABILITY AS A DEFENCE WITNESS

An accused is a competent *but not compellable* witness on his or her own behalf or on behalf of any co-accused (see the Criminal Evidence Act 1898, s. 1(a)).

This does not, of course, mean that co-accused X can only give evidence which is favourable to co-accused Y. Indeed one accused will often give evidence (pursuant to

s. 1(a)) which is strongly *against* another accused (see *Paul* [1920] 2 KB 83) (often called a cut-throat defence). However, the prosecution cannot *rely* on this in making out *their* case because they must generally prove a prima facie case before the defence case even begins (i.e. they must rely on witnesses who are competent for the prosecution and, as just noted, this does not include the accused).

4.1.3　THE COMPETENCE AND COMPELLABILITY OF THE SPOUSE OF AN ACCUSED

4.1.3.1　Introduction

Where there are co-accused there may, of course, be several spouses who are all affected by the rules considered here. It aids understanding of the rules to recognise that the individual co-accused are separate parties who may wish to call as a witness both their own spouse and the spouse of another accused. For convenience a spouse witness will be referred to in this section as X, the co-accused will be referred to as Y (X's spouse) and Z. The position is governed by PACE 1984, s. 80 as amended by the Youth Justice and Criminal Evidence Act 1999.

> **80.**—(2) *In any proceedings the wife or husband of a person charged in the proceedings shall, subject to subsection (4) below, be compellable to give evidence on behalf of that person.*
>
> *(2A) In any proceedings the wife or husband of a person charged in the proceedings shall, subject to subsection (4) below, be compellable—*
>
> *(a) to give evidence on behalf of any other person charged in the proceedings but only in respect of any specified offence with which that other person is charged; or*
>
> *(b) to give evidence for the prosecution but only in respect of any specified offence with which any person is charged in the proceedings.*
>
> *(3) In relation to the wife or husband of a person charged in any proceedings, an offence is a specified offence for the purposes of subsection (2A) above if—*
>
> *(a) it involves an assault on, or injury or a threat of injury to, the wife or husband or a person who was at the material time under the age of 16;*
>
> *(b) it is a sexual offence alleged to have been committed in respect of a person who was at the material time under that age; or*
>
> *(c) it consists of attempting or conspiring to commit, or of aiding, abetting, counselling, procuring or inciting the commission of, an offence falling within paragraph (a) or (b) above.*
>
> *(4) No person who is charged in any proceedings shall be compellable by virtue of subsection (2) or (2A) above to give evidence in the proceedings.*
>
> *(4A) References in this section to a person charged in any proceedings do not include a person who is not, or is no longer, liable to be convicted of any offence in the proceedings (whether as a result of pleading guilty or for any other reason).*
>
> *(5) In any proceedings a person who has been but is no longer married to the accused shall be compellable to give evidence as if that person and the accused had never been married.*
>
> *(6) Where in any proceedings the age of any person at any time is material for the purposes of subsection (3) above, his age at the material time shall for the purposes of that provision be deemed to be or to have been that which appears to the court to be or to have been his age at that time.*
>
> *(7) In subsection (3)(b) above 'sexual offence' means an offence under the Sexual Offences Act 1956, the Indecency with Children Act 1960, the Sexual Offences Act 1967, section 54 of the Criminal Law Act 1977 or the Protection of Children Act 1978.*

Note: Where a husband and wife are the co-accused, since, in that trial, they are both accused persons, they both fall within the common law rule (mentioned in **4.1.1** above and acknowledged in PACE 1984, s. 80(4)) that no accused is ever competent for the prosecution. In this section it will be assumed that the co-accused are *not* husband and wife.

The problems arise in relation to *non-compellability* (an accused's spouse is generally a *competent* witness for *any* party including the prosecution and any co-accused).

4.1.3.2 Non-compellability

The spouse of an accused (X) is generally *not* compellable for the prosecution. However, by virtue of s. 80(3), X *is* compellable for the prosecution if the offence charged against Y either involves an assault on or injury or threat of injury to X or a child who was at the time of the offence under 16 (s. 80(3)(a)), *or* is a sexual offence on such a child (s. 80(3)(b)), *or* is an inchoate or secondary form of any such offences (s. 80(3)(c)).

Since s. 80(3) covers a relatively narrow range of offences, X will often not be compellable for the prosecution. Where X is not compellable he or she should be informed of this by the court when he or she enters the witness box (see *Pitt* [1983] QB 25). If this warning is not given X cannot later be treated as a hostile witness; if the warning is given and X elects to testify then he or she may be treated as hostile.

By virtue of s. 80(2) X is compellable *for* Y (i.e. a wife, X, can be required by her husband, Y (the accused), to give evidence as a defence witness). However, Y may not wish to call X; in such cases, is X compellable for Y's co-accused, Z?

By virtue of s. 80(3) X is only compellable for Z if the offence charged against Y and Z involves either an assault on or injury or threat of injury to X or a child who was at the time of the offence under 16 (s. 80(3)(a)), *or* is a sexual offence on such a child (s. 80(3)(b)), *or* is an inchoate or secondary form of any such offences (s. 80(3)(c)) (i.e. X is only compellable for Z where X is also compellable for the prosecution (see above)).

These special rules about compellability still apply even if X and Y are living apart or separated. However as soon as the marriage is legally terminated the ex-spouse of an accused becomes compellable to the same extent as any other witness (e.g. *is* compellable to give evidence for the prosecution, including evidence about matters occurring during the marriage — see s. 80(5), *Khan* (1987) 84 Cr App R 44 and *Cruttenden* [1991] 3 All ER 242).

4.2 The Character of the Accused

The issue here relates to the extent to which one co-accused can use character evidence to advance his or her case against another. Subject to the rules to be considered here, this can be done either by using evidence of the other's *bad* character or by using evidence of his or her own *good* character.

4.2.1 BAD CHARACTER

There are two aspects to this. First, there is the question to what extent X can *cross-examine* Y on Y's bad character (assuming that Y testifies) in order to undermine Y's credibility (see **4.2.1.1** below). Secondly, it is necessary to consider the extent to which X can *adduce evidence* of Y's bad character as part of X's case, i.e., for the purpose of showing that because of Y's bad character it is more likely that Y is guilty or X is innocent (see **4.2.1.2** below).

4.2.1.1 Cross-examining a co-accused on bad character

Any accused starts off the trial with his or her shield against cross-examination on bad character (by any other party) intact. However, the shield may be lost in a variety of circumstances, e.g. by casting imputations on the character of prosecution witnesses. Undoubtedly the most important circumstance to be considered here is where accused Y has given evidence against co-accused X (see the Criminal Evidence Act 1898, s. 1(f)(iii)). In such a case X can cross-examine Y on Y's bad character in order to challenge credibility. The leading authority on s. 1(f)(iii) is *Murdoch* v *Taylor* [1965] AC 574. Here the House of Lords held:

   (a) 'evidence against' means evidence which supports the prosecution case in a material respect or which undermines the defence of the co-accused — it is not necessary to show that Y has any hostile intent against X (for further details on this see below);

(b) Y can be taken to 'give evidence' against X either when Y gives evidence in chief or when Y is being cross-examined (giving evidence against X does not include cross-examination of X by Y's counsel);

(c) the court has no discretion to prevent X cross-examining Y on bad character once s. 1(f) (iii) is brought into effect;

(d) when Y's bad character is revealed in cross-examination pursuant to s. 1(f) (iii) it only goes to the issue of Y's credibility.

Evidence given by Y which does no more than contradict something which X has said, without further advancing the prosecution's case against X in any significant degree is not evidence against X. Thus, in *Bruce* [1975] 1 WLR 1252, Bruce and others including X were charged with robbery. X said that Bruce and the others had formed an agreement to rob but he (X) was not part of it. Bruce simply testified that there was no robbery (i.e. his defence was a bare denial). Had Bruce given evidence against X? The Court of Appeal held that Bruce had not given evidence against X. *Bruce* falls to be compared with *Hatton* (1976) 64 Cr App R 88. Hatton conceded part of the prosecution's case (whereas Bruce denied it all). The Court of Appeal held that Hatton had given evidence against a co-accused who had put forward a different line of defence. It does not follow from *Bruce* that a bare denial will never trigger s. 1(f) (iii): it depends on the particular circumstances of the case. Where X and Y are jointly charged and on the facts it is clear that either X or Y must have committed the offence, a bare denial by Y may well amount to giving evidence against X (see *Davis* [1975] 1 WLR 345 and *Varley* (1982) 75 Cr App R 241). This may arise where Y is simply denying evidence already given against Y by X.

This area of law was reviewed by the Court of Appeal in *Crawford* [1998] 1 Cr App R 338 where Bingham CJ said that the essential question is:

> Did the evidence given by the defendant in the witness box [i.e. the defendant in danger of losing the shield], if accepted, damage in a significant degree the defence of the co-defendant?

The Court of Appeal held that X's defence could involve giving evidence against Y even though X's defence did not necessarily imply Y's guilt. X would still be giving evidence against Y if his defence made it less likely that Y's defence would be believed.

4.2.1.2 Adducing evidence of a co-accused's bad character

Background points

It is not generally permissible for *the prosecution* to adduce evidence of an accused's bad character in order to show that the accused in question is more likely to have committed the offence charged. However, this general rule (the rule against similar fact evidence) does not apply in the same way to evidence adduced by an accused. Thus an accused may generally adduce evidence of the character/propensity of prosecution witnesses if it is relevant, e.g., showing that the victim in an assault case has a propensity towards violence to support a defence of self-defence (there is a limited exception to this in relation to rape complainants).

The main issue

The main question to be addressed is whether one co-accused can adduce character (similar fact) evidence against another co-accused for the purpose of showing that the other is more likely to have committed the offence charged. The answer is, that such evidence may be admissible but only if it specifically advances the case of the accused who seeks to adduce it (see *Miller* [1952] 2 All ER 667). Because similar fact evidence is always likely to be prejudicial (whoever adduces it) the court will always scutinize the accused's claim that it is relevant carefully (even though the court has no *discretion* to exclude it). Thus in *Neale* (1977) 65 Cr App R 304, N, being charged jointly with X with arson, ran the defence that at the time of the fire in question he (N) was asleep.

The Court of Appeal held that N could not prove that X had admitted starting several other fires by himself because this evidence of X's bad character was irrelevant to N's defence. However, where it is clear that one or both of two accused (X and Y) must have committed the offence, i.e., both accused can be placed at the scene of the crime and each blames the other (disclaiming any responsibility), then character evidence may be adduced by one against the other (see *Lowery* v *R* [1974] AC 85; *Douglass* (1989) 89 Cr App R 264 and *Kracher* [1985] Crim LR 819).

4.2.2 GOOD CHARACTER

The accused has always been able to adduce evidence of his or her *good* character as evidence of innocence, i.e., to show that he or she was *less* likely to have committed the offence charged and, where relevant, to support his or her credibility. (Care must be taken, however, as a claim to good character may be rebutted by evidence of bad character even if the accused does not testify.)

In *Vye* [1993] 1 WLR 471, the Court of Appeal confirmed that a trial judge should specifically direct the jury about evidence of good character, i.e., that (a) it supports the accused's credibility (if that is in issue), and (b) it is evidence of propensity which is inconsistent with guilt.

The full direction is required even though the accused with good character, X, is tried jointly with an accused with bad character, Y. However, if Y's bad character is revealed to the jury pursuant to s. 1(f)(ii) or s. 1(f)(iii) the judge will also be required to direct the jury that while Y's bad character is admissible to impeach Y's credit it *cannot* be used to show that Y is more likely to have committed the offence charged (see *Cain* [1994] 2 All ER 398). Even when the jury remain unaware of the bad character of accused Y, X will get the full direction on good character (see *Shepherd* [1995] Crim LR 153). An intelligent jury will doubtless draw inferences about Y's character from the fact that the judge gives a direction about X's character but no direction about Y's character.

4.3 Confessions

There are essentially two main issues about confessions which are of particular relevance to trials involving co-accused. These are:

(a) the admissibility of a confession by Y, to be used against Y as part of *X's* case (see **4.3.1** below);

(b) the admissibility of a confession by X which implicates Y, as part of the *prosecution* case against Y (see **4.3.2** below).

4.3.1 Y'S CONFESSION AS EVIDENCE FOR X AGAINST Y

Usually where Y has made a confession the prosecution will make use of it in their case against Y and unless it is excluded either under PACE 1984, s. 76(2) or by discretion the question of its admissibility for X will not arise. The question does however arise where the prosecution either:

(a) are barred from using the confession by a court ruling pursuant to s. 76(2) or by an exercise of discretion; or

(b) simply choose not to use it (e.g. by conceding that they would be barred); or

(c) are unaware of its existence.

The Court of Appeal in *Rowson* [1986] QB 174 (confirmed by the Privy Council in *Lui Mei Lin* v *R* [1989] AC 288) held that if Y gives evidence on the issues which is inconsistent with Y's confession, then X can cross-examine Y using the confession (or relevant part of the confession) as a previous inconsistent statement. The decision of the House of Lords in *Myers* [1998] 1 Cr App R 153 holds that X may go further than this and rely on Y's confession for all purposes, i.e., not solely to undermine Y's credibility.

The Court of Appeal in *Myers* ([1996] 2 Cr App R 335) had certified that a point of law of public importance was involved in their decision, namely:

> In a joint trial of two defendants A and B, is an out of court confession by A *which is conceded to be inadmissible as evidence for the Crown* nevertheless admissible at the instigation of B in support of B's defence?

The House of Lords answered this question in the affirmative; however the House of Lords said that B could only rely on A's confession if it was voluntary.

Thus, X can give evidence of a confession by accused Y as evidence against Y so long as it is voluntary and relevant to X's defence. This is consistent with s. 76(1) which provides that a confession is technically admissible against the person making it so long as it is not excluded by reference to s. 76(2) and this provision is only directed at the prosecution. Moreover the discretion to exclude a confession only applies 'against' the prosecution.

4.3.2 A CONFESSION BY ONE ACCUSED WHICH IMPLICATES ANOTHER

Section 76(1) confirms that a confession is only admissible evidence against the accused who made it. In general, therefore, a confession by one accused is no evidence against a co-accused, i.e., accused X is *not* treated as the agent of accused Y for the purpose of making confessions. This, of course, leads to difficulties in joint trials where the confession of one accused contains statements which are adverse to another. The obvious solution is to edit the confession; however, this will not generally be permitted because the accused who made the confession is entitled to object (so far as he or she is concerned, if the confession is to be admitted at all it should be admitted in its entirety (see *Pearce* (1979) Cr App R 365)). Where the 'confessor' agrees to the editing it seems that it will be allowed. However, the court has no discretion to allow editing against the confessor's wishes (see *Lobban* v *R* [1995] 1 WLR 877). If editing is not permitted although the jury will hear X's confession (including the parts implicating Y) Y cannot be cross-examined by counsel for X about X's confession (see *Gray, The Times*, 9 March 1998). Moreover, the judge should always direct the jury that a confession by X which implicates co-accused Y is not admissible evidence against Y (see *Gunewardene* [1951] 2 KB 600). If such a direction is unlikely to overcome the prejudice to Y, separate trials should be considered (see *Lake* (1977) 64 Cr App R 17 and *O'Boyle* (1991) 92 Cr App R 202).

Where co-accused are charged with conspiracy or, on the facts, there is a clear allegation that the co-accused acted to a common purpose, statements by one 'conspirator' *made in furtherance of the common purpose* are admissible against another. It is important to recognise the limits of this exception to the general rule. Statements which are incidental to the common purpose are not admissible. Thus, once the crime is complete and the common purpose has ceased the exception cannot apply. It would not, for example, apply when a conspirator is being interviewed by the police. The exception and its limits are illustrated by *Blake & Tye* (1844) 6 QB 126. The accused were charged with a conspiracy to avoid customs duty. As part of the plan, T had made false entries referring to B in the official records of the relevant transaction. These records were used against both accused. T had also written B's name in his personal record of the transaction. This document was admissible against T but not against B.

Where no conspiracy is charged (and the indictment charges separate substantive offences) it is essential that what is alleged is that the accused *were* acting in concert (see *Liggins, Riding, Gray and Rowlands* [1995] Crim LR 45 and commentary). There must be evidence of the common purpose apart from the statement. However, the statement can be admitted conditionally. If at the end of the prosecution's case there is no independent evidence of common purpose the statement must be ruled inadmissible against the other accused mentioned (see *Donat* (1986) 82 Cr App R 173 and

Governor of Pentonville Prison, ex parte Osman [1989] 3 All ER 701). The independent evidence of a common purpose may it seems consist solely in circumstantial evidence against the accused in question (see *Jones* [1997] 2 Cr App R119).

It appears that, even though it was not actually necessary to make the statement in order to pursue the common purpose, if the statement is in fact made in pursuance of the common purpose then it will be admissible under these principles (see *Devonport* [1996] 1 Cr App R 221).

A useful example of the principles under consideration is to be found in *Murray* [1997] 2 Cr App R 136. In this case X made telephone arrangements with an undercover officer relating to the supply of heroin. X said that Y (Murray) was his boss. After a subsequent arrangement for supplying heroin was made, X and Y were seen together at the venue for the proposed supply. Murray (Y) was convicted of being concerned in offering to supply heroin. On appeal he argued that X's statements to the police officer implicating Murray should have been ruled inadmissible. The Court of Appeal, dismissing Murray's appeal, held that the statements of X were clearly in the course and furtherance of the common purpose and there was other evidence of conspiracy or joint enterprise between X and Y.

FIVE

IDENTIFICATION EVIDENCE

The importance of the Police and Criminal Evidence Act (PACE) 1984, Code D in terms of its impact on obtaining and presenting identification evidence cannot be overstated. It regulates the obtaining of both eyewitness identification evidence and fingerprints and body samples. The full text of Code D can be found in the **Evidence Manual**, **Appendix 3**. The following is an attempt to explain the key points of the Code in relation to these two forms of identification evidence.

Although non-compliance with the Code will not *necessarily* lead to the exclusion of identification evidence under PACE 1984, s. 78, the courts take a strict approach to breaches of Code D in respect of both types of identification evidence. In *Quinn* [1995] 1 Cr App R 480 the police had, in good faith, improvised on (the then existing) Code rules on identity parades. The Court of Appeal held that, although it could not interfere with the judge's decision not to apply s. 78 (because it could not say that no judge could reasonably have reached that decision), the judge *should* have drawn the jury's attention to the breaches of the Code and directed them to consider whether the breaches were such as to cause them to have doubts about the safety of the identification. Lord Taylor CJ observed that 'where a detailed regime was laid down in a statutory Code it was not for police . . . to substitute their own procedure for what was laid down'. (Note: the Code has now been adapted so as to include the police improvisation which had occurred improperly in this case.) In *Nathaniel* [1995] 2 Cr App R 565 the police had retained and provided as evidence a blood sample from N when under the relevant rules the sample should have been destroyed. The Court of Appeal held that the sample should have been excluded under s. 78. As Lord Taylor CJ observed:

> Parliament would not have gone to all the trouble of laying down this strict regime for obtaining/retaining samples if it did not intend it to be observed. . . . To allow that blood sample to be used in evidence . . . when the sample had been retained in breach of statutory duty and in breach of the undertakings to the (accused) must in their Lordship's view have had an adverse effect on the fairness of the proceedings.

In *Allen* [1995] Crim LR 643 the Court of Appeal, in holding that identification evidence obtained in breach of Code D should have been excluded by s. 78, went on to say that where a judge found that Code D had been breached, but nonetheless refused to apply s. 78, the judge should state why he or she did not apply s. 78.

5.1 Eyewitness Identification: Code D, Paragraph 2

In the following sections, note the distinction between cases where the identity of the suspect is known (i.e., there is sufficient information known to the police to justify the arrest of a particular person for suspected involvement in the offence — see Code D, note 2D) and where the identity of the suspect is not known. The rules in the former are much stricter than those in the latter.

31

5.1.1 WHERE THE SUSPECT'S IDENTITY IS KNOWN

5.1.1.1 Identity parade

(a)   By Code D, para. 2.3, if the suspect disputes an identification, an identification parade shall be held, if the suspect consents, unless:

   (i)   the identification officer considers that it is not practicable to assemble sufficient people who resemble the suspect to make a parade fair (para. 2.4); or

   (ii)   the officer in charge of the investigation considers, whether because of fear on the part of the witness or for some other reason, that a group identification (see **5.1.1.2**) is more satisfactory than a parade (para. 2.7); or

   (iii)   the officer in charge of the investigation considers, whether because of the refusal of the suspect to take part in a parade or group ID, or other reasons, that a video film identification (see **5.1.1.3**) would be the most satisfactory course of action (para. 2.10).

(b)   Annex A, para. 2, provides that the parade may be conducted in a room equipped with a screen permitting witnesses to see members of the parade without being seen.

(c)   The fact that the identifying witness has previously identified the suspect to the police does not necessarily obviate the need to hold an identity parade (see *Brown* [1991] Crim LR 368 and *Macmath* [1997] Crim LR 586). However, in *Popat* [1998] 2 Cr App R 208, the Court of Appeal held that if the suspect had been 'properly and adequately' identified by the witness it would be unnecessary to hold an identification parade. This decision was doubted in the subsequent Court of Appeal case of *Forbes*, *The Times*, 5 May 1999, but *Forbes* was itself criticised and *Popat* affirmed as the correct authority in *Popat (No. 2)*, *The Times*, 7 September 1999 and *Ryan*, *The Times*, 13 October 1999.

5.1.1.2 Group identification

(a)   If the suspect refuses or, having agreed, fails to attend a parade, or a parade is unsatisfactory for any of the reasons mentioned in (a) in **5.1.1.1**, the witness should be allowed to see the suspect either in a group ID or video ID; a confrontation should only be resorted to if none of the other procedures is practicable (paras 2.6 and 2.13). (For video and confrontation see **5.1.1.3** and **5.1.1.4**.)

(b)   A group ID is where the suspect is viewed by a witness amongst an informal group of people. Although the suspect should be asked to consent to a group ID, where a suspect refuses to co-operate with it, it can be held covertly if this is practicable and the identification officer exercises his or her discretion to permit it (see paras 2.7 to 2.9 and Annex E). In *Tiplady*, *The Times*, 23 February 1995, the Court of Appeal held, on the facts, that the foyer of a magistrates' court *was* a suitable place in which to hold a group ID.

5.1.1.3 Video identification

This is where the witness is shown a prepared video film of a known suspect. Although the suspect should be asked to consent to a video ID, if the suspect refuses to co-operate the identification officer has a discretion to proceed if it is practicable to do so (see paras 2.10 to 2.12 and Annex B).

5.1.1.4 Confrontation

This is where the suspect is shown to the witness and the witness is asked: 'Is this the person?'. Before the confrontation the identification officer must tell the witness that the person he or she saw may or may not be the person he or she is to confront. The suspect's consent is *not* required. There is no power for the police to use reasonable force to make a suspect submit to a confrontation — see *Jones (Derek), The Times,* 21 April 1999.

5.1.2   WHERE THE IDENTITY OF THE SUSPECT IS NOT KNOWN

5.1.2.1   Street identification

Code D, para. 2.17 provides that a police officer may take a witness to a particular neighbourhood or place to see whether he or she can identify the person who had been seen on the relevant occasion. Care should be taken not to direct the witness's attention to any individual. Such identifications normally take place shortly after the alleged offence. For an example of such identification see *Malashev* [1997] Crim LR 587.

5.1.2.2   Identification from police photographs

Identification can be made from photographs the police are permitted to retain of convicted persons. Code D, para. 2.18 provides that the showing of photographs must be done in accordance with Annex D. The key features of Annex D are:

(a)   The first description of the suspect given by the witness must be recorded before the showing of photographs.

(b)   The viewing should be in private; only one witness should be shown photographs at any one time and there should be no prompting.

(c)   The witness should be shown not less than 12 photographs at a time, which shall, as far as possible, all be of a similar type.

5.1.2.3   Films and photographs of incidents

Due to the increase in the number of security cameras this has, in recent years, become a particularly important source of identification evidence. However, until 1995, Code D made no special rules about it. This omission has been made good in para. 2.21A which provides that when the film etc. is shown to potential witnesses (including police officers) for the purpose of obtaining identification evidence it shall (a) be shown on an individual basis so as to avoid any possibility of collusion, and (b) the showing shall, as far as possible, follow the principles for video IDs or identification from (police) photographs (see **5.1.2.2**).

As soon as a street, photo or security film ID has been made, the identity of the suspect becomes known. At this stage the first part of Code D, para. 2 (identity parades etc.) comes into effect. Although street IDs etc. are technically admissible in their own right (see, e.g., *Rogers* [1993] Crim LR 386), it is submitted in the light of *Quinn* (1995) 1 Cr App R 480 that the safe course would be for the police to offer a parade (or, if more satisfactory, a Code alternative, such as a group identification). Then, if the accused refuses to co-operate, reliance may be placed on the street ID etc. at trial without any suggestion of a breach of the Code. See also *Macmath* [1997] Crim LR 586 and **5.1.1.1** above. As regards an identification from police photographs the requirement for a subsequent ID parade etc. is explicitly stated in Annex D, para. 5.

5.2   Fingerprints and Body Samples

5.2.1   FINGERPRINTS: CODE D, PARAGRAPH 3

The key points to note about Code D, para. 3 (based on the powers given in PACE 1984, s. 61 and set out in the **Evidence Manual** at **12.3.2.6**) are that the fingerprints of a person can be obtained *without the appropriate consent* if:

(a)   the person is detained at a police station and *either* a superintendent authorises it *or* the person has been charged with a recordable offence (or informed that he or she will be reported for such an offence) and has not previously had his or her fingerprints taken in relation to that offence; or

(b)   the person has been convicted of *any* recordable offence.

The definition of 'recordable offence' is obviously of considerable importance. The definition is to be found in the National Police Records (Recordable Offences) Regulations 1985 (SI 1985 No. 1941) — it includes *all* offences punishable by imprisonment and a variety of other offences. There is a very wide power to take a person's fingerprints without consent (especially when account is also taken of the related power to use reasonable force if necessary (PACE 1984, s. 117)). If a person has been convicted of a recordable offence but his or her fingerprints have not been taken, the police can (a) (within one month of the conviction) require the person to attend a police station in order that his or her fingerprints may be taken, and (b) arrest without warrant if the person fails to comply.

By PACE 1984, s. 65:

(a) 'fingerprints' includes palm prints.

(b) 'appropriate consent' means—

    (i) in relation to a person who has attained the age of 17 years, the consent of that person;

    (ii) in relation to a person who has not attained that age but has attained the age of 14 years, the consent of that person and his or her parent or guardian; and

    (iii) in relation to a person who has not attained the age of 14 years, the consent of his or her parent or guardian.

PACE 1984, s. 61(7A) (inserted by the Criminal Justice and Public Order Act (CJPOA) 1994) makes reference to a speculative search. This is defined in this context as a check against other fingerprints contained in records held by or on behalf of the police or held in connection with or as a result of an investigation of an offence — see PACE 1984, s. 65 (as amended by CJPOA 1994, s. 58(4)).

Once a person has been convicted of a recordable offence his or her fingerprints may be kept permanently in police records; however, where the person is cleared of an offence in respect to which his or her fingerprints were taken they must be destroyed as soon as practicable — see PACE 1984, s. 64.

5.2.2   BODY SAMPLES: CODE D, PARAGRAPH 5

Code D, para. 5 is based on PACE 1984, ss. 62 and 63 (set out in the *Evidence Manual* at **12.3.2.6**) — s. 62 deals with intimate samples and s. 63 deals with non-intimate samples.

'Intimate sample' means:

(a) a sample of blood, semen or any other tissue fluid, urine or pubic hair;

(b) a dental impression;

(c) a swab taken from a person's body orifice other than the mouth.

'Intimate search' means a search which consists of the physical examination of a person's body orifices other than the mouth.

'Non-intimate sample' means:

(a) a sample of hair other than pubic hair;

(b) a sample taken from a nail or from under a nail;

(c) a swab taken from any part of a person's body including the mouth but not any other body orifice;

(d)   saliva;

(e)   a footprint or a similar impression of any part of a person's body other than a part of his hand.

5.2.2.1   Obtaining intimate samples

An intimate sample may be taken from a person in police detention if a police officer of at least the rank of superintendent authorises it to be taken *and the appropriate consent is given*. An intimate sample may also be taken from a person who is not in police detention but from whom, in the course of the investigation of an offence, two or more non-intimate samples suitable for the same means of analysis have been taken which have proved insufficient if the appropriate consent is given. An officer may only give authorisation if he or she has reasonable grounds (a) for suspecting the involvement of the person from whom the sample is to be taken in a recordable offence; and (b) for believing that the same will tend to confirm or disprove his or her involvement.

Where the appropriate consent to the taking of an intimate sample is refused without good cause the court, in determining whether there is a case to answer, and the court or jury, in determining whether that person is guilty of the offence charged may draw such inferences from the refusal as appear proper.

For the definitions of recordable offence and appropriate consent see **5.2.1**.

5.2.2.2   Obtaining non-intimate samples

Although, *in general*, a non-intimate sample may not be taken from a person without the appropriate consent, a non-intimate sample may be taken from a person without the appropriate consent if he or she is in police detention or is being held in custody by the police on the authority of a court, and an officer of at least the rank of superintendent authorises it to be taken without the appropriate consent.

A non-intimate sample may also be taken from a person without appropriate consent (a) if he has been charged with a recordable offence and has not had a non-intimate sample taken from him in the course of the investigation of the offence; or (b) if he has been convicted of a recordable offence. The position with regard to obtaining non-intimate samples was further extended by the Criminal Evidence (Amendment) Act 1997.

The position with regard to obtaining non-intimate samples is now similar to the position relating to obtaining fingerprints (see **5.2.1**). Even where a non-intimate sample cannot be taken without the appropriate consent, the refusal without good cause to consent to giving a non-intimate sample can, at common law, form the basis for an inference of guilt (see *Smith* (1985) 81 Cr App R 286).

The original provisions (PACE 1984, ss. 63 and 63A) dealing with this topic have been subjected to such considerable amendment by the CJPOA 1994, the Criminal Procedure and Investigations Act 1996 and the Criminal Evidence (Amendment) Act 1997 (and are of such importance) that they are set out here (as amended) in full.

63.—(1)   Except as provided by this section, a non-intimate sample may not be taken from a person without the appropriate consent.

(2)   Consent to the taking of a non-intimate sample must be given in writing.

(3)   A non-intimate sample may be taken from a person without the appropriate consent if—

(a)   he is in police detention or is being held in custody by the police on the authority of a court; and

(b)   an officer of at least the rank of superintendent authorises it to be taken without the appropriate consent.

(3A)   A non-intimate sample may be taken from a person (whether or not he falls within subsection (3)(a) above) without the appropriate consent if—

(a)   he has been charged with a recordable offence or informed that he will be reported for such an offence; and

(b) either he has not had a non-intimate sample taken from him in the course of the investigation of the offence by the police or he has had a non-intimate sample taken from him but either it was not suitable for the same means of analysis or, though so suitable, the sample proved insufficient.

(3B) A non-intimate sample may be taken from a person without the appropriate consent if he has been convicted of a recordable offence.

(3C) A non-intimate sample may also be taken from a person without the appropriate consent if he is a person to whom section 2 of the Criminal Evidence (Amendment) Act 1997 applies (persons detained following acquittal on grounds of insanity or finding of unfitness to plead).

(4) An officer may only give an authorisation under subsection (3) above if he has reasonable grounds—

(a) for suspecting the involvement of the person from whom the sample is to be taken in a recordable offence; and

(b) for believing that the sample will tend to confirm or disprove his involvement.

(5) An officer may give an authorisation under subsection (3) above orally or in writing but, if he gives it orally, he shall confirm it in writing as soon as is practicable.

(6) Where—

(a) an authorisation has been given; and

(b) it is proposed that a non-intimate sample shall be taken in pursuance of the authorisation,

an officer shall inform the person from whom the sample is to be taken—

(i) of the giving of the authorisation; and

(ii) of the grounds for giving it.

(7) The duty imposed by subsection (6)(ii) above includes a duty to state the nature of the offence in which it is suspected that the person from whom the sample is to be taken has been involved.

(8) If a non-intimate sample is taken from a person by virtue of subsection (3) above—

(a) the authorisation by virtue of which it was taken; and

(b) the grounds for giving the authorisation,

shall be recorded as soon as is practicable after the sample is taken.

(8A) In a case where by virtue of subsection (3A), (3B) or (3C) above a sample is taken from a person without the appropriate consent—

(a) he shall be told the reason before the sample is taken; and

(b) the reason shall be recorded as soon as practicable after the sample is taken.

(8B) If a non-intimate sample is taken from a person at a police station, whether with or without the appropriate consent—

(a) before the sample is taken, an officer shall inform him that it may be the subject of a speculative search; and

(b) the fact that the person has been informed of this possibility shall be recorded as soon as practicable after the sample has been taken.

(9) If a non-intimate sample is taken from a person detained at a police station, the matters required to be recorded by subsection (8) or (8A) or (8B) above shall be recorded in his custody record.

(9A) Subsection (3B) above shall not apply to any person convicted before 10th April 1995 unless he is a person to whom section 1 of the Criminal Evidence (Amendment) Act 1997 applies (persons imprisoned or detained by virtue of pre-existing conviction for sexual offence etc.).

(10) Nothing in this section, except as provided in section 15(13) and (14) of, and paragraph 7(6C) and (6D) of Schedule 5 to, the Prevention of Terrorism (Temporary Provisions) Act 1989, applies to a person arrested or detained under the terrorism provisions.

63A.—(1) Where a person has been arrested on suspicion of being involved in a recordable offence or has been charged with such an offence or has been informed that he will be reported for such an offence, fingerprints or samples or the information derived from samples taken under any power conferred by this Part of this Act from the person may be checked against—

(a) other fingerprints or samples to which the person seeking to check has access and which are held by or on behalf of a police force (or police forces) falling within subsection (1A) below or are held in connection with or as a result of an investigation of an offence;

(b)   information derived from other samples if the information is contained in records to which the person seeking to check has access and which are held as mentioned in paragraph (a) above.

(1A)   Each of the following police forces falls within this subsection—

(a)   a police force within the meaning given by section 62 of the Police Act 1964 (which relates to England and Wales);

(b)   a police force within the meaning given by section 50 of the Police (Scotland) Act 1967;

(c)   the Royal Ulster Constabulary and the Royal Ulster Constabulary Reserve;

(d)   the States of Jersey Police Force;

(e)   the salaried police force of the Island of Guernsey;

(f)   the Isle of Man Constabulary.

(2)   Where a sample of hair other than pubic hair is to be taken the sample may be taken either by cutting hairs or by plucking hairs with their roots so long as no more are plucked than the person taking the sample reasonably considers to be necessary for a sufficient sample.

(3)   Where any power to take a sample is exercisable in relation to a person the sample may be taken in a prison or other institution to which the Prison Act 1952 applies.

(3A)   Where—

(a)   the power to take a non-intimate sample under section 63(3B) above is exercisable in relation to any person who is detained under Part III of the Mental Health Act 1983 in pursuance of—

(i)   a hospital order or interim hospital order made following his conviction for the recordable offence in question, or

(ii)   a transfer direction given at a time when he was detained in pursuance of any sentence or order imposed following that conviction, or

(b)   the power to take a non-intimate sample under section 63(3C) above is exercisable in relation to any person,

the sample may be taken in the hospital in which he is detained under that Part of that Act.

Expressions used in this subsection and in the Mental Health Act 1983 have the same meaning as in that Act.

(3B)   Where the power to take a non-intimate sample under section 63(3B) above is exercisable in relation to a person detained in pursuance of directions of the Secretary of State under section 53 of the Children and Young Persons Act 1933 the sample may be taken at the place where he is so detained.

(4)   Any constable may, within the allowed period, require a person who is neither in police detention nor held in custody by the police on the authority of a court to attend a police station in order to have a sample taken where—

(a)   the person has been charged with a recordable offence or informed that he will be reported for such an offence and either he has not had a sample taken from him in the course of the investigation of the offence by the police or he has had a sample so taken from him but either it was not suitable for the same means of analysis or, though so suitable, the sample proved insufficient; or

(b)   the person has been convicted of a recordable offence and either he has not had a sample taken from him since the conviction or he has had a sample taken from him (before or after his conviction) but either it was not suitable for the same means of analysis or, though so suitable, the sample proved insufficient.

(5)   The period allowed for requiring a person to attend a police station for the purpose specified in subsection (4) above is—

(a)   in the case of a person falling within paragraph (a), one month beginning with the date of the charge or of his being informed as mentioned in that paragraph or one month beginning with the date on which the appropriate officer is informed of the fact that the sample is not suitable for the same means of analysis or has proved insufficient, as the case may be;

(b)   in the case of a person falling within paragraph (b), one month beginning with the date of the conviction or one month beginning with the date on which the *appropriate officer is informed of the fact that the sample is not suitable for the same means of analysis or has proved insufficient, as the case may be.*

(6)   A requirement under subsection (4) above—

(a)   shall give the person at least 7 days within which he must so attend; and

(b)   may direct him to attend at a specified time of day or between specified times of day.

(7)   Any constable may arrest without a warrant a person who has failed to comply with a requirement under subsection (4) above.

(8)   In this section 'the appropriate officer' is—

(a)   in the case of a person falling within subsection (4)(a), the officer investigating the offence with which that person has been charged or as to which he was informed that he would be reported;

(b)   in the case of a person falling within subsection (4)(b), the officer in charge of the police station from which the investigation of the offence of which he was convicted was conducted.

5.2.2.3   A national DNA profile database

A database of DNA profiles of convicted persons (and records currently held in connection with or as a result of an investigation of an offence) can be used as a basis for linking suspects with 'new' offences — by way of a 'speculative search' (see para. 5.11A). However, since samples can be taken from persons who have not been convicted, the question arises: What if the person is acquitted or not proceeded against? Under para. 5.8 the general rule is that if samples are taken from a person (X) in the course of an investigation and the investigation does *not* result in the conviction (or formal cautioning) of X, X's samples must be destroyed as soon as practicable after X is 'eliminated from the enquiry' (whether by acquittal at trial or at an earlier stage).

However, under para. 5.8A and note 5F if somebody is convicted as a result of the investigation in which X's sample was taken, X's sample does not need to be destroyed but the information derived from X's sample (i.e., X's DNA profile) cannot be used in evidence against X or for any investigation. Even if nobody is convicted as a result of the investigation, although X's sample itself will be destroyed, the information derived from it can be retained (but it cannot be used in evidence against X or for any investigation). These are, to say the least, curious provisions which may have a fairly random effect in practice (see *Kelt* [1994] 1 WLR 765 and cf. *Nathaniel* [1995] 2 Cr App R 565).

SIX

EUROPEAN CONVENTION ON HUMAN RIGHTS

The European Convention on Human Rights (ECHR) was signed in 1950, and came into force in 1953. It was produced by the Council of Europe, of which the United Kingdom was one of the original ten members (now considerably expanded), in the aftermath of the Second World War and the Nuremberg Trials. There is of course no direct connection between the Council of Europe and the European Union (EU). By now, however, the Convention has been signed and ratified by all the member States of the EU, as well as a number of countries which are outside the EU and including a number of former communist States.

Like the EU, the Council of Europe has a Commission and a Court. These institutions are based in Strasbourg. The European Court of Justice has at times relied on the ECHR as an influence on the general principles of EU law, but the Convention has no formal role in determining EU law.

6.1   The Status of the ECHR in UK Law

The ECHR is an international treaty to which the United Kingdom is a signatory, and it is binding on all its signatories in international law. In some member countries of the Council of Europe, the ECHR has been made a directly enforceable part of the domestic legal system. That is not the case, however, as far as the United Kingdom is concerned. In this respect, the ECHR is in sharp contrast to the law of the EU, whose incorporation into English law can be seen from the enactment of the European Communities Act 1972. When the Convention was ratified, it was not considered necessary to enact legislation to give it effect in UK law, perhaps because it was assumed that the rights which it contained were already protected in this country. In virtually all the member countries of the Council of Europe, the ECHR has been made a directly enforceable part of the domestic legal system, and the question whether this should also be done by the United Kingdom has figured high on the political agenda for some years. As a result of the provisions of the Human Rights Act 1998, the ECHR will be incorporated into the domestic law of the United Kingdom in October 2000. Section 2(1) of the Act provides that a court or tribunal determining a question in connection with a Convention right 'must take into account any judgment, decision, declaration or opinion made or given by the European Court of Human Rights, the Commission, or the Committee of Ministers of the Council of Europe. Even more significantly, s. 3 states:

> **3.**—*(1) So far as it is possible to do so, primary legislation and subordinate legislation must be read and given effect in a way which is compatible with the Convention rights.*
> *(2) This section—*
> *(a) applies to primary legislation and subordinate legislation whenever enacted;*
> *(b) does not affect the validity, continuing operation or enforcement of any incompatible primary legislation; and*

(c) does not affect the validity, continuing operation or enforcement of any incompatible subordinate legislation if (disregarding any possibility of revocation) primary legislation prevents removal of the incompatibility.

Once incorporation takes effect therefore, the provisions of the ECHR will be applicable at all levels, including the magistrates' courts. Moreover, as a result of s. 3(1), the courts will be required to interpret legislation so as to uphold Convention rights unless the legislation is so clearly incompatible with the ECHR that it is impossible. In doing so, they will have to have regard to the substantial body of case law which has evolved as a result of the decisions of the various bodies set up under the auspices of the ECHR.

Meanwhile, the Convention may in any event be relied on in the interpretation of statute law, in line with the general statutory principle that Parliament does not intend to legislate contrary to the country's international treaty obligations. It is a matter of using the Convention as an aid to interpretation, rather than recognising the creation of new rights which appear in the ECHR but which Parliament has not intended to implement (see *Secretary of State for the Home Department, ex parte Brind* [1991] 1 All ER 720). As far as the common law is concerned, the position would appear to be similar in that where the law is either unclear or ambiguous, or concerns an issue not yet ruled on, the courts ought to consider the implications of the ECHR (see *Derby County Council* v *Times Newspapers* [1992] 3 All ER 65). There is also authority to the effect that a judicial discretion ought to be exercised with an eye to the provisions of the Convention. As it was put by Balcombe LJ in *Derby County Council* at p. 77:

> Article 10 has not been incorporated into English domestic law. Nevertheless it may be resorted to in order to help resolve some uncertainty or ambiguity in municipal law (per Lord Ackner in *Brind* v *Secretary of State for the Home Dept* [1991] 1 All ER 720 at 734. . . . Thus (1) art. 10 may be used for the purpose of the resolution of an ambiguity in English primary or subordinate legislation (see *Brind's* case [1991] 1 All ER 720 . . . per Lord Bridge of Harwich, Lord Roskill and Lord Ackner). (2) Article 10 may be used when considering the principles upon which the court should act in exercising a discretion, e.g. whether or not to grant an interlocutory injunction (see *Attorney-General* v *Guardian Newspapers Ltd* [1987] 3 All ER 316 at 355, 364 . . . per Lord Templeman and Lord Ackner); *Re W (a minor) (wardship; restriction on publication)* [1992] 1 All ER 794 at 797. . . . (3) Article 10 may be used when the common law (by which I include the doctrines of equity) is uncertain.

It is not possible, however, for an individual to complain of a breach of the ECHR before an English court (until the Human Rights Act 1998 comes into force). In the event of such a breach, the person aggrieved has the right of individual petition. This right was recognised by the United Kingdom in 1966, and has been renewed until January 2001. The machinery to enforce the right is supplied by the European Court of Human Rights.

If the petitioner is successful and the Court decides that English law falls short of the standards required by the Convention, then the government will usually introduce legislation, or adjust administrative practices, to remedy the defect which has been identified. The fact that such legislation is necessary, however, merely serves to underline the fact that English courts have to reach their decision in accordance with English law where such law is certain and unambiguous, even where it conflicts with the Convention (see Ralph Gibson LJ in *Derby County Council* at p. 83).

6.2   The Rights Contained in the ECHR

A number of the provisions of the Convention have relevance to criminal practice in this country. Extracts from the most important Articles in the Convention for our purposes are set out below, together with a commentary, where appropriate.

Article 3
No one shall be subjected to torture or to inhuman or degrading treatment or punishment.

Cases in which the UK has been involved where this Article has formed the basis of the petition have included:

(a) the use of corporal punishment as a criminal sanction (*Tyrer* v *UK*, Series A, vol. 26);

(b) extradition to face a possible death penalty in the United States of America (*Soering* v *UK*, Series A, vol. 161);

(c) the treatment of terrorist suspects (*Republic of Ireland* v *UK*, Series A, vol. 25).

Article 5
1. Everyone has the right to liberty and security of person. No one shall be deprived of his liberty save in the following cases and in accordance with a procedure prescribed by law:
(a) the lawful detention of a person after conviction by a competent court;
(b) the lawful arrest or detention of a person for non-compliance with the lawful order of a court or in order to secure the fulfilment of any obligation prescribed by law;
(c) the lawful arrest or detention of a person effected for the purpose of bringing him before the competent legal authority on a reasonable suspicion of having committed an offence or when it is reasonably considered necessary to prevent his committing an offence or fleeing after having done so;
(d) the detention of a minor by lawful order for the purpose of educational supervision or his lawful detention for the purpose of bringing him before the competent legal authority;
(e) the lawful detention of persons for the prevention of the spreading of infectious diseases, of persons of unsound mind, alcoholics or drug addicts or vagrants;
(f) the lawful arrest or detention of a person to prevent his effecting an unauthorised entry into the country or of a person against whom action is being taken with a view to deportation or extradition.
2. Everyone who is arrested shall be informed promptly, in a language which he understands, of the reasons for his arrest and of any charge against him.
3. Everyone arrested or detained in accordance with the provisions of paragraph 1(c) of this Article shall be brought promptly before a judge or other officer authorized by law to exercise judicial power and shall be entitled to trial within a reasonable time or to release pending trial. Release may be conditioned by guarantee to appear for trial.
4. Everyone who is deprived of his liberty by arrest or detention shall be entitled to take proceedings by which the lawfulness of his detention shall be decided speedily by a court and his release ordered if the detention is not lawful.
5. Everyone who has been the victim of arrest or detention in contravention of the provisions of this Article shall have an enforceable right to compensation.

There have been a number of cases brought against the UK, based upon this Article which involve the detention of suspected terrorists in the context of the situation in Northern Ireland (see, for example, *Brannigan and McBride* v *UK*, Series A, vol. 258-B).

In *Monnell and Morris* v *UK*, Series A, vol. 115, the applicants had been convicted of criminal offences, and applied for leave to appeal despite advice not to do so. The appeal was unsuccessful, and the Court of Appeal made a direction for loss of time (see **Criminal Litigation and Sentencing Manual**, **12.7.1**). The applicants claimed that those loss of time orders resulted in a deprivation of liberty contrary to Article 5. They argued that the loss of time was in effect a further period of imprisonment imposed not for an offence, but for seeking leave to appeal. The practice was alleged to be discriminatory, because people who were not detained at the time of applying for leave to appeal did not suffer from the danger of a direction for loss of time. The Court held that, despite the fact that persons who were at liberty did not run the same risk, the difference in treatment had an objective and reasonable justification because:

. . . Whilst the loss of time ordered by the Court of Appeal is not treated under domestic law as part of the applicants' sentences as such, it does form part of the period of detention which results from the overall sentencing procedure that follows conviction. As a matter of English law, a sentence of imprisonment passed by a Crown Court is to be served subject to any order which the Court of Appeal may, in the event of an unsuccessful application for leave to appeal, make as to loss of time. Section 29(1) of the [Criminal Appeal Act 1968] is couched in rather wide and flexible terms. However, the power of the Court of Appeal to order loss of time, as it is actually exercised, is a component of the machinery existing under English law to ensure that criminal appeals are considered within a reasonable time and, in particular, to reduce the time spent in custody by those with meritorious grounds waiting for their appeal to be heard.

As a result:

. . . there was a sufficient and legitimate connection, for the purposes of the deprivation of liberty permitted under sub-paragraph (a) of Article 5(1), between the conviction of each applicant and the additional period of imprisonment undergone as a result of the loss-of-time order made by the Court of Appeal. The time spent in custody by each applicant under this head is accordingly to be regarded as detention of a person after conviction by a competent court, within the meaning of sub-paragraph (a) of Article 5(1).

Article 6
1. In the determination of his civil rights and obligations or of any criminal charge against him, everyone is entitled to a fair and public hearing within a reasonable time by an independent and impartial tribunal established by law. Judgment shall be pronounced publicly but the press and public may be excluded from all or part of the trial in the interests of morals, public order or national security in a democratic society, where the interests of juveniles or the protection of the private life of the parties so require, or to the extent strictly necessary in the opinion of the court in special circumstances where publicity would prejudice the interests of justice.
2. Everyone charged with a criminal offence shall be presumed innocent until proved guilty according to law.
3. Everyone charged with a criminal offence has the following minimum rights:
(a) to be informed promptly, in a language which he understands and in detail, of the nature and cause of the accusation against him;
(b) to have adequate time and facilities for the preparation of his defence;
(c) to defend himself in person or through legal assistance of his own choosing or, if he has not sufficient means to pay for legal assistance, to be given it free when the interests of justice so require;
(d) to examine or have examined witnesses against him and to obtain the attendance and examination of witnesses on his behalf under the same conditions as witnesses against him;
(e) to have the free assistance of an interpreter if he cannot understand or speak the language used in court.

This article is of particular importance to criminal practice, and there have been a number of cases against the United Kingdom, based upon different issues which arise from it.

For example, in *X* v *UK* 15 EHRR CD 113, the decision of an English court to screen witnesses from the petitioner was held not to be an infringement of his rights under Article 6(1) or 6(3)(d). The accused must, however, in adversarial proceedings such as those in this country, have the right to participate fully. This includes the right to be present, to hear and to follow proceedings (*Standford* v *UK*, Series A, vol. 282). The right of participation also implies that the applicant should be able to understand the proceedings and conduct a defence (*V* v *UK* 15 EHRR CD 108). It is under the provisions of this Article that the effects of prejudicial press coverage may be considered, for example, if the campaign was so extreme that it deprived the accused of a fair trial.

A central principle contained in Article 6 is that of 'equality of arms'. The underlying notion is that the accused should be equal to the prosecution in procedural terms. This means that there should be defence access to the evidence gathered by the prosecution, given the superior resources available to the State in terms of investigation and interrogation. This has implications for the way in which the prosecution duty to disclose unused material is defined (see the article on 'Disclosure, Appeals and Procedural Traditions' by Field and Young, referred to in **6.6**, and the case of *Edwards v UK* (1993) 96 Cr App R 1). 'Equality of arms' also means that both parties to an action in an adversarial system must generally have the right to challenge and confront each other's witnesses, with the power to cross-examine.

Article 6(3)(c) has relevance to the availability of legal aid. In limiting the right to those without the means to pay for it, and to cases where the interests of justice require it, the provision is based upon premises similar to those of our own legal aid. However, the United Kingdom's provision of legal aid for appellants making oral representations to the High Court of Justiciary in Scotland has been successfully challenged in a series of cases before the Court (*Granger v UK* 12 EHRR 451; *Maxwell v UK* 15 EHRR CD 101 and 19 EHRR 97; *Boner v UK* 19 EHRR 246).

In *Murray v UK, The Times*, 9 February 1996, the UK was alleged to have violated the Convention in two respects:

(a) by denying the applicant access to legal advice for the first 48 hours of detention;

(b) by allowing inferences to be drawn from the applicant's silence (under the Northern Ireland predecessor of the provisions in ss. 34 and 35 of the Criminal Justice and Public Order Act 1994).

The Court upheld the complaint as far as (a) was concerned, but not with regard to (b).

Article 10
1. Everyone has the right to freedom of expression. This right shall include freedom to hold opinions and to receive and impart information and ideas without interference by public authority and regardless of frontiers. This Article shall not prevent States from requiring the licensing of broadcasting, television or cinema enterprises.
2. The exercise of these freedoms, since it carries with it duties and responsibilities, may be subject to such formalities, conditions, restrictions or penalties as are prescribed by law and are necessary in a democratic society, in the interests of national security, territorial integrity or public safety, for the prevention of disorder or crime, for the protection of health or morals, for the protection of the reputation or rights of others, for preventing the disclosure of information received in confidence, or for maintaining the authority and impartiality of the judiciary.

Cases have been brought against the United Kingdom alleging violations of this Article in repect of:

(a) blasphemous libel (*Gay News and Lemon v UK* 5 EHRR 123);

(b) contempt of court (e.g., the 'Spycatcher' case (*Observer and Guardian v UK* 14 EHRR 153));

(c) the Incitement to Disaffection Act 1934 (*Arrowsmith v UK* 3 EHRR 218).

Article 14
The enjoyment of the rights and freedoms set forth in this Convention shall be secured without discrimination on any ground such as sex, race, colour, language, religion,

political or other opinion, national or social origin, association with a national minority, property, birth or other status.

Article 14 prohibits discrimination only with respect to the enjoyment of the rights set out in the Convention. It follows that complaint about the violation of Article 14 can only be brought where some other Article of the Convention has allegedly been breached.

This Article has been invoked against the UK, e.g., in respect of:

(a) exclusion of a solicitor from interviews with terrorist suspects in Northern Ireland (*Murray* v *UK, The Times,* 9 February 1996);

(b) the legal treatment of transsexuals (*X, Y and Z* v *UK* App No. 21830/93 unreported);

(c) directions for loss of time for appellants in custody (*Monnell and Morris* v *UK,* dealt with under Article 5 above);

(d) the treatment of sado-masochistic acts between consenting males compared to boxing (*Laskey, Jaggard and Brown* v *UK,* Council of Europe Report, 26 October 1995).

Article 15
1. In time of war or other public emergency threatening the life of the nation, any High Contracting Party may take measures derogating from its obligations under this Convention to the extent strictly required by the exigencies of the situation, provided that such measures are not inconsistent with its other obligations under international law.
2. No derogation from Article 2, except in respect of deaths resulting from lawful acts of war, or from Articles 3, 4 (paragraph 1) and 7 shall be made under this provision.
3. Any High Contracting Party availing itself of this right of derogation shall keep the Secretary General of the Council of Europe fully informed of the measures which it has taken and the reasons therefor. It shall also inform the Secretary General of the Council of Europe when such measures have ceased to operate and provisions of the Convention are again being fully executed.

Article 16
Nothing in Articles 10, 11 and 14 shall be regarded as preventing the High Contracting Parties from imposing restrictions on the political activity of aliens.

These Articles (together with Articles 17 and 18, which are less frequently invoked) set out the restrictions on the scope of the Convention. The UK has made use of the right to derogate under Article 15, informing the Secretary General of derogations relating to the situation in Northern Ireland. The Commission and the Court are responsible for ensuring that the requirements of Article 15(1) are met, but the tendency has been to allow the contracting State a wide 'margin of appreciation' (see **6.4**) in judging, e.g., whether there is a public emergency threatening the life of the nation. There can in any event, by virtue of Article 15(2), be no derogation from certain of the Articles, e.g., Article 3.

6.3 Procedure under the ECHR

The procedure commences with a petition to the Secretary General of the Council of Europe, who forwards it to the Court. There is provision for legal aid to applicants in the Addendum to the Court's Rules of Procedure, although legal aid is in fact only granted in a small proportion of cases.

6.3.1   REQUIREMENTS FOR ADMISSIBILITY

When determining admissibility, the Court must be satisfied that the applicant has exhausted all domestic remedies, and has presented the petition within six months of the final decision reached through the pursuit of those remedies. In addition, the petition must raise a matter which is not substantially the same as one already ruled on by the Court, and has not been submitted to 'another procedure of international investigation or settlement' (art. 35(2)b). Further, the Court will rule inadmissible any application 'imcompatible with the provision' of the ECHR, 'manifestly ill-founded', or 'an abuse of the right of petition' (art. 35(3)).

6.3.2   EXHAUSTING DOMESTIC REMEDIES

As far as the requirement that the applicant exhaust domestic remedies is concerned, certain remedies may not be regarded as normal e.g., an application for *habeus corpus* is not considered as part of the normal appeal procedure (*X* v *UK* (1969) 12 *Yearbook* 298). Further, there is no obligation to pursue remedies which clearly offer no chance of success. Where an appeal would clearly fail because there is a binding domestic precedent which stands in the way of the applicant, then the case does not have to be pursued all the way to the House of Lords.

6.3.3   THE TIME LIMIT

The six month period within which the petition must be brought to the Court begins with the date when the final decision is taken (art. 35(1)). This has been defined as 'the date of a "final decision" taken in the exhaustion of an effective and sufficient domestic remedy, or from the date of the act or decision complained of where such an act or decision finally determines the applicant's position on the domestic level' (*Greenock Ltd* v *UK* (1985) 42 D & R 33 at 41). Time will usually cease to run on the date of the first letter to the Court indicating an intention to lodge an application, and the nature of the complaint (*Kelly* v *UK* (1985) 42 D & R 205), but the Court may look at the circumstances of the case to decide on the relevant date e.g., where pursuit of the case has been unreasonably delayed. Where the breach of the ECHR is a continuing one, then time will not begin to run until the continuing state of affairs ceases to exist (*Temple* v *UK* 8 EHRR 319).

6.3.4   SETTLEMENT

If the Court decides that the application is admissible, it proceeds to the next stage. It usually receives further evidence and submissions. At the same time, it will try to reach a 'friendly settlement' or negotiated agreement between the parties. Such a settlement may involve, for example, payment of compensation, or a change in the law or administrative practice which is the subject of the complaint.

If there is no settlement, the government and the applicant may make further written and oral submissions.

6.3.5   THE HEARING

The oral hearings are short, typically lasting a couple of hours. Speeches have to be written in advance to aid simultaneous translation.

The Court has a number of judges equivalent to the members of the Council of Europe, but it usually sits in chambers of nine judges. The procedure is in the main written, affidavits and other documents being filed with the Court in compliance with time limits. A date is fixed for a public oral hearing, in which the applicant, although not strictly a party to the proceedings, is in practice allowed to participate, represented by an advocate. The final judgment of the Court is by a majority, and dissenting judgments are common. It has the power to order a State which is in breach of the ECHR to make just compensation (art. 41). In addition, a judgment finding that a State's laws are in breach of the ECHR imposes a duty on the State in question to rectify the law.

6.4   The Approach of the European Court of Human Rights

The approach of the judges in Strasbourg is determined by the fact that they are engaged in interpreting what is in effect a Code containing a limited number of general provisions. Frequently, they are required to fill in the details to what is a very broad statement of rights and freedoms. In doing so, the approach which they adopt may be said to have the following characteristics:

(a) It is purposive, i.e., the Court searches for the purposes underlying the broad statement contained in the Convention. For example, in *Soering* v *UK*, Series A, vol. 161 at paragraph 87, the Court stated:

In interpreting the Convention regard must be had to its special character as a treaty for the collective enforcement of human rights and fundamental freedoms (see the *Ireland* v *United Kingdom* judgment of 18 January 1978, Series A, No. 25, p. 90 §239). Thus, the object and purpose of the Convention as an instrument for the protection of individual human beings require that its provisions be interpreted and applied so as to make its safeguards practical and effective (see, *inter alia*, the *Artico* judgment of 13 May 1980, Series A, No. 37 p. 16 §33). In addition, any interpretation of rights and freedoms guaranteed has to be consistent with 'the general spirit of the Convention, an instrument designed to maintain and promote the ideals and values of a democratic society' (see the *Kjeldsen, Busk, Madsen and Pedersen* judgment of 7 December 1976, Series A, No. 23, p. 27 §53).

(b) It is evolutionary, interpreting the Convention in the light of current thinking and the social climate (e.g. in *Tyrer* v *UK*, Series A, vol. 26, where the practice of corporal punishment as part of the criminal justice system on the Isle of Man was examined and held to be a breach of Article 3, the Court stated that 'the Convention is a living instrument which . . . must be interpreted in the light of present-day conditions').

(c) It produces decisions which are based on the specific set of facts which it is considering, rather than laying down propositions of general application e.g., often the Court will emphasise that it is interpreting the Convention specifically in relation to the facts before it.

(d) It recognises the principle of proportionality: that restrictions on human rights or penalties imposed for infringement of the law should be proportional to their aims.

(e) It has based itself on the principle of the margin of appreciation. This principle derives from a recognition of the legal and social diversity existing within the States which are signatories to the ECHR. It leaves individual States a measure of discretion in the way in which they implement the principles of the Convention. In interpreting an article, the Court will concentrate on the broad picture and the limits of acceptable conduct, rather than prescribing exactly how a State should comply with its treaty obligations.

6.5   Reporting of ECHR Cases

The edited *European Human Rights Reports* are published by Sweet & Maxwell (cited as EHRR).

The Publications of the European Court of Human Rights include the following:

— Series A is the Judgments of the Court.

— Series B is the Reports of the Commission.

— Decisions and Reports of the Commission (cited as D & R).

6.6   Further Reading

The following books and articles may prove helpful in exploring the growing impact of the Convention's provisions on our criminal justice system:

Ashworth, A., 'Article 6 and the Fairness of Trials' [1999] Crim LR 261.

Farran, S., *The UK Before the European Court of Human Rights: Case Law and Commentary* (Blackstone Press, 1996).

Field and Young, 'Disclosure, Appeals and Procedural Traditions: *Edwards* v *United Kingdom*' [1994] Crim LR 264.

Manchester, Salter, Moodie and Lynch, *Exploring the Law* (Sweet & Maxwell, 1996) (see ch. 3).

Munday, 'Inferences from Silence and European Human Rights Law' [1996] Crim LR 370.

Nash and Furse, 'Self Incrimination, Corporate Misconduct and the Convention on Human Rights' [1995] Crim LR 855.

Nicholson and Reid, 'Arrest for Breach of the Peace and the European Convention on Human Rights' [1996] Crim LR 764.

Sharpe, S., 'Article 6 and the Disclosure of Evidence in Criminal Trials' [1999] Crim LR 273.

Stone, R., *Textbook on Civil Liberties* (Blackstone Press, 1997) (see section 1.5).

Uglow, S., 'Covert Surveillance and the European Convention on Human Rights' [1999] Crim LR 287.

Wadham, J. and Mountfield, H., *Human Rights Act 1998* (Blackstone Press, 1999).

PART II
SUBSTANTIVE LAW

SEVEN

DANGEROUS DRUGS

7.1 'Controlled Drugs'

The Misuse of Drugs Act 1971 applies to 'controlled drugs'. Section 2 of the Act defines this term as the substances listed in sch. 2 to the Act. Schedule 2 divides controlled drugs into three classes: A (e.g. cocaine, lysergide (LSD) and diamorphine (heroin)), B (e.g. amphetamine, cannabis and cannabis resin), and C (e.g. those drugs mentioned in **7.5**). The relevance of this distinction is that offences involving class A drugs attract a more severe sentence than offences involving class B drugs, and class B drug offences are more serious than class C drug offences. This distinction is based on the degree of harm a particular drug can do.

Whether or not the particular substance in question is a controlled drug has to be determined by expert evidence (*Hunt* [1987] AC 352; *Hill* (1993) 96 Cr App R 456). However, it was said in *Chatwood* [1980] 1 WLR 874, that an admission by the defendant that the substance is a controlled drug is prima facie evidence as to the nature of the substance, and so such an admission can found a case to answer.

To be controlled, the substance must be listed in sch. 2. So the coco-leaf (from which cocaine may be extracted) is specifically listed. The 'magic mushroom' is not listed *per se* and so in its natural state is not a controlled drug. However, when it is 'prepared' (sch. 2, Part 1, para. 5), so as to produce psilocin (which is listed in sch. 2) it does become a controlled drug (*Hodder* v *DPP* [1989] Crim LR 261).

Note that cannabis and cannabis resin are listed separately, and so the prosecution must specify which is alleged (*Best* (1979) 70 Cr App R 21).

7.2 The Offences

7.2.1 IMPORT/EXPORT

Section 3 of the Misuse of Drugs Act 1971 prohibits the export and import of controlled drugs. However, the section by itself does not create an offence. The offence is committed under s. 50(3) of the Customs and Excise Management Act 1979, which creates the offence of importing or being concerned with the importing of any goods contrary to any prohibition with intent to evade that prohibition or s. 170(2) of the same Act which creates the offence of being knowingly concerned in the fraudulent evasion (or attempted evasion) of any prohibition. The latter offence covers both import and (unlike s. 50) export of prohibited goods. In *Latif and Shahzad* [1996] 1 All ER 353, S approached a shopkeeper in Pakistan who was acquainted with local drug dealers but who was also a paid informer used by the US Drugs Enforcement Agency. It was agreed that S would deliver to the shopkeeper 20 kg of heroin for export to London. S was to take delivery of the heroin in London and then arrange for its distribution. The shopkeeper reported this to a local British drugs liaison officer. The officer arranged for a British customs officer to take the heroin to London. The two appellants went to London. A customs officer delivered to them packages which looked like the packages of heroin. The two appellants were then arrested. The House of Lords held that, although S had not committed the full offence of evading the prohibition on the importation of heroin, he had committed two attempts to do so: one, in Pakistan, when he delivered the heroin to the shopkeeper for export to London, and the second when he tried to collect the heroin from the undercover customs officer for distribution in the United Kingdom. L was a party to the second occasion. Since s. 170(2) covers both evasion and attempted evasion, S and L were both guilty of an offence under that section.

In *Attorney-General's Reference (No. 1 of 1998), The Times*, 2 October 1998, the defendant had agreed to look after a parcel which was due to arrive from Holland. He knew that the parcel might contain controlled drugs. The parcel (which did indeed contain drugs) duly arrived. The defendant had taken no action in relation to the parcel but was charged with being concerned in the fraudulent evasion of the prohibition on the importation of controlled drugs (contrary to s. 170(2)(b) of the Customs and Excise Management 1979). It was held by the Court of Appeal that the question for the jury was whether, at any time before or after the arrival of the controlled drugs in the UK, the defendant could be said to have been knowingly concerned in their illegal import-ation. A person could be knowingly concerned without doing anything to bring about the importation. Further, even if there is uncertainty as to whether the illegal import-ation will take place or not, a person can still be knowingly concerned in the illegal importation if that importation in fact takes place. The 'vice' is being prepared to assist or participate in the enterprise if the circumstances enabling that enterprise to take place arise.

7.2.2 PRODUCTION

Section 4 of the Misuse of Drugs Act 1971 creates these offences:

(a) producing a controlled drug (s. 4(2)(a)). Section 37(1) defines 'producing' as including manufacture or cultivation. Growing cannabis can be charged under this section or under s. 6 which deals specifically with cannabis;

(b) being concerned in the production of a controlled drug by another person (s. 4(2)(b)) (this is a sort of statutory conspiracy).

Converting one controlled drug into another controlled drug amounts to production (e.g., converting cocaine hydrochloride into freebase cocaine, i.e., 'crack') (*Russell* (1991) 94 Cr App R 351).

7.2.3 SUPPLY

Under s. 4(3)(a) Misuse of Drugs Act 1971, it is an offence to supply or offer to supply a controlled drug to another person (i.e. drug dealing).

The meaning of 'supply' was considered by the House of Lords in *Maginnis* [1987] 1 All ER 907. It was held (Lord Goff dissenting) that a person who was in unlawful possession of a controlled drug which had been deposited with him by another person for safekeeping had the necessary intent to supply it to another if it was the defendant's intention to return it to the person who had given it to him for that other person's purposes. The handing over must be for the recipient to use the thing handed over for his or her own purposes, but it was not necessary that the supply be made out of the defendant's own personal resources. It follows that a person who hands another a drug for temporary safekeeping and intending to reclaim it does not commit an offence, since the person looking after it cannot use it for his own purposes (*Dempsey* (1985) 82 Cr App R 291).

If the defendant offers to supply one controlled drug, thinking mistakenly that it is another controlled drug, the offence is still made out. If the defendant offers to supply what he or she believes to be a controlled drug but which in fact is not a controlled drug, the offence is nonetheless committed (*Haggard* v *Mason* [1976] 1 WLR 187).

Further, an offence is committed even if the defendant did not in fact intend to supply the drug he was offering to supply (*Gill* (1993) 97 Cr App R 215).

Under s. 4(3)(b), it is an offence to be concerned in the supplying of a controlled drug to another person. Under s. 4(3)(c), it is an offence to be concerned in the making of an offer to supply a controlled drug to another person.

The last two offences require the prosecution to prove:

(a) supply/offer to supply (by someone other than the defendant);

(b) that the defendant is a participant in the supply/offer;

(c) that the defendant knows the nature of the enterprise.

See *Hughes* (1985) 81 Cr App R 344.

'Another person' in this context cannot be someone who is charged in the same count, though it may be someone who is charged under a different count in the same indictment (*Connelly* [1992] Crim LR 296 (CA)).

A person may be concerned by being involved at a distance in the making of an offer to supply a controlled drug (*Blake* (1978) 68 Cr App R 1) (one person introducing another to someone who could supply a controlled drug).

7.2.4 POSSESSION/POSSESSION WITH INTENT TO SUPPLY

Section 5(2) of the Misuse of Drugs Act 1971 creates the offence of being in possession of a controlled drug. Section 5(3) creates the offence of being in possession of a controlled drug with intent to supply it to another person.

The greater the quantity of drugs seized, the less likely it is that they were for the defendant's personal use, and so a charge of possession with intent to supply is more likely.

The only definition of 'possession' given by the 1971 Act is that contained in s. 37(3). This says that a person is in possession of something even if it is in the custody of someone else provided that it is subject to the control of the possessor. However, this section is dealing with the fairly unusual situation where custody and control are separated.

Perhaps the leading case on possession (decided under similar legislation to the 1971 Act) is *Warner v Metropolitan Police Commissioner* [1968] 2 All ER 356. All five Law Lords agreed that the appeal should be dismissed, but their reasoning differed. The defendant was stopped by police. His vehicle contained two packages. One contained perfume, the other a controlled drug. His defence was that he thought both packages contained perfume. The question that had to be decided was whether he could be said to be in possession of the drugs.

Lord Morris defined possession as:

> [being] knowingly in control of something in circumstances which [show] that [the defendant] was assenting to being in control of it . . . The conception [to be explained to the jury] will be that of being knowingly in control of a thing in circumstances which have involved an opportunity (whether availed of or not) to learn or discover, at least in a general way, what the thing is . . . If there is assent to the control of a thing, either having the means of knowledge of what the thing is or contains or being unmindful whether there are means of knowledge or not, then ordinarily there will be possession. (p. 375)

Lord Pearce said (at p. 388):

> I think that the term 'possession' is satisfied by a knowledge only of the existence of the thing itself and not its qualities, and that ignorance or mistake as to its qualities is not an excuse . . . Though I reasonably believe the tablets which I possess to be aspirin, yet if they turn out to be heroin I am in possession of heroin tablets.

In *Boyesen* [1982] 2 All ER 161 (HL), Lord Scarman said (at p. 163) possession 'connotes a physical control or custody of a thing plus knowledge that you have it in your custody or control. You may possess a thing without knowing or comprehending its nature; but you do not possess it unless you know you have it'.

In *McNamara* (1988) 87 Cr App R 246, Lord Lane CJ derived the following propositions from *Warner* v *MPC* (at pp. 250–1):

(a) 'a man does not have possession of something which has been put into his pocket or his house without his knowledge';

(b) 'a mere mistake as to the quality of a thing under the defendant's control is not enough to prevent him being in possession' (e.g. being in possession of heroin but believing it to be cannabis or even aspirin);

(c) 'if the defendant believes that the thing is of a wholly different nature from that which in fact it is, then the result . . . would be otherwise' (e.g. being in possession of heroin but believing it to be sugar);

(d) 'in the case of a container or a box, the defendant's possession of the box leads to the strong inference that he is in possession of the contents . . . But if the contents are quite different in kind from what he believed, he is not in possession of [them].' Considering this latter situation, Lord Lane CJ adopted the words of Lord Pearce in *Warner* v *MPC* (at p. 389). It would be for the defendant to prove (or raise a real doubt in the matter) either:

    (i) '[he] had no right to open [the box] and no reason to suspect that its contents were illicit or were drugs', or

    (ii) 'although he was the owner he had no knowledge of (including a genuine mistake as to) its actual contents or of their illicit nature and that he received them innocently and also that he had had no reasonable opportunity since receiving the package of acquainting himself with its actual contents'.

See also *Lewis* (1988) 87 Cr App R 270, where the defendant was an infrequent visitor to a house of which he was the tenant but was nonetheless held to be in possession of drugs found on the premises.

Where more than one person has the right to draw on drugs which form a common pool, all those having such control may be charged with possession (*Searle* [1971] Crim LR 592). Everyone who has the right to say what is done with the drugs possesses them (*Strong, The Times*, 26 January 1990).

The issue in *Boyesen* (mentioned above) was whether one can be said to be in possession of a quantity of a controlled drug which is so minute that it is not 'usable'. The answer given by the House of Lords was yes, provided that the prosecution are able to prove possession and provided that the drug is 'visible, tangible, measureable and capable of manipulation' (per Lord Scarman, at p. 166).

7.2.4.1 Proving intent to supply

In *Grant* [1996] 1 Cr App R 73 it was held by the Court of Appeal that the finding of money (in the defendant's home or in his possession) together with a substantial quantity of drugs is capable of being relevant to the issue of intent to supply drugs. However, the judge must direct the jury that any innocent explanation for the money put forward by the defendant would have to be rejected by them before they could regard the money as evidence of intent to supply drugs. If there is, in the view of the jury, any possibility of the money being in the defendant's possession for reasons other than drug dealing, then the money cannot be probative of an intent to supply drugs. If, however, the jury concludes that the finding of the money indicates not past drug dealing but on-going drug dealing, the money (together with the drugs) may be probative of intent. See also *Gordon* [1995] 2 Cr App R 61.

In *Wilkinson* (1997, unreported) the Court of Appeal upheld the decision of the trial judge that a pager, mobile telephone, plastic bags and a small amount of money were admissible as part of the paraphernalia of drug dealing. The Court of Appeal emphasised that it is important to remember that the jury are concerned only with the question of whether the defendant intended to supply the drugs found in his possession to someone else. Evidence which is *merely* probative of propensity to commit an offence (such as evidence of past drug dealing) is inadmissible. However, evidence which is *also* relevant to the intention of the defendant as regards the drugs found in his possession is admissible. Therefore, if the defendant has money which the prosecution allege was the profit of an earlier supply of drugs, that money can be part of the evidence that he also intended to sell the drugs which were found in his possession. However, the jury must be directed that the money can only be regarded as evidence supporting the allegation that the defendant intended to sell the drugs in his possession if they first reject any explanation which the defendant puts forward for his possession of the money.

7.2.5 EXPERT EVIDENCE

As well as expert evidence proving that the substance in question is indeed a controlled drug (see **7.1**), a police officer in the drugs squad is entitled to give expert evidence on the street value of drugs and on the use of paraphernalia by drug dealers (e.g. giving evidence that certain equipment is commonly used by drug dealers to produce crack cocaine). However, in *Jeffries* [1997] Crim LR 819 it was held that a police officer was not entitled to say that, in her opinion, a list containing dates, names and figures related to the sale of drugs: to do so would amount to her giving as her opinion the fact that the defendant is guilty as charged.

7.3 Statutory Defences

The dicta on the meaning of possession set out in **7.2.4** must be related to the defences contained in the Misuse of Drugs Act 1971, s. 28. Section 28(2), which applies, *inter alia* to s. 4(2) and (3) and s. 5(2) and (3), creates the defence for the defendant to show (on the balance of probabilities) that 'he neither knew of nor suspected nor had any reason to suspect the existence of some fact alleged by the prosecution which it is necessary for the prosecution to prove if he is to be convicted of the offence charged'.

Section 28(3) further provides that where the prosecution have to prove that a particular substance was a controlled drug, it is *not* a defence for the defendant to show that he did not realise that it was the particular controlled drug alleged by the prosecution; however, it *is* a defence for the defendant to show that he did not realise (and could not reasonably have realised) that the substance was a controlled drug at all. So, it is a statutory defence to a charge of possession of cocaine to say 'I reasonably believed the substance to be aspirin' but it is not a defence to say 'I thought it was cannabis'.

In dealing with the relationship between the definition of possession (a matter for the prosecution to prove) and the s. 28 defence (whereof the burden rests on the defence), Lord Lane CJ in *McNamara* (**7.2.4**) considered the question of possession of the contents of a box. He said (at pp. 251–2) that the prosecution have the initial burden of proving that the defendant had, and knew he had, the box in his control and also that the box contained something. They must also prove that the box in fact contained the controlled drug alleged. The burden then passes to the defendant to show that the statutory defence in s. 28 applies.

The s. 28 defence is only available in respect of offences under the 1971 Act. It is not therefore available in a case where common law conspiracy is charged instead (*McGowan* [1990] Crim LR 399).

As well as the general defence in s. 28, s. 5(4) makes it a defence to a charge of being in possession of a controlled drug that the defendant was in possession of the drug in order to deliver it to someone who could lawfully take custody of it. The defendant bears the burden of proving this defence (on the balance of probabilities). The defence will only succeed if it is shown that the defendant's purpose was to act in accordance with s. 5(4) (*Dempsey* (1985) 82 Cr App R 291 (CA)).

7.4 Occupiers of Premises

Section 8 of the Misuse of Drugs Act 1971 applies to a person who is the occupier of premises or concerned in the management of the premises. The occupier is the person who has a legal right to exercise sufficient control over the premises as to be able to prevent the forbidden activities from taking place.

Such a person commits an offence if he or she knowingly permits or allows specified activities to take place on the premises including:

(a)   producing a controlled drug;

(b)   supplying/offering to supply a controlled drug;

(c)   smoking cannabis, cannabis resin or opium.

In *Bett* [1999] 1 All ER 600 the defendant was charged with permitting premises to be used for supplying a controlled drug (contrary to s. 8(b) of the Misuse of Drugs Act 1971). The trial judge directed the jury that it had to be proved that the defendant knowingly permitted the premises to be used for supplying *a* controlled drug but that it was not necessary to prove that he knew the particular identity or class of the drug that was in fact being supplied. The Court of Appeal upheld this direction.

7.5 Permitted Uses of Controlled Drugs

Many of the controlled drugs have legitimate medical uses (e.g. morphine, a class A drug, is a painkiller and drugs such as Lorazepam, Diazepam and Temazepam, all class C drugs, are very commonly prescribed sleeping tablets). So s. 7 of the 1971 Act requires the making of regulations to permit doctors, dentists, pharmacists and veterinary surgeons to produce and supply controlled drugs. The regulations in question are the Misuse of Drugs Regulations 1985 (SI 1985 No. 2066) (as amended). Effectively, these regulations permit the appropriate use of drugs for medicinal purposes or which are contained in a medicinal product.

Accordingly, one must first check sch. 2 of the Misuse of Drugs Act 1971 to see if the drug in question is a controlled drug and then check the 1985 Regulations to see if the particular use of the particular drug in question is authorised.

7.6 Enforcement

7.6.1 SEARCH AND SEIZURE

The Misuse of Drugs Act 1971, s. 23(2) says that a constable who has reasonable grounds to suspect that a person is in possession of a controlled drug may detain and search that person, stop and search a vehicle in which the constable suspects that drugs may be found, and seize and detain anything found in the course of the search which appears to be evidence of an offence under the Act. See also **Chapter 3**.

Section 23(3) empowers a justice of the peace to grant a search warrant if satisfied by information given on oath that there are reasonable grounds for suspecting that controlled drugs are on any premises, or that there is on the premises a document relating to unlawful dealing in controlled drugs.

7.6.2   PENALTIES: SENTENCING GUIDELINES

The maximum sentences are set out in the Misuse of Drugs Act 1971, sch. 4.

Cases involving class A drugs attract more severe sentences than those involving class B drugs, which in turn attract more severe sentences than cases involving class C drugs. Importation and production are generally regarded as the most serious offences, followed by supply and possession with intent to supply, followed by possession for personal use. A custodial sentence is usually appropriate for all drugs offences except those involving possession for personal use. All acts of supply are seen as serious. For example in *Luke* [1999] 1 Cr App R (S) 389, the defendant was a university student. He supplied cannabis to some friends. He made no profit from the transaction and the cannabis was intended for personal use by the recipients. The Court of Appeal held that a sentence of immediate custody was appropriate.

Factors relevant to determining the sentence include the following:

(a)   First and foremost, the type and quantity of the drug. The severest sentences are reserved for cases involving class A drugs (see *Richardson, The Times*, 18 March 1994, where the Lord Chief Justice speaks of the harm done by hard drugs). Guidelines in cases of importing drugs were laid down by the Court of Appeal in *Aramah* (1982) 76 Cr App R 190 and *Bilinski* (1987) 86 Cr App R 146. Those guidelines are based on the street value of the drug in question. However, in *Aranguren and others* (1994) 99 Cr App R 347 the Court of Appeal issued fresh guidelines for class A drugs, such as heroin and cocaine, to the effect that the sentence should be based on the weight of the drugs seized rather than their street value. The purity of the drug is to be taken into account in determining its weight. Guidelines for sentencing in cases involving Ecstasy were given in *Warren & Beeley* [1996] 1 Cr App R 120, for cases involving LSD in *Hurley* [1998] 1 Cr App R (S) 299, for cases involving importation of cannabis in *Ronchetti* [1998] Crim LR 227, and for cases involving importation of amphetamine in *Wijs* [1998] 2 Cr App R (S) 436. In *Chamberlain, The Independent*, 19 May 1997, the Court of Appeal said that being concerned in the management of premises used for the production of a controlled drug should, for sentencing purposes, be considered analogous to importing controlled drugs, thus attracting sentences at the higher end of the scale.

(b)   If the defendant has provided information to the authorities, this will result in a lower sentence (partly because it shows remorse). However, regard will be had to the actual value of the assistance and to the risk of possible reprisals faced by the offender or his family (*Richardson*, supra); the information must actually be useful to the authorities, assisting in the speedy arrest of other offenders and the prevention of further distribution of drugs (*M, The Times*, 1 March 1994).

(c)   The court must consider not only what the defendant in fact did, but also what he thought he was doing. If the defendant thinks he is importing cannabis when in fact it is heroin, the sentence should be reduced (*Bilinski*, supra). Similarly, if the defendant thinks he is importing high-quality heroin when in fact its purity is only 1%, the sentence will take account of the low purity of the heroin (*Afzal and Arshad, The Times*, 25 June 1991). In *Purcell* [1996] 1 Cr App R (S) 190 the appellant believed that he was carrying 'speed' (amphetamine sulphate, a class B drug). Later analysis showed that the substance was not, in fact, a controlled drug. He was convicted of attempting to import a controlled drug. In light of this (and the fact that he confessed at the earliest opportunity, and that, as a courier, he would have received very little profit) the Court of Appeal reduced his sentence from three years to two years.

(d) The degree of organisation and planning, and any steps taken to avoid detection will be relevant to the sentence (*Kouadio, The Times,* 21 February 1991).

(e) How 'high up in the drug operation' the defendant was is also relevant to the sentence (*Hussain, The Times,* 27 June 1990).

7.6.3 FORFEITURE

Section 27(1) of the 1971 Act allows the court to order forfeiture (and destruction, if appropriate) of 'anything shown to the satisfaction of the court to relate to the offence'. In *Cuthbertson* [1980] 2 All ER 401, Lord Diplock said (at p. 406) that forfeiture orders apply to 'tangible' items such as 'the drugs involved, apparatus for making them, vehicles used for transporting them [as in *Bowers* (1994) 15 Cr App R (S) 315], or cash ready to be, or having just been handed over for them'.

The point was made in *Cuthbertson* that the aim of forfeiture orders was not to strip drug traffickers of the profits of their crime. That objective is achieved instead through the Drug Trafficking Act 1994.

7.7 Drug Trafficking Act 1994

7.7.1 CONFISCATION ORDERS

The objective of this Act (which consolidates the Drug Trafficking Offences Act 1986 and the relevant provisions of the Criminal Justice Act 1993) is primarily to confiscate the proceeds of drug trafficking, and so remove the profit element. The Act empowers the Crown Court to make a confiscation order. The Crown Court may make such an order following conviction on indictment or upon a committal for sentence under s. 38 of the Magistrates' Courts Act 1980 (but not any other committal for sentence) (s. 2(7)). The procedure to be followed by the Court is set out in the Act itself and in the Crown Court (Amendment) (No. 2) Rules 1994 (SI 1994 No. 3153).

Where there are several defendants, each one must be considered separately to determine whether a confiscation order should be made and, if so, its amount (*Porter* (1990) 12 Cr App R (S) 377).

For the Act to apply, the defendant must have been convicted of a drug trafficking offence. Such offences are defined by s. 1(3) as including offences under ss. 4(2), 4(3) and 5(3) of the 1971 Act (production, supply and possession with intent to supply) or ss. 50(2) or (3) or 170 of the Customs and Excise Management Act 1979 (illegal import or export) (see **7.2**).

The Crown Court proceeds under the 1994 Act if the prosecutor asks it to do so or, even though the prosecutor has not asked the court to do so, the court considers that it is appropriate to proceed under the Act (s. 2(1)).

The court then has to determine (under s. 2(2)) whether the defendant has 'benefited from drug trafficking' (i.e. from the commission of the drug trafficking offences for which he or she is to be sentenced). Benefit is defined by s. 2(3) so as to mean receiving payment or other reward in connection with drug trafficking, whether carried on by the defendant or by someone else. In *Osei* (1988) 10 Cr App R (S) 289, it was held that 'payment' means any payment whether reward or to enable the defendant to deal in drugs. This means that money which the defendant has received and then spent in order to continue drug trafficking will still be regarded as part of the benefit received by the defendant; in other words the Act applies to gross receipts, not net profit. See also *Smith* [1989] 2 All ER 948 (at p. 951, per Lord Lane CJ) and *Banks* [1997] 2 Cr App R (S) 110. However, in assessing the value of the benefit received by the defendant, the court should not ignore the fact that some expenses must have been incurred (*Comiskey* (1990) Cr App R (S) 562). See also *Akengin* (1995) 16 Cr App R (S) 499, where a distinction was drawn between drugs which are a reward for drug trafficking carried on by the defendant, and drugs which were purchased with money obtained from earlier dealings and which were not a reward for past services.

In *Butler* [1993] Crim LR 320, it was held that if the court accepts that there is no history of drug trafficking and the drugs in respect of which the defendant has been convicted were purchased on a single occasion, it would be wrong to say that the defendant has benefited from drug trafficking; so a confiscation order cannot be made in such a case.

In *Berry, The Times*, 20 October 1999, the defendant was convicted of a drug trafficking offence and a confiscation order was made under the Drug Trafficking Act 1994. The Court of Appeal held that in the absence of any evidence from the defendant as to what he paid or received for drugs which he had been convicted of supplying, but where the only possible inference from the evidence was that he had supplied the drugs in bulk, it was not appropriate for the judge, in deciding the amount by which the defendant had benefited from the drug trafficking, to infer that he had received the street value of the drugs. Some discount from the street value fell, on the balance of probabilities, to be made to reflect the fact that the defendant was probably selling wholesale.

Where the court finds that the defendant has benefited from drug trafficking, it then has to consider the amount to be recovered (s. 2(4)).

It is for the prosecution to prove that the defendant has benefited from drug trafficking and the amount of the benefit. Section 2(8) of the Act provides that the standard of proof required to determine whether the defendant has benefited from drug trafficking (and, if so, the amount to be recovered by way of confiscation order) is the civil standard (i.e. the balance of probabilities). This provision reverses the decision of the Court of Appeal in *Dickens* [1990] 2 All ER 626, that the standard of proof required was the criminal standard.

The evidence on which this decision will be based will come in part from the trial, if there has been one, in part from the statements tendered by the parties to the court under s. 11 of the Act, and in part from evidence adduced before the court in a hearing to determine whether an order should be made under the 1994 Act.

7.7.2   STATUTORY ASSUMPTIONS

Under s. 4(2), in deciding whether the defendant has benefited from drug trafficking and, if so, in assessing the value of the defendant's proceeds (that is, under s. 4(1), the payments or other rewards received by the defendant in connection with drug trafficking by the defendant or another person), the court has to make a series of assumptions, set out in s. 4(3), unless s. 4(4) applies.

Section 4(2) says that the court 'shall' (i.e. must) make the assumptions. The effect of this is to reverse the decisions of the Court of Appeal in *Dickens* (**7.7.1**), *Redbourne* [1993] 2 All ER 753 and *Rose* [1993] 2 All ER 761, that there must be prima facie evidence that the defendant has benefited from drug trafficking before the assumptions or any of them can be made.

The assumptions which may be made by the court are contained in s. 4(3):

(a)   that any property—

    (i)   held by the defendant after the date of his or her conviction or

    (ii)   transferred to the defendant during the period of six years prior to the institution of the proceedings (i.e. the date of charge where the defendant was arrested without warrant, or the date of the issue of the arrest warrant where the defendant was arrested pursuant to a warrant)

    is a payment or reward for drug trafficking;

(b) that any expenditure by the defendant during the time set out in (a) was met out of payments received in connection with drug trafficking;

(c) that (for the purpose of valuing the property in question) no one but the defendant has an interest in the property.

In *Brett, The Times*, 13 October 1997, it was held that the rebuttable presumption which relates to any property held by the defendant at the time of his conviction applies even if the property was obtained more than six years before proceedings were commenced for the present offence.

In *Gooch (No. 2)* [1999] 1 Cr App R (S) 283, it was held that where the offence of which the defendant has been convicted is one which was added to the indictment under s. 2 of the Administration of Justice (Miscellaneous Provisions) Act 1933, the proceedings are to be regarded as having been instituted on the date when the defendant was first charged in the proceedings which eventually led to his conviction (not the date when the indictment was preferred).

Section 4(4) provides that the court shall not make any of the assumptions contained in s. 4(3) if either:

(a) that assumption is shown to be incorrect in the defendant's case; or

(b) the court is satisfied that there would be a serious risk of injustice to the defendant if the assumption were to be made.

It is for the defendant to show, on the balance of probabilities (*Redbourne*, above, at p. 759; *Dickens*, above, at p. 629), that the assumption is incorrect or would cause injustice. Each item of property and expenditure must be looked at separately, since the defendant may be able to rebut the assumption for some but not other items.

Lord Lane in *Dickens* went on to say that if any of the assumptions survive (i.e. are not rebutted by the defendant), 'they will, together with any evidence which the judge may accept, assist the judge to decide whether . . . the prosecution have made out their case' (pp. 629–30). In *Redbourne*, Staughton LJ (at p. 760) interpreted Lord Lane's words as dealing with two separate situations. If the defendant fails to rebut an assumption, then that assumption stands as fact and there is no need for further evidence as regards that item of property or expenditure. As regards items where assumptions have been rebutted or which were never covered by assumptions in the first place, the judge will have to ask if the evidence enables the conclusion that the particular item in question represents benefit from drug trafficking.

It is clear from all this that the benefit from drug trafficking caught by the Act is not confined to benefit derived from the offences of which the defendant has just been convicted.

In *Delaney and Hanrahan*, 14 May 1999, unreported, it was argued that similar assumptions under the confiscation provisions contained in the Criminal Justice Act 1988 infringe Article 6(2) of the European Convention on Human Rights. The Court of Appeal rejected this argument. It was held that the presumption of innocence is not violated where a defendant has the opportunity to rebut the assumptions.

In *Richards* [1992] 2 All ER 572, it was held by the Court of Appeal that a confiscation order cannot be made unless it is shown that the defendant knew that the payment or reward was received in connection with drug trafficking, since without such knowledge it could not be said that the defendant had benefited from the drug trafficking.

7.7.3 THE PROSECUTOR'S STATEMENT

As well as the assumptions contained in s. 4, there are also evidential provisions contained in s. 11 of the Act.

Section 11(1) of the Act requires the prosecutor to give to the court a statement of matters considered by the prosecution to be relevant in connection with determining whether the defendant has benefited from drug trafficking or assessing the value of the defendant's proceeds of drug trafficking. This statement ('the prosecutor's statement') may be followed by a further statement if necessary (s. 11(4)).

A copy of the statement must be served on the defendant (s. 11(5)). The court may then require the defendant:

(a) to indicate the extent to which he or she accepts each allegation in the statement, and

(b) so far as he or she does not accept any such allegation, to give particulars of any matters on which he or she proposes to rely.

Section 11(7) provides that if the defendant accepts an allegation in the prosecutor's statement, then that acceptance may be treated as conclusive. However, in *Emmett* [1997] 4 All ER 737, the House of Lords rejected the view of the Court of Appeal in *Tredwen* (1994) 99 Cr App R 154 that the acceptance is conclusive for all purposes. The House of Lords went on to hold that, despite s. 11(7), the Court of Appeal is entitled to entertain an appeal against a confiscation order where the basis of that appeal is that the defendant's acceptance of the allegations in the prosecutor's statement was induced by a mistake of law or fact.

In *Dickens* (per Lord Lane CJ, at p. 630), it was said that 'it is clear from these provisions that, where the prosecution statement is not accepted by the defendant, the prosecution, if they wish to rely on any of its contents, must adduce evidence to establish them'.

It should be noted that s. 11(8) provides that if the defendant fails to indicate which parts of the prosecutor's statement are accepted (and in so far as they are not accepted, giving an indication of matters which will be relied upon by the defence), the defendant may be treated as accepting any prosecution allegation in respect of which he or she has failed to comply with the requirements. This provision does not apply, however, to any allegation that the defendant has benefited from drug trafficking or that any payment received was received in connection with drug trafficking. This latter proviso (s. 11(8)(b)) is 'designed to preserve the defendant's right to rebut the assumption under s. 4(4) from the fact of the present holding of an asset or its transfer within six years prior to the institution of proceedings' (per Parker LJ in *Re Thomas* [1992] 4 All ER 814, at p. 818 *et seq*).

7.7.4 THE AMOUNT OF THE ORDER

Section 5(1) provides that the amount of the confiscation order shall be the court's assessment of the value of the defendant's proceeds of drug trafficking.

However, s. 5(3) goes on to say that if the court is satisfied that the amount that might be realised at the time the confiscation order is made is less than the value of the proceeds of drug trafficking, then the confiscation order shall be for the lesser (i.e. the realisable) amount (s. 5(3)(a)). If it appears (on the basis of the information presently before the court) that the amount which might be realised is nil, then the court should make a nominal confiscation order (s. 5(3)(b)).

In *Ilseman* (1990) 12 Cr App R (S) 408, it was held that s. 5(3) places a burden on the defence to show that the amount which might be realised is less than the value of the proceeds from drug trafficking (per Taylor LJ, at p. 404). Presumably the relevant burden, being on the defence, is on the balance of probabilities.

7.7.5 REALISABLE PROPERTY

The term 'realisable property' is defined in s. 6(2) as meaning '(a) any property held by the defendant, and (b) any property held by a person to whom the defendant has directly or indirectly made a gift caught by this Act'. Section 8(1) says that a gift is caught by the Act if it was made by the defendant at any time during the six years prior to the institution of the proceedings or else was a gift (whenever made) of property received by the defendant in connection with drug trafficking or otherwise representing benefit from drug trafficking.

'Gift' is defined in s. 8(2)(a) so as to include a transaction by which property is transferred by the defendant at significantly less than its true value.

Section 6(5)(a) says that property is held by any person if he or she holds any interest in it. So any property in which the defendant has an interest at the time of conviction will be regarded as proceeds of drug trafficking unless the defendant can show the contrary. 'If at the time of her conviction, the defendant is in possession of property or has a sufficient control over it to be able to dispose of it, it can be assumed in the absence of contrary evidence to be her proceeds of drug trafficking' (per Glidewell LJ in *Chrastny (No. 2)* [1992] 1 All ER 193, at p. 199). Thus, if property is owned by the defendant and someone else (e.g. a spouse) who is not a co-defendant, a confiscation order may be made in respect of the whole of the property (see p. 201).

The practical effect of this is that the court can order the sale of jointly owned property. The defendant's interest (i.e. share) in that property will then be confiscated. In *Gregory, The Times*, 31 October 1995, the Court of Appeal emphasised the need for caution where a confiscation order is being made in respect of a jointly owned matrimonial home. Great care must be taken to assess the extent of the defendant's interest in the proceeds of sale and regard must be had to the costs likely to be incurred in effecting the sale; where the defendant's family is still in occupation, the court should consider whether it is appropriate to make an immediate order for sale.

Where assets are jointly owned, the appropriate course is for the court to start by considering the value of the beneficial interests of the defendant and the co-owners (in the same way as the court assesses the value of beneficial interests when ordering the sale of land which is subject to a trust for sale). The court should then go on to decide whether there are any gifts caught by the anti-avoidance provisions in s. 6 of the Act. See *Buckman* [1997] Crim LR 67.

However, where the property is owned jointly by two co-defendants, the proper course is to make two separate confiscation orders so as to apportion the confiscation between the two defendants; a single joint confiscation order would be unlawful (*Porter* [1990] 3 All ER 784, at p. 786).

Section 6(1) says that in putting a value on the amount of property that may be realised, the court should take the total value of all realisable property held by the defendant at the time of the confiscation order, less the total value of any obligations having priority at that time (e.g. a mortgage), together with the total value of gifts caught by the Act.

In *Chrastny (No. 2)* it was held that realisable property included legitimately acquired property. All the court has to do is to decide what profit the defendant has made out of drug trafficking and what assets (however acquired) are presently available so as to confiscate the profit made. '[T]he statute seeks to ensure that anybody who has benefited from drug trafficking shall to the extent to which he or she can do so be deprived of the whole of that benefit' (Glidewell LJ, ibid., p. 202).

In other words, realisable property means all property currently owned by the defendant and property formerly owned by the defendant but disposed of without proper consideration, whether that property was acquired through drug trafficking or not.

In *Harvey, The Times*, 14 October 1998, the Court of Appeal had to consider a case where the Crown Court was determining the amount of realisable property owned by a defendant for the purposes of a confiscation order under s. 74 of the Criminal Justice Act 1988. The provisions of the 1988 Act are very similar to those of the Drug Trafficking Act 1994. It was held that the court has to make findings on matters which may not be certain, for example the market value of property in which the defendant has an interest and the amount required to discharge any incumbrance on that interest: this includes consideration of whether the incumbrance might not be enforced for any reason.

The value of any drugs seized from the defendant cannot be regarded as realisable property (*Thacker* (1995) 16 Cr App R (S) 461). Similarly, in *Satchell* [1996] 2 Cr App R (S) 258, the Court of Appeal said that the sentencer had rightly assumed that the cost of the drugs found in the offender's possession was to be regarded as part of the value of his proceeds from drug trafficking. However, the Court went on to hold that, when applying the statutory assumptions the court had to take account of the fact that nothing could be realised from the proceeds of drugs which were about to be forfeited (on the ground of double jeopardy). This latter aspect was disapproved in *Dore* [1997] 2 Cr App R (S) 152. In that case it held that where drugs are found in the offender's possession and they were purchased with the proceeds of earlier drug trafficking, there is no principle of double jeopardy which requires the court to leave that amount out of account when assessing the value of the offender's benefit from drug trafficking.

7.7.6 POSTPONED DETERMINATIONS

Under s. 3(1) of the Act, where the court requires further information before determining whether the defendant has benefited from drug trafficking or determining the amount to be recovered under the Act, it may postpone making the determination for such period as it may specify. There may be more than one postponement, if the information is not available when expected (s. 3(2)). The total postponement should not exceed six months from the date of conviction, unless there are exceptional circumstances (s. 3(3)). This postponement may be sought by the prosecutor, the defence or may be made by the court of its own motion (s. 3(5)). Where the defendant is appealing against conviction, determination may be postponed, this time for a maximum of three months (unless there are exceptional circumstances) from the disposal of the appeal (s. 3(4) and (6)). See *Coles, The Independent*, 30 April 1998.

Where the court exercises its discretion to postpone determining the application of the Act, it may nevertheless proceed to sentence the defendant for the offences of which he has been convicted, although if the court does so it must not impose a fine or make a forfeiture order, since these orders might nullify the effect of a confiscation order (s. 3(7) and (9)).

7.7.7 PROCEDURE

The procedure for a hearing under the Drug Trafficking Act 1994 is as follows:

(a) If the defendant accepts in full the contents of the prosecutor's s. 11 statement, the court makes an order in the terms sought by the prosecution.

(b) If the defendant disputes material particulars in the prosecutor's statement, the prosecutor will make a brief opening speech and will then call evidence. Usually it is the police officer who prepared the s. 11 statement who will be called to give evidence. The defence may, of course, cross-examine any witnesses called by the Crown. The defendant may then give evidence (subject to cross-examination by the prosecution) and may call other witnesses. Counsel for the prosecution and the defence may then address the court and the judge will come to a decision.

In summary, the issues which have to be determined before a confiscation order can be made are as follows:

1. Has the defendant been convicted by the Crown Court or committed by the magistrates' court to be sentenced in respect of a drug trafficking offence? If so, proceed to 2.

2. Has the defendant benefited from drug trafficking? If so, proceed to 3.

3. What is the value of that benefit?

4. Does that value exceed the realisable assets against which an order can be made? If not, make an order for the sum found in 3; if so, make an order for the amount of the realisable assets.

7.7.8 ENFORCEMENT

Section 9(1) of the Act provides that a confiscation order is enforceable in the same way as a fine imposed by the Crown Court (so that the defendant will go to prison if the order is not satisfied). The Crown Court must fix a term of imprisonment in default (using the table set out in the Powers of Criminal Courts Act 1973, s. 31(3A)) (*Popple* (1992) 14 Cr App R (S) 60). As with a fine, the court may allow time to pay and may direct payment by instalments. In *Ellis, The Times*, 25 March 1996, it was held by the Court of Appeal that the confiscation order is valid even if the court fails to observe the mandatory requirement of fixing a term of imprisonment in default of payment.

If the amount due under the confiscation order is not paid, a magistrates' court will be asked to issue a warrant compelling the attendance of the defendant (who will usually have to be produced from prison since most defendants convicted of drug trafficking offences receive custodial sentences). The justices must consider the defendant's means before committing him to prison for non-payment under the confiscation order as it may be that the value of the defendant's realisable assets has gone down or that the confiscation order could be enforced in some other way (*Harrow Justices, ex parte DPP* [1991] 3 All ER 873). A term of imprisonment for non-payment of the confiscation order will be served after the defendant has completed the custodial sentence imposed for the original offence (s. 9(2)).

In *Liverpool Justices, ex parte Ansen* [1998] 1 All ER 692 it was held by the Divisional Court that where the offender fails to satisfy a confiscation order made under the Drug Trafficking Act 1994, the magistrates should give the prosecution an opportunity to make representations at the means inquiry which has to take place before the defendant can be committed to prison for his or her default. The Court went on to hold that, for the purposes of this legislation, the fact that an asset might be difficult to realise is not relevant.

Section 9(5) provides that if the defendant serves a term of imprisonment in default of paying any amount under a confiscation order, this will not prevent the confiscation order from continuing in effect as far as other methods of enforcement are concerned — so the money is still regarded as due and owing.

7.7.9 ANCILLARY POWERS CONFERRED BY THE 1994 ACT

Section 25 of the Drug Trafficking Act 1994 provides that where proceedings in respect of a drug trafficking offence have been instituted against a defendant but those proceedings have not been concluded (or the defendant is about to be charged with a drug trafficking offence) and there is reasonable cause to believe that the defendant has benefited from drug trafficking, then the High Court may make a restraint order or a charging order.

7.7.9.1 Restraint order

A restraint order, which is sought (under s. 26) by the prosecution on an *ex parte* application to a judge in chambers, prohibits any person from dealing with the property covered by the order. The order applies to 'realisable property', which term is defined in s. 6 of the Act (see **7.7.5**). The restraint order must be discharged at the conclusion of the proceedings.

7.7.9.2 Charging order

The other power available to the High Court is to make a charging order. This power, conferred by s. 27 of the Act, applies both before and after the making of a confiscation order. Again, the application is made *ex parte* by the prosecution to a judge in chambers. The order operates in the same way as a charging order made in civil proceedings and is a means of securing payment. It applies to land and to stock of companies (other than building societies) incorporated in England and Wales. The charging order must be discharged at the conclusion of the proceedings or if a payment into court is made to cover the sum secured by the charging order.

7.7.9.3 Appointment of a receiver

Under s. 29 of the Act, where a restraint order or a charging order or a confiscation order has been made, the court may also appoint a receiver to take possession of or manage property to which the order applies, and to realise that property so as to enforce the confiscation order.

7.7.9.4 Disclosure by defendant of assets

In *Re Thomas (disclosure order)* [1992] 4 All ER 814, the Court of Appeal (Civil Division) held that the High Court, when making a restraint order under s. 26 of the Act, preventing the defendant from dealing with assets, had power also to make an order requiring the defendant to swear an affidavit disclosing the full value, nature and whereabouts of all his or her assets so as to render the restraint order effective. To take account of the privilege against self-incrimination it would be made a condition of the order for disclosure that nothing said by the defendant in compliance with the order was to be used as evidence in the prosecution of an offence alleged to have been committed by the defendant.

7.7.10 OTHER PROVISIONS

The Drug Trafficking Act 1994, s. 32 deals with the situation where the defendant is adjudged bankrupt; s. 19 deals with the situation where the defendant has died or absconded. The detail of these provisions is beyond the scope of this Manual.

7.7.11 REVISITING THE QUESTION OF CONFISCATION

Section 13 of the Drug Trafficking Act 1994 provides that where the court did not proceed under s. 2 of the Act but new evidence has come to light which the prosecution believe would have led the court to do so had that evidence been available earlier, the prosecution may apply for a confiscation order (s. 13(2)). No application may be made later than six years following the date of the defendant's conviction (s. 13(10)).

The court will consider making an order if it is appropriate, in all the circumstances of the case, to do so. In such a case, regard must be had to any fine which has been imposed on the defendant in respect of the original offence(s) (s. 13(6)). Section 13(8) states that the court may take account of any payment or reward received by the defendant since conviction, but only if the prosecution can show (on the civil standard) that it was received by the defendant in connection with drug trafficking carried on before that date.

Section 14 of the 1994 Act says that where the court decided that the defendant had not benefited from drug trafficking, the prosecution may apply to the Crown Court to reconsider this question if there is new evidence which the prosecution believe would enable the court to conclude that the defendant had in fact benefited from drug trafficking. The court would then go on to consider the amount to be recovered from the defendant. No application may be made more than six years after the date of the defendant's conviction (s. 14(7)).

Section 15 of the 1994 Act enables the prosecution to ask the Crown Court to reconsider the value of the defendant's proceeds from drug trafficking if there is evidence to suggest that the value was greater than that originally assessed by the court. The court may increase the amount payable under the confiscation order if it agrees with the contentions of the prosecution. The value may be greater either because the real value was higher than the court appreciated on the first occasion or because the value of the proceeds has subsequently increased (s. 15(4)). Payments received by the defendant since the date of the first order may be taken into account, but only if the prosecution show that the payment was received by the defendant in connection with drug trafficking carried on before that date (s. 15(10)). The prosecution can apply only within the period of six years from the date of the original conviction (s. 15(15)).

Section 16 of the Drug Trafficking Act 1994 applies where a confiscation order is made under the Drug Trafficking Act 1994 for an amount which is less than the amount by which the offender is held to have benefited from the drug trafficking, because his realisable assets are less than the amount of that benefit. The section allows the prosecution to apply to the High Court for a certificate that the realisable amount is greater than the amount originally specified by the court in the confiscation order. This would normally be used where the offender is found to have assets which were not discovered at the original determination. However, in *Tivnan* [1999] 1 Cr App R (S), it was held that the prosecution can apply to the court for an increase in the amount of the order if the offender acquires assets after the original order was made, even if there is no evidence that those assets were acquired by criminal means. The Court also confirmed that there is no time limit within which such an application may be made.

The Drug Trafficking Act 1994, s. 17, allows the defendant to make an application to the High Court for a certificate that the realisable property now available to the defendant is insufficient to meet the outstanding amount of the confiscation order. If the High Court is satisfied that this is the case, it will issue a certificate. The defendant may then apply to the Crown Court for a reduction in the amount of the order to such lesser amount as the Crown Court thinks just in all the circumstances of the case.

In *Re S, The Times*, 1 November 1994, Dyson J held that an application for variation involves a two-stage process. First, the court has to decide whether the value of the defendant's realisable property, at the time of the application, is adequate to pay the amount still due under the confiscation order. Any assets which the defendant has dissipated are not included in this valuation. If the value of the defendant's realisable assets is insufficient to meet the balance due under the confiscation order, the court goes to the second stage. The second stage enables the court to consider whether a variation of the order is required in the interests of fairness; where the defendant has dissipated assets since the original order was made, the court can (at this stage) consider the reason for that dissipation.

7.7.12 RELATIONSHIP BETWEEN CONFISCATION ORDER AND OTHER SENTENCE

The confiscation order is regarded as a sentence for the purpose of the defendant being able to appeal to the Court of Appeal, but in addition to making a confiscation order, the court should impose some other sentence too. See *Johnson* (1990) 91 Cr App R 332.

If information about drugs offences other than those in respect of which the defendant is to be sentenced comes to light during the course of the enquiry as to the making of a confiscation order (which precedes the passing of sentence), the information about the commission of other offences is irrelevant to the sentence to be imposed unless the defendant asks for those other offences to be taken into consideration, or accepts that the offences of which he has been convicted are examples of a larger number of offences, or they make the present offence(s) more serious by showing, for example, planning or the hallmarks of professionalism. See *Bragason* (1988) 10 Cr App R (S) 258 (at p. 261, per McCullough J). The judge may take the view from the evidence called in respect of the confiscation order that the offence(s) of which the defendant has been convicted are not isolated, depriving the defendant of the argument in mitigation of sentence that the conviction is in respect of an isolated incident (*Harper* (1989) 11 Cr App R (S) 240 per Farquarson J, at p. 243).

According to s. 2(5)(c) of the 1994 Act, having made the confiscation order, the court should disregard its effect when deciding on the appropriate sentence for the offence(s) of which the defendant has been convicted. However, s. 2(5)(b) provides that account should be taken of the confiscation order before a fine or other order involving payment of money by the defendant is made. It follows that if all the defendant's assets are to be made the subject of a confiscation order, the confiscation order should nevertheless be made and a fine would then be wrong in principle.

EIGHT

PUBLIC ORDER OFFENCES

8.1   Introduction

Offences relating to public order have been created by a number of statutes. The main statutes dealt with in this chapter are the Criminal Law Act 1977, the Sporting Events (Control of Alcohol etc.) Act 1985, the Public Order Act 1986, the Football Spectators Act 1989, the Football (Offences) Act 1991, the Criminal Justice and Public Order Act 1994 and the Crime and Disorder Act 1998.

8.2   Riot

Riot is the most serious offence against public order and is triable only on indictment. It is defined by the Public Order Act 1986, s. 1, as follows:

> *(1)   Where 12 or more persons who are present together use or threaten unlawful violence for a common purpose and the conduct of them (taken together) is such as would cause a person of reasonable firmness present at the scene to fear for his personal safety, each of the persons using unlawful violence for the common purpose is guilty of riot.*
> *(2)   It is immaterial whether or not the 12 or more use or threaten unlawful violence simultaneously.*
> *(3)   The common purpose may be inferred from conduct.*
> *(4)   No person of reasonable firmness need actually be, or be likely to be, present at the scene.*
> *(5)   Riot may be committed in private as well as in public places.*

Section 1(6) of the Act provides for a maximum penalty of a term of 10 years, or a fine or both.

Section 6(1) of the Act provides that a person is guilty of riot only if he intends to use violence or is aware that his conduct may be violent. Section 6(7) provides that s. 6(1) does not affect the determination for the purposes of riot of the number of persons who use or threaten violence, thus one of 12 or more persons may be guilty of riot even though the *mens rea* of riot cannot be proved against the remaining persons.

As for aiding and abetting, see *Jefferson, Skerritt, Keogh and Readman* [1994] 1 All ER 270.

'Violence' is defined in s. 8 of the Act as follows:

> *In this Part—*
>   *. . .*
>   *'violence' means any violent conduct, so that—*
>   *(a)   except in the context of affray, it includes violent conduct towards property as well as violent conduct towards persons, and*

(b)   it is not restricted to conduct causing or intended to cause injury or damage but includes any other violent conduct (for example, throwing at or towards a person a missile of a kind capable of causing injury which does not hit or falls short).

The Act makes special provision for the intoxicated defendant in s. 6(5) and (6) as follows:

(5)   For the purposes of this section a person whose awareness is impaired by intoxication shall be taken to be aware of that of which he would be aware if not intoxicated, unless he shows either that his intoxication was not self-induced or that it was caused solely by the taking or administration of a substance in the course of medical treatment.

(6)   In subsection (5) 'intoxication' means any intoxication, whether caused by drink, drugs or other means, or by a combination of means.

8.3   Violent Disorder

Violent disorder is an offence which is triable either way. Section 2(5) of the Public Order Act 1986 provides that it is punishable on indictment with a term of five years, or a fine or both, or on summary conviction, with six months' imprisonment, or a fine not exceeding the statutory maximum or both.

The offence is defined in s. 2 of the Act as follows:

(1)   Where three or more persons who are present together use or threaten unlawful violence and the conduct of them (taken together) is such as would cause a person of reasonable firmness present at the scene to fear for his personal safety, each of the persons using or threatening unlawful violence is guilty of violent disorder.

(2)   It is immaterial whether or not the three or more use or threaten unlawful violence simultaneously.

(3)   No person of reasonable firmness need actually be, or be likely to be, present at the scene.

(4)   Violent disorder may be committed in private as well as in public places.

There is no need for a common purpose. Each of at least three persons must be using or threatening unlawful violence. See *Mahroof* (1989) 88 Cr App R 317, *Fleming* (1989) 153 JP 517, *Worton* (1990) 154 JP 201, *McGuigan* [1991] Crim LR 719, *Rothwell and Barton* [1993] Crim LR 626.

8.4   Affray

Affray is an offence which is triable either way. Section 3(7) of the Public Order Act 1986 provides that it is punishable on indictment with a term of three years, or a fine or both, or on summary conviction, with six months' imprisonment, or a fine not exceeding the statutory maximum or both.

The offence is defined in s. 3 of the Act as follows:

(1)   A person is guilty of affray if he uses or threatens unlawful violence towards another and his conduct is such as would cause a person of reasonable firmness present at the scene to fear for his personal safety.

(2)   Where two or more persons use or threaten the unlawful violence, it is the conduct of them taken together that must be considered for the purposes of subsection (1).

(3)   For the purposes of this section a threat cannot be made by the use of words alone.

(4)   No person of reasonable firmness need actually be, or be likely to be, present at the scene.

(5)   Affray may be committed in private as well as in public places.

(6)   A constable may arrest without warrant anyone he reasonably suspects is committing affray.

In the context of this offence, 'violence' relates to persons and does not include violent conduct towards property. See s. 8 and *Davison* [1992] Crim LR 31, *Charles* (1989) 11 Cr App R (S) 125, *Walsh* (1990) 12 Cr App R (S) 243, *DPP* v *Cotcher* [1993] COD 181, *Dixon* [1993] Crim LR 579, *Robinson* [1993] Crim LR 581 and *Stanley and Knight* [1993] Crim LR 618. Note further that it is the 'hypothetical, reasonable bystander who must be put in fear for his personal safety, not the victim himself', per Simon Brown LJ in *Sanchez* (1996) 160 JP 321 at p. 323.

See further, *Thind* [1999] Crim LR 842, where the Court of Appeal held that the conviction was not unsafe even though the judge's summing up had not made it sufficiently clear that the person put in fear had to be the hypothetical bystander.

8.5 Fear or Provocation of Violence

The offence under s. 4 of the Public Order Act 1986 is triable summarily only and is punishable with six months' imprisonment, or a fine not exceeding level 5 or both. The offence is defined as follows:

> (1) *A person is guilty of an offence if he—*
> (a) *uses towards another person threatening, abusive or insulting words or behaviour, or*
> (b) *distributes or displays to another person any writing, sign or other visible representation which is threatening, abusive or insulting,*
> *with intent to cause that person to believe that immediate unlawful violence will be used against him or another by any person, or to provoke the immediate use of unlawful violence by that person or another, or whereby that person is likely to believe that such violence will be used or it is likely that such violence will be provoked.*
> (2) *An offence under this section may be committed in a public or a private place, except that no offence is committed where the words or behaviour are used, or the writing, sign or other visible representation is distributed or displayed, by a person inside a dwelling and the other person is also inside that or another dwelling.*
> (3) *A constable may arrest without warrant anyone he reasonably suspects is committing an offence under this section.*

The four ways in which the offence may be committed were set out in *Winn* v *DPP* (1992) 156 JP 881. See also *Loade* v *DPP* [1990] 1 QB 1052, *Horseferry Road Metropolitan Stipendiary Magistrate, ex parte Siadatan* [1991] 1 QB 260, *O'Brien* [1993] Crim LR 70, *Afzal* [1993] Crim LR 791, *Rukwira and others* v *DPP* [1993] Crim LR 882 and *Swanston* v *DPP, The Times*, 23 January 1997.

8.5.1 INTENTIONAL HARASSMENT, ALARM OR DISTRESS

The offence under s. 4A of the Public Order Act 1986 is triable summarily only and is punishable with six months' imprisonment, or a fine not exceeding level 5, or both. The offence is defined as follows:

> **4A.**—*(1) A person is guilty of an offence if, with intent to cause a person harassment, alarm or distress, he—*
> (a) *uses threatening, abusive or insulting words or behaviour, or disorderly behaviour, or*
> (b) *displays any writing, sign or other visible representation which is threatening, abusive or insulting,*
> *thereby causing that or another person harassment, alarm or distress.*
> (2) *An offence under this section may be committed in a public or a private place, except that no offence is committed where the words or behaviour are used, or the writing, sign or other visible representation is displayed, by a person inside a dwelling and the person who is harassed, alarmed or distressed is also inside that or another dwelling.*
> [(3) provides a specific defence.]

(4)   A constable may arrest without warrant anyone he reasonably suspects is committing an offence under this section.

(5)   A person guilty of an offence under this section is liable on summary conviction to imprisonment for a term not exceeding 6 months or a fine not exceeding level 5 on the standard scale or both.

The following statutory defence is provided in s. 4A(3) as follows:

(3)   It is a defence for the accused to prove—

(a)   that he was inside a dwelling and had no reason to believe that the words or behaviour used, or the writing, sign or other visible representation displayed, would be heard or seen by a person outside that or any other dwelling, or

(b)   that his conduct was reasonable.

Note: Section 4A of the Public Order Act 1986 has been inserted by s. 154 of the Criminal Justice and Public Order Act 1994 (CJPOA 1994).

8.6   Harassment, Alarm or Distress

The offence under s. 5 of the Public Order Act 1986 is triable summarily only and is punishable with a fine not exceeding level 3. The offence is defined as follows:

(1)   A person is guilty of an offence if he—

(a)   uses threatening, abusive or insulting words or behaviour, or disorderly behaviour, or

(b)   displays any writing, sign or other visible representation which is threatening, abusive or insulting,
within the hearing or sight of a person likely to be caused harassment, alarm or distress thereby.

[(2) and (3) concern the place of commission of the offence and a specific defence.]

(4)   A constable may arrest a person without warrant if—

(a)   he engages in offensive conduct which a constable warns him to stop, and

(b)   he engages in further offensive conduct immediately or shortly after the warning.

(5)   In subsection (4) 'offensive conduct' means conduct the constable reasonably suspects to constitute an offence under this section, and the conduct mentioned in paragraph (a) and the further conduct need not be of the same nature.

See *Lodge* v *DPP, The Times*, 26 October 1988, *DPP* v *Orum* [1989] 1 WLR 88, *Ball* (1990) 90 Cr App R 378, *Chappell* v *DPP* (1989) 89 Cr App R 82, *Groom* v *DPP* [1991] Crim LR 713, *DPP* v *Clarke* (1992) 94 Cr App R 359, *Chambers and Edwards* v *DPP* [1995] Crim LR 896 and *Vigon* v *DPP* (1998) 162 JP 115.

A specific defence is set out in s. 5(3) as follows:

(3)   It is a defence for the accused to prove—

(a)   that he had no reason to believe that there was any person within hearing or sight who was likely to be caused harassment, alarm or distress, or

(b)   that he was inside a dwelling and had no reason to believe that the words or behaviour used, or the writing, sign or other visible representation displayed, would be heard or seen by a person outside that or any other dwelling, or

(c)   that his conduct was reasonable.

See *Kwasi Poku* v *DPP* [1993] Crim LR 705 and *Morrow and others* v *DPP and others* [1994] Crim LR 58.

8.7   Racially Aggravated Public Order Offences

Section 31 of the Crime and Disorder Act 1998 creates racially aggravated public order offences. The offences are defined as follows:

31.—(1)   A person is guilty of an offence under this section if he commits—

(a)   an offence under section 4 of the Public Order Act 1986 (fear or provocation of violence);

(b)   an offence under section 4A of that Act (intentional harassment, alarm or distress); or

(c)   an offence under section 5 of that Act (harassment, alarm or distress), which is racially aggravated for the purposes of this section.

(2)   A constable may arrest without warrant anyone whom he reasonably suspects to be committing an offence falling within subsection (1)(a) or (b) above.

(3)   A constable may arrest a person without warrant if—

(a)   he engages in conduct which a constable reasonably suspects to constitute an offence falling within subsection (1)(c) above;

(b)   he is warned by that constable to stop; and

(c)   he engages in further such conduct immediately or shortly after the warning. The conduct mentioned in paragraph (a) above and the further conduct need not be of the same nature.

(4)   A person guilty of an offence falling within subsection (1)(a) or (b) above shall be liable—

(a)   on summary conviction, to imprisonment for a term not exceeding six months or to a fine not exceeding the statutory maximum, or to both;

(b)   on conviction on indictment, to imprisonment for a term not exceeding two years or to a fine, or to both.

(5)   A person guilty of an offence falling within subsection (1)(c) above shall be liable on summary conviction to a fine not exceeding level 4 on the standard scale.

(6)   If, on the trial on indictment of a person charged with an offence falling within subsection (1)(a) or (b) above, the jury find him not guilty of the offence charged, they may find him guilty of the basic offence mentioned in that provision.

(7)   For the purposes of subsection (1)(c) above, section 28(1)(a) above shall have effect as if the person likely to be caused harassment, alarm or distress were the victim of the offence.

8.8   Offences of Stirring Up Racial Hatred

Sections 18 to 23 of the Public Order Act 1986 create six distinct offences. They are triable either way and are punishable on indictment with a term of two years' imprisonment or a fine or both, or on summary conviction, with six months' imprisonment, or a fine not exceeding the statutory maximum or both. Proceedings require the consent of the Attorney-General (s. 27(3)).

8.8.1   USE OF WORDS OR BEHAVIOUR OR DISPLAY OF WRITTEN MATERIAL STIRRING UP RACIAL HATRED

The s. 18 offence is defined as follows:

(1)   A person who uses threatening, abusive or insulting words or behaviour, or displays any written material which is threatening, abusive or insulting, is guilty of an offence if—

(a)   he intends thereby to stir up racial hatred, or

(b)   having regard to all the circumstances racial hatred is likely to be stirred up thereby.

'Racial hatred' is defined by s. 17 as follows:

In this part 'racial hatred' means hatred against a group of persons in Great Britain defined by reference to colour, race, nationality (including citizenship) or ethnic or national origins.

The *mens rea* of the offence is referred to in s. 18(5):

A person who is not shown to have intended to stir up racial hatred is not guilty of an offence under this section if he did not intend his words or behaviour, or the written material, to be, and was not aware that it might be, threatening, abusive or insulting.

Section 18(2) stipulates where the offence may be committed and s. 18(4) sets out a statutory defence:

> *(2) An offence under this section may be committed in a public or a private place, except that no offence is committed where the words or behaviour are used, or the written material is displayed, by a person inside a dwelling and are not heard or seen except by other persons in that or another dwelling.*
>
> *(4) In proceedings for an offence under this section it is a defence for the accused to prove that he was inside a dwelling and had no reason to believe that the words or behaviour used, or the written material displayed, would be heard or seen by a person outside that or any other dwelling.*

8.8.2 PUBLISHING OR DISTRIBUTING WRITTEN MATERIAL STIRRING UP RACIAL HATRED

The Public Order Act 1986, s. 19 offence is defined as follows:

> *(1) A person who publishes or distributes written material which is threatening, abusive or insulting is guilty of an offence if—*
> *(a) he intends thereby to stir up racial hatred, or*
> *(b) having regard to all the circumstances racial hatred is likely to be stirred up thereby.*

This offence is an arrestable offence in accordance with s. 24(2) of the Police and Criminal Evidence Act 1984 (s. 155 of the CJPOA 1994).

8.8.3 PUBLIC PERFORMANCE OF PLAY STIRRING UP RACIAL HATRED

The Public Order Act 1986, s. 20 offence is defined as follows:

> *(1) If a public performance of a play is given which involves the use of threatening, abusive or insulting words or behaviour, any person who presents or directs the performance is guilty of an offence if—*
> *(a) he intends thereby to stir up racial hatred, or*
> *(b) having regard to all the circumstances (and, in particular, taking the performance as a whole) racial hatred is likely to be stirred up thereby.*

The following statutory defences are provided in s. 20:

> *(2) If a person presenting or directing the performance is not shown to have intended to stir up racial hatred, it is a defence for him to prove—*
> *(a) that he did not know and had no reason to suspect that the performance would involve the use of the offending words or behaviour, or*
> *(b) that he did not know and had no reason to suspect that the offending words or behaviour were threatening, abusive or insulting, or*
> *(c) that he did not know and had no reason to suspect that the circumstances in which the performance would be given would be such that racial hatred would be likely to be stirred up.*
>
> *(3) This section does not apply to a performance given solely or primarily for one or more of the following purposes—*
> *(a) rehearsal,*
> *(b) making a recording of the performance, or*
> *(c) enabling the performance to be included in a programme service,*
> *but if it is proved that the performance was attended by persons other than those directly concerned with the giving of the performance or the doing in relation to it of the things mentioned in paragraph (b) or (c), the performance shall, unless the contrary is shown, be taken not to have been given solely for the purposes mentioned above.*
>
> *(4) For the purposes of this section—*
> *(a) a person shall not be treated as presenting a performance of a play by reason only of his taking part in it as a performer,*

(b) a person taking part as a performer in a performance directed by another shall be treated as a person who directed the performance if without reasonable excuse he performs otherwise than in accordance with that person's direction, and

(c) a person shall be taken to have directed a performance of a play given under his direction notwithstanding that he was not present during the performance;

and a person shall not be treated as aiding or abetting the commission of an offence under this section by reason only of his taking part in a performance as a performer.

8.8.4 DISTRIBUTING, SHOWING OR PLAYING A RECORDING STIRRING UP RACIAL HATRED

The Public Order Act 1986, s. 21 offence is defined as follows:

(1) A person who distributes, or shows or plays, a recording of visual images or sounds which are threatening, abusive or insulting is guilty of an offence if—

(a) he intends thereby to stir up racial hatred, or

(b) having regard to all the circumstances racial hatred is likely to be stirred up thereby.

The following statutory defence is provided in s. 21:

(3) In proceedings for an offence under this section it is a defence for an accused who is not shown to have intended to stir up racial hatred to prove that he was not aware of the content of the recording and did not suspect, and had no reason to suspect, that it was threatening, abusive or insulting.

(4) This section does not apply to the showing or playing of a recording solely for the purpose of enabling the recording to be included in a programme service.

8.8.5 BROADCASTING OR INCLUDING PROGRAMME IN CABLE PROGRAMME SERVICE STIRRING UP RACIAL HATRED

The Public Order Act 1986, s. 22 offence is defined as follows:

(1) If a programme involving threatening, abusive or insulting visual images or sound is included in a programme service, each of the persons mentioned in subsection (2) is guilty of an offence if—

(a) he intends to stir up racial hatred, or

(b) having regard to all the circumstances racial hatred is likely to be stirred up thereby.

(2) The persons are—

(a) the person providing the programme service,

(b) any person by whom the programme is produced or directed, and

(c) any person by whom offending words or behaviour are used.

The following statutory defences are provided in s. 22:

(3) If the person providing the service, or a person by whom the programme was produced or directed, is not shown to have intended to stir up racial hatred, it is a defence for him to prove that—

(a) he did not know and had no reason to suspect that the programme would involve the offending material, and

(b) having regard to the circumstances in which the programme was included in a programme service, it was not reasonably practicable for him to secure the removal of the material.

(4) It is a defence for a person by whom the programme was produced or directed who is not shown to have intended to stir up racial hatred to prove that he did not know and had no reason to suspect—

(a) that the programme would be included in a programme service, or

(b) that the circumstances in which the programme would be so included would be such that racial hatred would be likely to be stirred up.

(5) It is a defence for a person by whom offending words or behaviour were used and who is not shown to have intended to stir up racial hatred to prove that he did not know and had no reason to suspect—

(a) that a programme involving the use of the offending material would be included in a programme service, or

(b) that the circumstances in which a programme involving the use of the offending material would be so included, or in which a programme so included would involve the use of the offending material, would be such that racial hatred would be likely to be stirred up.

(6) A person who is not shown to have intended to stir up racial hatred is not guilty of an offence under this section if he did not know, and had no reason to suspect, that the offending material was threatening, abusive or insulting.

8.8.6 POSSESSION OF RACIALLY INFLAMMATORY MATERIAL STIRRING UP RACIAL HATRED

The Public Order Act 1986, s. 23 offence is defined as follows:

(1) A person who has in his possession written material which is threatening, abusive or insulting, or a recording of visual images or sound which are threatening, abusive or insulting, with a view to—

(a) in the case of written material, its being displayed, published, distributed, or included in a programme service, whether by himself or another, or

(b) in the case of a recording, its being distributed, shown, played, or included in a programme service, whether by himself or another,
is guilty of an offence if he intends racial hatred to be stirred up thereby or, having regard to all the circumstances, racial hatred is likely to be stirred up thereby.

(2) For this purpose regard is to be had to such display, publication, distribution, showing, playing, or inclusion in a programme service as he has, or it may reasonably be inferred that he has, in view.

A statutory defence is provided in s. 23(3):

(3) In proceedings for an offence under this section it is a defence for an accused who is not shown to have intended to stir up racial hatred to prove that he was not aware of the content of the written material or recording and did not suspect, and had no reason to suspect, that it was threatening, abusive or insulting.

8.9 Football and Sporting Offences

8.9.1 THROWING OF OBJECTS, CHANTING OF INDECENT OR RACIALIST NATURE, GOING ONTO PLAYING AREA

Sections 2, 3 and 4 of the Football (Offences) Act 1991 create offences which are triable summarily only. The maximum penalty is a fine not exceeding level 3 on the standard scale (s. 5(2)). They provide as follows:

2. It is an offence for a person at a designated football match to throw anything at or towards—

(a) the playing area, or any area adjacent to the playing area to which spectators are not generally admitted, or

(b) any area in which spectators or other persons are or may be present, without lawful authority or lawful excuse (which shall be for him to prove).

3.—(1) It is an offence to take part at a designated football match in chanting of an indecent or racialist nature.

(2) For this purpose—

(a) 'chanting' means the repeated uttering of any words or sounds in concert with one or more others; and

(b) 'of racialist nature' means consisting of or including matter which is threatening, abusive or insulting to a person by reason of his colour, race, nationality (including citizenship) or ethnic or national origins.

4. *It is an offence for a person at a designated football match to go onto the playing area, or any area adjacent to the playing area to which spectators are not generally admitted, without lawful authority or lawful excuse (which shall be for him to prove).*

8.9.2 ALCOHOL OFFENCES AT SPORTING EVENTS

Section 1 of the Sporting Events (Control of Alcohol etc.) Act 1985 creates offences which are triable summarily only and are punishable by a fine not exceeding level 4 on the standard scale in the case of an offence under s. 1(2), level 3 in the case of an offence under s. 1(3), and level 2 in the case of an offence under s. 1(4). The offences are defined as follows:

(2) A person who knowingly causes or permits intoxicating liquor to be carried on a vehicle to which this section applies is guilty of an offence—
(a) if the vehicle is a public service vehicle and he is the operator of the vehicle or the servant or agent of the operator, or
(b) if the vehicle is a hired vehicle and he is the person to whom it is hired or the servant or agent of that person.
(3) A person who has intoxicating liquor in his possession while on a vehicle to which this section applies is guilty of an offence.
(4) A person who is drunk on a vehicle to which this section applies is guilty of an offence.

Section 2 offences are also triable summarily only and are punishable by a fine not exceeding level 3 on the standard scale, or by imprisonment for a term not exceeding three months or both in the case of an offence under s. 2(1), and a fine not exceeding level 2 in the case of an offence under s. 2(2). The offences are defined as follows:

(1) A person who has intoxicating liquor or an article to which this section applies in his possession—
(a) at any time during the period of a designated sporting event when he is in any area of a designated sports ground from which the event may be directly viewed, or
(b) while entering or trying to enter a designated sports ground at any time during the period of a designated sporting event at that ground, is guilty of an offence.
(2) A person who is drunk in a designated sports ground at any time during the period of a designated sporting event at that ground or is drunk while entering or trying to enter such a ground at any time during the period of a designated sporting event at that ground is guilty of an offence.

8.9.3 RESTRICTION ORDERS

The Football Spectators Act 1989 provides that a court by or before which a person has been convicted of certain offences may make a restriction order against him. The relevant offences are set out in sch. 1. See also the Football Spectators (Designation of Football Matches in England and Wales) Order 1993 (SI 1993 No. 1691) which came into force on 1 August 1993.

8.10 Offences Relating to Public Processions and Assemblies

8.10.1 FAILURE TO GIVE NOTICE TO THE POLICE

A person organising a public procession is required by s. 11 of the Public Order Act 1986 to satisfy requirements concerning the giving of notice of the procession to the police.

The offence under s. 11(7) of the Public Order Act 1986 is triable summarily only and is punishable with a fine not exceeding level 3. The offence is defined as follows:

(7)   Where a public procession is held each of the persons organising it is guilty of an offence if—
(a)   the requirements of this section as to notice have not been satisfied, or
(b)   the date when it is held, the time when it starts, or its route, differs from the date, time or route specified in the notice.

The following statutory defences are provided in s. 11(8) and (9):

(8)   It is a defence for the accused to prove that he did not know of, and neither suspected nor had reason to suspect, the failure to satisfy the requirements or (as the case may be) the difference of date, time or route.
(9)   To the extent that an alleged offence turns on a difference of date, time or route, it is a defence for the accused to prove that the difference arose from circumstances beyond his control or from something done with the agreement of a police officer or by his direction.

8.10.2   FAILURE TO COMPLY WITH CONDITIONS IMPOSED ON PUBLIC PROCESSION

The three offences under the Public Order Act 1986, s. 12 are triable summarily and are defined in s. 12(4) to (6) as follows:

(4)   A person who organises a public procession and knowingly fails to comply with a condition imposed under this section is guilty of an offence, but it is a defence for him to prove that the failure arose from circumstances beyond his control.
(5)   A person who takes part in a public procession and knowingly fails to comply with a condition imposed under this section is guilty of an offence, but it is a defence for him to prove that the failure arose from circumstances beyond his control.
(6)   A person who incites another to commit an offence under subsection (5) is guilty of an offence.

The penalty for the s. 12(4) offence is imprisonment for a term not exceeding three months, or a fine not exceeding level 4 or both.

The penalty for the s. 12(5) offence is a fine not exceeding level 3 and for the s. 12(6) offence, imprisonment for a term not exceeding three months, or a fine not exceeding level 4 or both.

8.10.3   CONTRAVENING PROHIBITION OF PUBLIC PROCESSION

The three offences under s. 13 of the 1986 Act are triable summarily and are defined in s. 13(7) to (9) as follows:

(7)   A person who organises a public procession the holding of which he knows is prohibited by virtue of an order under this section is guilty of an offence.
(8)   A person who takes part in a public procession the holding of which he knows is prohibited by virtue of an order under this section is guilty of an offence.
(9)   A person who incites another to commit an offence under subsection (8) is guilty of an offence.

The penalty for each of the s. 13(7) and (9) offences is imprisonment for a term not exceeding three months or a fine not exceeding level 4 or both, and for the s. 13(8) offence is a fine not exceeding level 3.

8.10.4   FAILURE TO COMPLY WITH CONDITIONS IMPOSED ON PUBLIC ASSEMBLY

The three offences under the Public Order Act 1986, s. 14 are triable summarily only and are defined in s. 14(4) to (6) as follows:

(4)   A person who organises a public assembly and knowingly fails to comply with a condition imposed under this section is guilty of an offence, but it is a defence for him to prove that the failure arose from circumstances beyond his control.

(5)   A person who takes part in a public assembly and knowingly fails to comply with a condition imposed under this section is guilty of an offence, but it is a defence for him to prove that the failure arose from circumstances beyond his control.

(6)   A person who incites another to commit an offence under subsection (5) is guilty of an offence.

The penalty for the s. 14(4) and (6) offences is imprisonment for a term not exceeding three months, or a fine not exceeding level 4 or both, and for the s. 14(5) offence, a fine not exceeding level 3. See *DPP* v *Baillie* [1995] Crim LR 426.

8.11   Bomb Hoaxes

An offence under s. 51(1) of the Criminal Law Act 1977 is triable either way and is punishable on indictment with a term of seven years' imprisonment, and on summary conviction with a term not exceeding six months' imprisonment, or a fine not exceeding the statutory maximum or both (s. 51(4)).

The offence is defined as follows:

(1)   A person who—
(a)   places any article in any place whatever, or
(b)   dispatches any article by post, rail or any other means whatever of sending things from one place to another,
with the intention (in either case) of inducing in some other person a belief that it is likely to explode or ignite and thereby cause personal injury or damage to property is guilty of an offence.
In this subsection 'article' includes substance.
(2)   A person who communicates any information which he knows or believes to be false to another person with the intention of inducing in him or any other person a false belief that a bomb or other thing liable to explode or ignite is present in any place or location whatever is guilty of an offence.

See *Browne* (1984) 6 Cr App R (S) 5, *Dunbar* (1987) 9 Cr App R (S) 393 and *Wilburn* (1992) 13 Cr App R (S) 309.

8.12   Offences in Relation to Collective Trespass or Nuisance on Land

8.12.1   POWERS REGARDING TRESPASS

Section 61(1)–(3) of the Criminal Justice and Public Order Act 1994 (CJPOA 1994) enable a senior police officer to make a direction for two or more trespassers to leave land.

***61.**—(1)   If the senior police officer present at the scene reasonably believes that two or more persons are trespassing on land and are present there with the common purpose of residing there for any period, that reasonable steps have been taken by or on behalf of the occupier to ask them to leave and—*
(a)   that any of those persons has caused damage to the land or to property on the land or used threatening, abusive or insulting words or behaviour towards the occupier, a member of his family or an employee or agent of his, or
(b)   that those persons have between them six or more vehicles on the land,
he may direct those persons, or any of them, to leave the land and to remove any vehicles or other property they have with them on the land.

(2)   Where the persons in question are reasonably believed by the senior police officer to be persons who were not originally trespassers but have become trespassers on the land, the officer must reasonably believe that the other conditions specified in subsection (1) are satisfied after those persons became trespassers before he can exercise the power conferred by that subsection.

(3)   A direction under subsection (1) above, if not communicated to the persons referred to in subsection (1) by the police officer giving the direction, may be communicated to them by any constable at the scene.

The offence under s. 61(4) is defined as follows:

(4)   If a person knowing that a direction under subsection (1) above has been given which applies to him—
(a)   fails to leave the land as soon as reasonably practicable, or
(b)   having left again enters the land as a trespasser within the period of three months beginning with the day on which the direction was given,
he commits an offence and is liable on summary conviction to imprisonment for a term not exceeding three months or a fine not exceeding level 4 on the standard scale, or both.

Section 61(5) confers a power of arrest without a warrant on a police officer in uniform.

The following statutory defence is provided in s. 61(6):

(6)   In proceedings for an offence under this section it is a defence for the accused to show—
(a)   that he was not trespassing on the land, or
(b)   that he had a reasonable excuse for failing to leave the land as soon as reasonably practicable or, as the case may be, for again entering the land as a trespasser.

Section 61(9) defines various terms including 'common land', 'occupier', 'trespass' and 'vehicle'.

8.12.2   POWERS REGARDING RAVES

Section 63(1)–(5) of the CJPOA 1994 enables a police officer of at least the rank of superintendent to give a direction for persons to leave land if two or more of them are preparing for a rave, or ten or more of them are waiting for, or attending a rave.

***63.**—(1)   This section applies to a gathering on land in the open air of 100 or more persons (whether or not trespassers) at which amplified music is played during the night (with or without intermissions) and is such as, by reason of its loudness and duration and the time at which it is played, is likely to cause serious distress to the inhabitants of the locality; and for this purpose—*
(a)   such a gathering continues during intermissions in the music and, where the gathering extends over several days, throughout the period during which amplified music is played at night (with or without intermissions); and
(b)   'music' includes sounds wholly or predominantly characterised by the emission of a succession of repetitive beats.
(2)   If, as respects any land in the open air, a police officer of at least the rank of superintendent reasonably believes that—
(a)   two or more persons are making preparations for the holding there of a gathering to which this section applies,
(b)   ten or more persons are waiting for such a gathering to begin there, or
(c)   ten or more persons are attending such a gathering which is in progress,
he may give a direction that those persons and any other persons who come to prepare or wait for or to attend the gathering are to leave the land and remove any vehicles or other property which they have with them on the land.
(3)   A direction under subsection (2) above, if not communicated to the persons referred to in subsection (2) by the police officer giving the direction, may be communicated to them by any constable at the scene.

(4)   Persons shall be treated as having had a direction under subsection (2) above communicated to them if reasonable steps have been taken to bring it to their attention.

(5)   A direction under subsection (2) above does not apply to an exempt person.

The offence under s. 63(6) is defined as follows:

(6)   If a person knowing that a direction has been given which applies to him—
(a)   fails to leave the land as soon as reasonably practicable, or
(b)   having left again enters the land within the period of 7 days beginning with the day on which the direction was given,
he commits an offence and is liable on summary conviction to imprisonment for a term not exceeding three months or a fine not exceeding level 4 on the standard scale, or both.

Section 63(8) confers a power of arrest without a warrant on a police officer in uniform.

The following statutory defence is provided in s. 63(7):

(7)   In proceedings for an offence under this section it is a defence for the accused to show that he had a reasonable excuse for failing to leave the land as soon as reasonably practicable or, as the case may be, for again entering the land.

Section 63(9) provides that licensed gatherings are not included in the section and an 'exempt person' is defined in s. 63(10) as an occupier, any member of his family, his employee or agent and any person whose home is on the land.

Section 65(1)–(3) enables a police officer in uniform to stop a person on his way to a rave within a radius of five miles of the site of the rave and to direct him not to proceed to the rave.

65.—*(1)   If a constable in uniform reasonably believes that a person is on his way to a gathering to which section 63 applies in relation to which a direction under section 63(2) is in force, he may, subject to subsections (2) and (3) below—*
(a)   stop that person, and
(b)   direct him not to proceed in the direction of the gathering.
(2)   The power conferred by subsection (1) above may only be exercised at a place within 5 miles of the boundary of the site of the gathering.
(3)   No direction may be given under subsection (1) above to an exempt person.

The offence under s. 65(4) is defined as follows:

(4)   If a person knowing that a direction under subsection (1) above has been given to him fails to comply with that direction, he commits an offence and is liable on summary conviction to a fine not exceeding level 3 on the standard scale.

Section 65(5) confers a power of arrest without a warrant on a police officer in uniform.

Powers of entry, seizure, retention and charges in respect of seized property are provided by ss. 64, 66 and 67.

8.12.3   AGGRAVATED TRESPASS

The offence of aggravated trespass is triable summarily only and carries a maximum penalty of three months' imprisonment, or a fine not exceeding level 4, or both (s. 68(3)).

It is defined in s. 68 of the CJPOA 1994 as follows:

68.—*(1)   A person commits the offence of aggravated trespass if he trespasses on land in the open air and, in relation to any lawful activity which persons are engaging*

in or are about to engage in on that or adjoining land in the open air, does there anything which is intended by him to have the effect—
(a) of intimidating those persons or any of them so as to deter them or any of them from engaging in that activity,
(b) of obstructing that activity, or
(c) of disrupting that activity.
(2) Activity on any occasion on the part of a person or persons on land is 'lawful' for the purposes of this section if he or they may engage in the activity on the land on that occasion without committing an offence or trespassing on the land.

Section 68(4) confers a power of arrest without a warrant on a police officer in uniform.

Section 69 enables a senior police officer present to direct disruptive or intending disruptive trespassers to leave land.

69.—(1) If the senior police officer present at the scene reasonably believes—
(a) that a person is committing, has committed or intends to commit the offence of aggravated trespass on land in the open air; or
(b) that two or more persons are trespassing on land in the open air and are present there with the common purpose of intimidating persons so as to deter them from engaging in a lawful activity or of obstructing or disrupting a lawful activity, he may direct that person or (as the case may be) those persons (or any of them) to leave the land.
(2) A direction under subsection (1) above, if not communicated to the persons referred to in subsection (1) by the police officer giving the direction, may be communicated to them by any constable at the scene.

The offence under s. 69(3) is defined as follows:

(3) If a person knowing that a direction under subsection (1) above has been given which applies to him—
(a) fails to leave the land as soon as practicable, or
(b) having left again enters the land as a trespasser within the period of three months beginning with the day on which the direction was given, he commits an offence and is liable on summary conviction to imprisonment for a term not exceeding three months or a fine not exceeding level 4 on the standard scale, or both.

Section 69(5) confers a power of arrest without a warrant on a police officer in uniform.

The following statutory defence is provided in s. 69(4):

(4) In proceedings for an offence under subsection (3) it is a defence for the accused to show—
(a) that he was not trespassing on the land, or
(b) that he had a reasonable excuse for failing to leave the land as soon as practicable or, as the case may be, for again entering the land as a trespasser.

8.12.4 TRESPASSORY ASSEMBLIES

Section 14A of the Public Order Act 1986 (as inserted by s. 70 of the CJPOA 1994) enables a chief officer of police to apply to a district council for an order prohibiting trespassory assemblies.

The offences in s. 14B are defined as follows:

14B.—(1) A person who organises an assembly the holding of which he knows is prohibited by an order under section 14A is guilty of an offence.
(2) A person who takes part in an assembly which he knows is prohibited by an order under section 14A is guilty of an offence.

(3)   In England and Wales, a person who incites another to commit an offence under subsection (2) is guilty of an offence.

Offences under s. 14B(1) and (3) are triable summarily only and are punishable with imprisonment for a term not exceeding three months or a fine not exceeding level 4, or both, and in the case of an offence under s. 14B(2) with a fine not exceeding level 3 (s. 14B(5)–(7)).

In *DPP* v *Jones* [1999] 2 WLR 625, the defendants had taken part in a peaceful, non-obstructive assembly on the highway adjacent to the monument at Stonehenge in respect of which there was in force an order under s. 14A. The House of Lords held that the public had a right to use the highway for such reasonable and usual activities, including peaceful assembly, as were consistent with the primary right to use it for passage and repassage, and that a peaceful assembly for a reasonable period that did not unreasonably obstruct the highway was not necessarily unlawful, nor did it necessarily constitute a trespassory assembly. Each case had to be decided in the light of its particular facts, and the right of public assembly could, in certain circumstances, be exercised on the highway provided that it caused no obstruction to persons passing along the highway and that the tribunal of fact made a finding that it had been a reasonable user.

Section 14C of the Public Order Act 1986 (inserted by s. 71 of the CJPOA 1994) enables a police officer in uniform to stop persons on their way to trespassory assemblies and to direct them not to proceed in that direction.

14C.—(1)   If a constable in uniform reasonably believes that a person is on his way to an assembly within the area to which an order under section 14A applies which the constable reasonably believes is likely to be an assembly which is prohibited by that order, he may, subject to subsection (2) below—
> *(a)   stop that person, and*
> *(b)   direct him not to proceed in the direction of the assembly.*
> *(2)   The power conferred by subsection (1) may only be exercised within the area to which the order applies.*

The offence under s. 14C is triable summarily only and is punishable with a fine not exceeding level 3 (s. 14C(5)).

The offence is defined as follows:

(3)   A person who fails to comply with a direction under subsection (1) which he knows has been given to him is guilty of an offence.

Section 14C(4) confers a power of arrest without a warrant on a police officer in uniform.

8.12.5   REMOVAL OF UNAUTHORISED CAMPERS

Section 77 of the CJPOA 1994 enables a local authority to give a direction for removal of unauthorised campers from land.

77.—(1)   If it appears to a local authority that persons are for the time being residing in a vehicle or vehicles within that authority's area—
> *(a)   on any land forming part of a highway;*
> *(b)   on any other unoccupied land; or*
> *(c)   on any occupied land without the consent of the occupier,*
the authority may give a direction that those persons and any others with them are to leave the land and remove the vehicle or vehicles and any other property they have with them on the land.
> *(2)   Notice of a direction under subsection (1) must be served on the persons to whom the direction applies, but it shall be sufficient for this purpose for the direction to specify the land and (except where the direction applies to only one person) to be addressed to all occupants of the vehicles on the land, without naming them.*

The offence under s. 77(3) is defined as follows:

> *(3)   If a person knowing that a direction under subsection (1) above has been given which applies to him—*
>
> *(a)   fails, as soon as practicable, to leave the land or remove from the land any vehicle or other property which is the subject of the direction, or*
>
> *(b)   having removed any such vehicle or property again enters the land with a vehicle within the period of three months beginning with the day on which the direction was given,*
>
> *he commits an offence and is liable on summary conviction to a fine not exceeding level 3 on the standard scale.*

Guidance relating to the making of removal directions and to service of notices of directions was provided by the Divisional Court in *Wealden DC, ex parte Wales, The Times*, 22 September 1995.

Section 78(1)–(3) enables a local authority to apply to a magistrates' court for an order requiring the removal of vehicles or property from the land where a direction has been breached.

> **78.**—*(1)   A magistrates' court may, on a complaint made by a local authority, if satisfied that persons and vehicles in which they are residing are present on land within that authority's area in contravention of a direction given under section 77, make an order requiring the removal of any vehicle or other property which is so present on the land and any person residing in it.*
>
> *(2)   An order under this section may authorise the local authority to take such steps as are reasonably necessary to ensure that the order is complied with and, in particular, may authorise the authority, by its officers and servants—*
>
> *(a)   to enter upon the land specified in the order; and*
>
> *(b)   to take, in relation to any vehicle or property to be removed in pursuance of the order, such steps for securing entry and rendering it suitable for removal as may be so specified.*
>
> *(3)   The local authority shall not enter upon any occupied land unless they have given to the owner and occupier at least 24 hours' notice of their intention to do so, or unless after reasonable inquiries they are unable to ascertain their names and addresses.*

The offence under s. 78(4) is defined as follows:

> *(4)   A person who wilfully obstructs any person in the exercise of any power conferred on him by an order under this section commits an offence and is liable on summary conviction to a fine not exceeding level 3 on the standard scale.*

Section 78(5) provides that it is not necessary for the names of the occupants of vehicles on the land in question to be named in any summonses sent to them.

For an article commenting on the public order provisions of the CJPOA 1994, see Dr A. T. H. Smith 'The Public Order Elements' [1995] Crim LR 19.

NINE

OFFENSIVE WEAPONS

9.1 Introduction

This chapter deals with some of the more common offences relating to weapons that a junior practitioner is likely to come across in early practice. It does not deal with firearms legislation, which is extensive, and for which reference should be made to textbooks or practitioner works.

9.2 Prevention of Crime Act 1953

Section 1 provides:

> *(1) Any person who without lawful authority or reasonable excuse, the proof whereof shall lie on him, has with him in any public place any offensive weapon shall be guilty of an offence.*

This is an offence that is triable either way, and is punishable on indictment with a term of four years' imprisonment or a fine or both, or on summary conviction with six months' imprisonment or a fine not exceeding the prescribed sum or both. Section 1(2) permits the court on conviction of an offence under s. 1 to make an order for the forfeiture or disposal of any weapon in respect of which the offence was committed.

It should be noted that generally offences relating to weapons are used to deal with those people who *carry* weapons with them: those who actually *use* a weapon to inflict, say, an assault, are usually charged with the relevant substantive assault charge. A person who, on the spur of the moment, uses a lawfully carried article to attack another is unlikely to have committed an offence under s. 1 (although that person is likely to be liable for some form of assault). On this point see, e.g., *Jura* [1954] 1 QB 503, *Ohlson* v *Hylton* [1975] 1 WLR 724, *Bates* v *Bulman* [1979] 1 WLR 1190, and *Veasey* [1999] Crim LR 158.

9.2.1 'HAS WITH HIM'

It must be proved that the defendant had the article with him knowingly, although forgetting that the article is in one's possession is not an excuse (*McCalla* (1988) 87 Cr App R 372). However, on the question of whether forgetfulness can amount to reasonable excuse (see **9.2.4**), see *Glidewell, The Times*, 14 May 1999.

9.2.2 'PUBLIC PLACE'

Public place is defined as including any highway and any other premises or place to which at the material time the public have or are permitted to have access, whether on payment or otherwise (s. 1(4)).

9.2.3 'OFFENSIVE WEAPON'

Section 1(4) defines an offensive weapon as:

. . . any article made or adapted for use for causing injury to the person, or intended by the person having it with him for such use by him or by some other person.

The Court of Appeal in *Simpson* (1983) 78 Cr App R 115 explained this as meaning that there were three categories of offensive weapon: articles made for causing injury to the person (often known as weapons offensive *per se*); articles adapted for that purpose; and articles not so made or adapted, but which were carried with an intention to use to cause injury to the person.

The distinction between the first two categories and the third one is important, for in the third category the prosecution is required to prove the accused had the requisite intent to cause injury. In the first two categories such additional intent is not needed.

The question of whether an article is offensive *per se* is usually a question of fact for the jury to decide; however, in some cases the judge can take judicial notice that an article is offensive *per se* and direct the jury accordingly. For examples of both types of situation see *Gibson* v *Wales* [1983] 1 WLR 393 and *Simpson* (1983) 78 Cr App R 115 (flick knives), *DPP* v *Hynde* (1997) 161 JP 671 (butterfly knives, on similar legislation), *Houghton* v *Chief Constable of Greater Manchester* (1986) 84 Cr App R 319 (a police truncheon), *Copus* v *DPP* [1989] Crim LR 577 (a rice flail) and *Butler* [1988] Crim LR 696 (a sword stick).

Articles adapted for causing injury would include articles such as a deliberately broken bottle. Articles that are not made or adapted for use for causing injury to the person (e.g., a baseball bat or sandbag) can still class as offensive weapons if the prosecution can show that the article was carried with the intention of using it to cause injury.

9.2.4 'LAWFUL AUTHORITY OR REASONABLE EXCUSE'

If a person has with him an offensive weapon in a public place with lawful authority or reasonable excuse, no offence is committed. The burden of proving lawful authority or reasonable excuse lies with the defendant: it is not for the prosecution to disprove it as part of its case. As with other legal burdens of proof cast on the defence, the standard of proof is on a balance of probabilities.

What constitutes lawful authority or reasonable excuse will depend on the circumstances of each case. Some people are permitted by the nature of their employment to carry offensive weapons at times, a common example being a police officer carrying a baton. A more common claim made by a defendant is that of reasonable excuse: carrying a police truncheon as part of a police uniform worn at a fancy dress party may amount to reasonable excuse (*Houghton* v *Chief Constable of Greater Manchester* (1986) 84 Cr App R 319). A defendant who carried a machete and a catapult in order to kill squirrels to feed wild birds which he kept under licence was held to have reasonable excuse (*Southwell* v *Chadwick* (1986) 85 Cr App R 235). On whether lack of knowledge that an object is an offensive weapon amounts to a reasonable excuse, see *Densu* [1998] Crim LR 345.

Often the defendant says that he carried the article in self-defence, and claims this to amount to reasonable excuse. A number of cases have considered this point, and the answer is ultimately one of degree. A person who habitually carries a weapon with him on his person or in his vehicle on the off chance that he may be attacked is unlikely to satisfy the test. However, carrying an offensive weapon following an assault which might be repeated may amount to reasonable excuse. See *Evans* v *Hughes* (1972) 56 Cr App R 813, *Peacock* [1973] Crim LR 639 and *Malnik* v *DPP* [1989] Crim LR 451.

9.3 Criminal Justice Act 1988

9.3.1 SECTION 139

Section 139 of the 1988 Act states:

(1) Subject to subsections (4) and (5) below, any person who has an article to which this section applies with him in a public place shall be guilty of an offence.

(2)   Subject to subsection (3) below, this section applies to any article which has a blade or is sharply pointed except a folding pocketknife.

(3)   This section applies to a folding pocketknife if the cutting edge of its blade exceeds 3 inches.

This section creates a triable either way offence for offences committed from 4 July 1996 (if prior to this, it is summary only), and is punishable on indictment with a term of imprisonment of up to two years and/or a fine, and on summary conviction by a term of six months' imprisonment and/or a fine not exceeding the prescribed amount.

Certain articles that are carried may not fall within the ambit of the Prevention of Crime Act 1953, s. 1, but may come within the scope of the Criminal Justice Act 1988, s. 139, e.g., a sheath knife for which there is no evidence of the specific intent necessary to make it an offensive weapon.

A folding pocket knife which locks in position when opened does not come within the term 'folding pocketknife' used by the section (*Harris* v *DPP* (1992) 96 Cr App R 235, followed in *Deegan* [1998] Crim LR 562).

A screwdriver has been held not to be a bladed article within the meaning of s. 139 (*Davis* [1998] Crim LR 564).

'Public place' includes any place to which at the material time the public have or are permitted access, whether on payment or otherwise (s. 139(7)).

Section 139(4) makes it a defence for the defendant to prove that he had good reason or lawful authority for having the article with him in a public place. Note the words 'good reason' are used, rather than the arguably wider 'reasonable excuse' phrase used in the Prevention of Crime Act 1953, s. 1. A failure to leave to the jury the issue of whether self-defence amounted to good reason has resulted in the conviction being quashed (see *Emmanuel* [1998] Crim LR 347).

Section 139(5) additionally provides that, without prejudice to the generality of subsection (4), it shall be a defence for the accused to prove that he had the article for use at work; for religious reasons; or as part of any national costume. For an example of an attempt to rely on the 'use at work' defence, see *Manning* [1998] Crim LR 198.

9.3.2   SECTION 139A

Section 139A provides an additional triable either way offence of having an article within the meaning of s. 139 or an offensive weapon within the meaning of the Prevention of Crime Act 1953, s. 1 on school premises. This is subject to the defence of good reason or lawful authority, and to the use at work/religious reasons/national dress defence, as well as an additional one of having the article on the premises for educational purposes. Punishment depends on whether the article comes within s. 139, in which case punishment is the same as s. 139 itself, or whether it comes within the Prevention of Crime Act 1953, s. 1, in which case punishment is the same as s. 1.

Section 139B provides search and seizure powers for the police to enter school premises and search people thereon.

9.4   Other Offences

In addition to the commonly used offences under the Prevention of Crime Act 1953 and the Criminal Justice Act 1988 there are a number of other pieces of legislation that seek to restrict the carrying, manufacture, sale, hire, purchase and use of weapons. These include the Restriction of Offensive Weapons Act 1959, ss. 141 and 141A of the Criminal Justice Act 1988 (introduced by the Offensive Weapons Act 1996), the Crossbows Act 1987 and the Knives Act 1997. Reference to practitioner works such as *Archbold* or *Blackstone's Criminal Practice* should be made for details of these offences.

TEN

ROAD TRAFFIC OFFENCES: GENERAL

10.1 Introduction

This chapter deals with the offences of dangerous driving, careless (or inconsiderate) driving, failing to stop after an accident and failing to report an accident. The various offences related to drinking and driving are dealt with in **Chapter 11**. Between them, these offences constitute a representative sample of the road traffic offences likely to confront counsel in early practice.

The standard reference work for practitioners is Wilkinson, *Road Traffic Offences* (London: FT Law & Tax). Section C of *Blackstone's Criminal Practice* is devoted to driving offences. A concise account is given in McMahon, *A Practical Approach to Road Traffic Law* (London: Blackstone Press, 1994).

There is one point which is of general application to road traffic offences, but has particular relevance to dangerous and careless driving. The Highway Code is often used by the courts as a guide to what constitutes safe or careful driving. The position in law is that a failure to observe a provision of the Code does not of itself constitute an offence. Any such failure may, however, be relied upon by any party to civil or criminal proceedings as tending to prove or disprove liability in those proceedings (Road Traffic Act 1988, s. 38(7)). In practice it is common for advocates, and the court, to place reliance upon the Code's provisions in evaluating the evidence in the case.

10.2 Dangerous Driving

The offence of dangerous driving is defined in s. 2A of the Road Traffic Act 1988 (RTA), which was inserted by the RTA 1991. It reads as follows:

> **2A.**—(1) *For the purposes of sections 1 and 2 above a person is to be regarded as driving dangerously if (and, subject to subsection (2) below, only if)—*
>   (a)   *the way he drives falls far below what would be expected of a competent and careful driver, and*
>   (b)   *it would be obvious to a competent and careful driver that driving in that way would be dangerous.*
>   (2)   *A person is also to be regarded as driving dangerously for the purposes of sections 1 and 2 above if it would be obvious to a competent and careful driver that driving the vehicle in its current state would be dangerous.*
>   (3)   *In subsections (1) and (2) above 'dangerous' refers to danger either of injury to any person or of serious damage to property; and in determining for the purposes of those subsections what would be expected of, or obvious to, a competent and careful driver in a particular case, regard shall be had not only to the circumstances of which he could be expected to be aware but also to any circumstances shown to have been within the knowledge of the accused.*

(4)   In determining for the purposes of subsection (2) above the state of a vehicle, regard may be had to anything attached to or carried on or in it and to the manner in which it is attached or carried.

The offence of dangerous driving was not in fact an entirely new one. It was on the statute books until 1977, when it was replaced by 'reckless driving'. The offence of reckless driving, which was not statutorily defined, gave rise to voluminous case law as the courts attempted to grapple with the concept of recklessness. In its revived form, the offence of dangerous driving is arguably somewhat more widely drawn than the concept of reckless driving, and is subject to a statutory definition.

The core of that definition is contained in s. 2A(1), and it poses two questions in relation to the allegedly dangerous driving:

(a)   Did the driving fall far below the standard which would be expected of a competent and careful driver? Clearly the word upon which the defence will frequently focus in argument is 'far', and its presence in the definition appears to be one of the features which distinguishes this offence from that of careless driving (see **10.3**).

(b)   Would it be obvious to that hypothetical competent and careful driver that driving in such a way would be dangerous? The key words in this formulation would seem to be 'obvious' and 'dangerous'. As far as 'dangerous' is concerned, some assistance is provided by the opening words to s. 2A(3), which tie the concept to danger of injury to the person or serious damage to property. In view of the fact that the word 'danger' is unqualified, it would seem that danger to any person, even though slight, would suffice, provided that it is not *de minimis*.

The prosecution must prove both elements (a) and (b) above before s. 2A(1) is satisfied (*Aitken* v *Lees* 1994 SLT 182).

As can be seen from the wording of s. 2A(3), in interpreting s. 2A(1) and (2), regard must be had:

(a)   to circumstances of which a competent and careful driver could be expected to be aware; and

(b)   to circumstances which are shown to be within the (actual) knowledge of the accused.

10.2.1   EVIDENCE OF DANGEROUS DRIVING

What, then, constitutes evidence of dangerousness to measure against the statutory definition? Obviously, it depends upon the particular facts of the case, and precedents are of little, if any, assistance. Some guidance can be gleaned from the *Driving Offences Charging Standard* which was agreed by the police and the Crown Prosecution Service in January 1996, and forms part of the CD-ROM version of *Blackstone's Criminal Practice*. It must be stressed, however, that the *Charging Standard* provides guidance for police and prosecutors, and is not authoritative as far as the courts are concerned. The *Charging Standard* gives the following as examples of driving which may support an allegation of dangerous driving (see para. 7.7):

- racing or competitive driving;

- prolonged, persistent or deliberate bad driving;

- speed which is highly inappropriate for the prevailing road or traffic conditions;

- aggressive or intimidatory driving, such as sudden lane changes, cutting into a line of vehicles or driving much too close to the vehicle in front, especially when the purpose is to cause the other vehicle to pull to one side to allow the accused to overtake;

- disregard of traffic lights and other road signs, which, on an objective analysis, would appear to be deliberate;

- failure to pay proper attention, amounting to something significantly more than a momentary lapse;

- overtaking which could not have been carried out with safety;

- driving a vehicle with a load which presents a danger to other road users.

10.2.2   NOTICE OF INTENDED PROSECUTION

Dangerous driving, like careless driving, is one of the offences to which s. 1 of the Road Traffic Offenders Act 1988 (RTOA) applies. This states:

> *1.—(1)   Subject to section 2 of this Act, a person shall not be convicted of an offence to which this section applies unless—*
>
> *(a)   he was warned at the time the offence was committed that the question of prosecuting him for some one or other of the offences to which this section applies would be taken into consideration, or*
>
> *(b)   within 14 days of the commission of the offence a summons . . . for the offence was served on him, or*
>
> *(c)   within 14 days of the commission of the offence a notice of the intended prosecution specifying the nature of the alleged offence and the time and place where it is alleged to have been committed, was—*
>
> *(i)   in the case of an offence under section 28 or 29 of the Road Traffic Act 1988 (cycling offences), served on him,*
>
> *(ii)   in the case of any other offence, served on him or on the person, if any, registered as the keeper of the vehicle at the time of the commission of the offence.*
>
> *(1A)   A notice required by this section to be served on that person may be served on that person*
>
> *(a)   by delivering it to him;*
>
> *(b)   by addressing it to him and leaving it at his last known address;*
>
> *(c)   by sending it by registered post, recorded delivery service or first class post addressed to him at his last known address.*
>
> *(2)   A notice shall be deemed for the purposes of subsection (1)(c) above to have been served on a person if it was sent by registered post or recorded delivery service addressed to him at his last known address, notwithstanding that the notice was returned undelivered or was for any other reason not received by him.*
>
> *(3)   The requirement of subsection (1) above shall in every case be deemed to have been complied with unless and until the contrary is proved.*
>
> *(4)   Schedule 1 to this Act shows the offences to which this section applies.*

The offences in respect of which there is an obligation under s. 1 include a number of the most common road traffic offences, e.g., dangerous driving (contrary to RTA 1988, s. 2), careless driving (s. 3), leaving a vehicle in a dangerous position (s. 22), dangerous cycling (s. 28), careless cycling (s. 29), failing to comply with traffic directions (s. 35) or signs (s. 36).

The warning must have been understood by the defendant. In *Gibson v Dalton* [1980] RTR 410, Donaldson LJ (as he then was) put it like this (pp. 413–4):

> The obligation on the prosecutor is to warn the accused, not merely to address a warning to him or to give a warning. The mischief to which this section is directed is clear. It is that motorists are entitled to have it brought to their attention at a relatively early stage there is likely to be a prosecution in order that they may recall and, it may be, record the facts as they occurred at the time . . . But a warning which does not get through to the accused person is of no value at all.

> If, viewing the matter objectively, one would expect that the words addressed to the accused person would have been heard and understood by him, then prima facie he

was warned within the meaning of the statute. But it is only a prima facie case. It is open to the defendant to prove, if he can, that he did not understand or hear or appreciate the warning and therefore that he was not warned.

Section 2 of the RTOA, however, lays down certain circumstances in which no notice of intended prosecution is required:

2.—(1) *The requirement of section 1(1) of this Act does not apply in relation to an offence if, at the time of the offence or immediately after it, an accident occurs owing to the presence on a road of the vehicle in respect of which the offence was committed.*
  (2) . . .
  (3) *Failure to comply with the requirement of section 1(1) of this Act is not a bar to the conviction of the accused in a case where the court is satisfied—*
    (a) *that neither the name and address of the accused nor the name and address of the registered keeper, if any, could with reasonable diligence have been ascertained in time for a summons, or, as the case may be, a complaint to be served or for a notice to be served or sent in compliance with the requirement, or*
    (b) *that the accused by his own conduct contributed to the failure.*
  (4) *Failure to comply with the requirement of section 1(1) of this Act in relation to an offence is not a bar to the conviction of a person of that offence by virtue of the provision of—*
    (a) *section 24 of this Act, or*
    (b) *any of the enactments mentioned in section 24(6);*
  but a person is not to be convicted of an offence by virtue of any of those provisions if section 1 applies to the offence with which he was charged and the requirement of section 1(1) was not satisfied in relation to the offence charged.

As can be seen, there is no requirement to warn of an intended prosecution in the case of an accident. If the accident was so trivial that the defendant was unaware of it, however, a notice will still be necessary (*Bentley* v *Dickinson* [1983] RTR 356).

The rationale was set out by Bingham LJ in *DPP* v *Pidhajeckvj* [1991] RTR 136:

The point of a notice is to alert the driver to the risk of prosecution so that he can promptly investigate the facts and prepare his defence. Ordinarily there is no need for such a notice where there has been an accident, because the driver is alerted to the situation and the possibility of proceedings. But there is a need where the driver is unaware of any accident, because then he has nothing to alert him to the possibility of proceedings.

The point which arose in *Pidhajeckvj* was whether a notice was required where the accident was so serious that its effects resulted in amnesia (contrast *Bentley* where it was so trivial that the defendant could not remember it). The Divisional Court in *Pidhajeckvj* held that this situation was distinguishable from that in *Bentley*. Where the defendant could not remember the details after an accident, but it was apparent that one had occurred, the exemption still applied and no notice of intended prosecution was required. As Bingham LJ put it:

Parliament cannot have intended oral warnings to be given to the unconscious survivors of serious motor accidents, not the giving of written notices to survivors so badly injured as to be unable to read them or understand their effect.

Note that there is a presumption in favour of compliance (see RTOA 1988, s. 1(3)). In other words, the prosecution do not have to prove a warning as part of their case. Hence, if the defence challenge the prosecution on this basis, they bear the burden of proof on a balance of probabilities. This can be a difficult onus to discharge, since it requires evidence from both the driver and the keeper of the vehicle in order to establish that neither of them was served in accordance with RTOA, s. 1(1)(c)(i). The prosecution may of course make an admission that one or other was not served. Once the defence establishes that there was no service, the prosecution can prove that a notice was sent to the last known address by recorded or registered delivery.

10.2.3 ALTERNATIVE VERDICT

Section 24 of the RTOA 1988 lays down a series of alternative verdicts which can be brought in in road traffic cases. The relevant part reads as follows:

24.—(1) Where—

(a) a person charged with an offence under a provision of the Road Traffic Act 1988 specified in the first column of the Table below (where the general nature of the offences is also indicated) is found not guilty of that offence, but

(b) the allegations in the indictment or information (or in Scotland complaint) amount to or include an allegation of an offence under one or more of the provisions specified in the corresponding entry in the second column,

he may be convicted of that offence or of one or more of those offences.

Offence charged	Alternative
Section 1 (causing death by dangerous driving)	Section 2 (dangerous driving) Section 3 (careless, and inconsiderate, driving)
Section 2 (dangerous driving)	Section 3 (careless, and inconsiderate, driving)
Section 3A (causing death by careless driving when under influence of drink or drugs)	Section 3 (careless, and inconsiderate, driving) Section 4(1) (driving when unfit to drive through drink or drugs) Section 5(1)(a) (driving with excess alcohol in breath, blood or urine) Section 7(6) (failing to provide specimen)
Section 4(1) (driving or attempting to drive when unfit to drive through drink or drugs)	Section 4(2) (being in charge of a vehicle when unfit to drive through drink or drugs)
Section 5(1)(a) (driving or attempting to drive with excess alcohol in breath, blood or urine)	Section 5(1)(b) (being in charge of a vehicle with excess alcohol in breath, blood or urine)
Section 28 (dangerous cycling)	Section 29 (careless, and inconsiderate, cycling)

(2) Where the offence with which a person is charged is an offence under section 3A of the Road Traffic Act 1988, subsection (1) above shall not authorise his conviction of any offence of attempting to drive.

(3) Where a person is charged with having committed an offence under section 4(1) or 5(1)(a) of the Road Traffic Act 1988 by driving a vehicle, he may be convicted of having committed an offence under the provision in question by attempting to drive.

(4) Where by virtue of this section a person is convicted before the Crown Court of an offence triable only summarily, the court shall have the same powers and duties as a magistrates' court would have had on convicting him of that offence.

. . .

(6) This section has effect without prejudice to section 6(3) of the Criminal Law Act 1967 (alternative verdicts on trial on indictment) . . . and section 23 of this Act.

As will be apparent, the offence of careless, and inconsiderate, driving is an alternative which the magistrates can find where they decide not to convict the accused of dangerous driving.

10.2.4 PUNISHMENT

Dangerous driving is punishable:

(a) on indictment, with two years' imprisonment, or an unlimited fine or both;

(b)   after summary trial, six months' imprsonment or a fine of £5,000 or both.

There is a minimum disqualification period of 12 months, unless special reasons (see **12.4**) can be established by the defence. Where the driver is disqualified, retesting by way of an extended driving test is mandatory. Endorsement is obligatory in the absence of special reasons (3 to 11 points unless the defendant is disqualified, in which case there is endorsement but without penalty points).

10.2.5   CAUSING DEATH BY DANGEROUS DRIVING

Section 1 of the RTA 1988 creates the offence of causing death by dangerous driving — the aggravated form of the offence under s. 2. It is an indictable only offence, with increased penalties (maximum ten years' imprisonment, minimum two-year disqualification subject to special reasons).

10.2.6   SENTENCING GUIDELINES

In *Boswell* (1984) 6 Cr App R (S) 257, the Court of Appeal laid down guidelines for the offences of reckless driving and causing death by reckless driving, which would appear to be applicable to the equivalent dangerous driving offences. The Lord Chief Justice indicated that the following features should figure in the determination of sentence:

> The following, amongst others, may be regarded as aggravating features: first of all, the consumption of alcohol or drugs, and that may range from a couple of drinks to . . . a 'motorised pub crawl'. Secondly, the driver who races: competitive driving against another vehicle on the public highway; grossly excessive speed; showing off. Thirdly, the driver who disregards warnings from his passengers, a feature which occurs quite frequently in this type of offence. Fourthly, prolonged, persistent and deliberate course of very bad driving . . ., a person who over a lengthy stretch of road ignores traffic signals, jumps red lights, passing other vehicles on the wrong side, driving with excessive speed, driving on the pavement and so on. Next, other offences committed at the same time and related offences, that is to say, driving without ever having had any licence, driving whilst disqualified, driving whilst a learner driver without a supervising driver and so on. Next, previous convictions for motoring offences, particularly offences which involve bad driving or offences involving the consumption of excessive alcohol before driving. In other words the man who demonstrates that he is determined to continue driving badly despite past experience. Next, where several people have been killed as a result of the particular incident of reckless driving. Then, behaviour at the time of the offence, for example, failure to stop, or, even more reprehensible, the driver who tries to throw off the victim from the bonnet of the car by swerving in order that he may escape. Finally causing death in the course of reckless driving carried out in an attempt to avoid detection or apprehension.

> . . . the mitigating features may be numbered as follows amongst others. First of all the piece of reckless driving which might be described in the vernacular as a 'one-off', a momentary reckless error of judgment: briefly dozing off at the wheel (see *Beeby* (1983) 5 Cr App R (S) 56 . . .); sometimes failing to notice a pedestrian on a crossing. Next, a good driving record will serve the defendant in good stead. Good character generally will also serve him in good stead. A plea of guilty will always be taken into account by the sentencing court in favour of the defendant. Sometimes the effect on the defendant, if he is genuinely remorseful, if he is genuinely shocked. That is sometimes coupled with . . . a possible mitigating factor, namely, where the victim was either a close relative of the defendant or a close friend and the consequent emotional shock was likely to be great.

The judgment goes on to indicate that the absence of aggravating features may make a non-custodial disposition appropriate, but that the presence of an aggravating feature or features would generally lead to a custodial penalty. In recent years, sentences for causing death by dangerous driving have become increasingly severe. In *Barber* [1997] 1 Cr App R (S) 65, the Court of Appeal suggested that in bad cases, particularly where alcohol or racing was involved, a prison sentence upwards of five years would be appropriate.

In *Duncan* [1994] RTR 93, the Court of Appeal issued guidance on the sentencing principles for causing death by dangerous driving. *D*, aged 19, held a provisional driving licence and drove unsupervised in excess of 30 mph over the speed limit, carrying four passengers. He swerved to avoid a parked van, lost control and struck a tree. Two of the passengers were killed. The court took the view that an important aggravating factor was that *D* should not have been driving at all without supervision, particularly when putting the passengers at risk by his inexperience and grossly excessive speed. The fact that he was showing off, and engaging in sustained conduct were aggravating factors, as were the fact that two deaths were caused, and other people injured. These matters had to be viewed in a climate in which levels of sentencing had risen. Three years' detention in a young offender institution and four years' disqualification was upheld.

10.3   Careless Driving

Section 3 of the RTA 1988 states:

> **3.**   *If a person drives a mechanically propelled vehicle on a road or other public place without due care and attention, or without reasonable consideration for other persons using the road or place, he is guilty of an offence.*

As will be seen from the statute, the offence is not defined, but it may take one of two forms:

(a)   Driving without due care and attention. The test is whether the defendant has failed to exercise 'the degree of care and attention which a reasonable prudent driver would exercise' (*Simpson* v *Peat* [1952] 2 QB 447).

(b)   Driving without reasonable consideration. The test is whether other road users were inconvenienced by the defendant's inconsiderate driving.

The *Driving Offences Charging Standard* (see **10.2.1** for comment on its status) gives the following as examples of driving which may support an allegation of careless driving:

(a)   Acts of driving caused by more than momentary inattention and where the safety of road users is affected, such as:

- overtaking on the inside;

- driving inappropriately close to another vehicle;

- driving through a red light;

- emerging from a side road into the path of another vehicle;

- turning into a minor road and colliding with a pedestrian.

(b)   Conduct which clearly caused the driver not to be in a position to respond in the event of an emergency on the road, for example:

- using a hand held mobile telephone while the vehicle is moving, especially when at speed;

- tuning a car radio;

- reading a newspaper/map;

- selecting and lighting a cigarette/cigar/pipe;

- talking to and looking at a passenger which causes the driver more than momentary inattention;

- leg and/or arm in plaster;

- fatigue/nodding off.

The *Charging Standard* makes the point, however, that it is the manner of the driving rather than the explanation for it which is crucial in deciding whether to charge careless driving. The list detailed above really consists of a series of examples which explain the driver's conduct, and usually where they occur, a charge of careless driving will be appropriate, but the manner of driving must be considered in the context of the other facts in the case to decide the most appropriate way forward (see para. 5.6 of the *Charging Standard*). In addition, the *Charging Standard* suggests that the public interest will tend to be against a prosecution for careless driving where:

- the incident is of a type such as frequently occurs at parking places, roundabouts, junctions or in traffic queues, involving minimal carelessness such as momentary inattention or a minor error of judgment;

- only the person at fault suffered injury and damage, if any, which was mainly restricted to the vehicle or property owned by that person.

As far as the second limb of the offence, inconsiderate driving, is concerned, the accused must be shown to have fallen below the standard of a reasonable, prudent and competent driver *and* to have done so without reasonable consideration for others. It follows that a person who drives without reasonable consideration for other road users can be convicted of driving without due care and attention, but the reverse does not necessarily apply. The *Charging Standard* (para. 6.4) suggests that an allegation of inconsiderate driving is appropriate 'when the driving amounts to a clear act of selfishness, impatience or aggressiveness' resulting in 'some inconvenience to other road users, for example, forcing other drivers to move over and/or brake as a consequence'. It gives the following examples of conduct appropriate to a charge of driving without reasonable consideration:

- flashing of lights to *force* other drivers in front to give way;

- misuse of any lane to avoid queuing or gain some other advantage over other drivers;

- unnecessarily remaining in an overtaking lane;

- unnecessarily slow driving or braking without good cause;

- driving with undipped headlights which dazzle oncoming drivers;

- driving through a puddle causing pedestrians to be splashed.

The usual basis on which the prosecution puts its case under s. 3, however, is an allegation of careless driving. In determining whether the defendant fell short of the necessary standard, the court must not judge him or her with hindsight. An illustration is provided by *Bristol Crown Court, ex parte Jones* [1986] RTR 259. The defendant's lights suddenly failed when he was driving at night. He pulled on to the motorway's hard shoulder and collided with an unlit parked vehicle of which he was unaware. It was held that his behaviour was reasonable, and the offence was not proved.

Where the defendant is unable to explain an accident, the facts of the case may lead to an irresistible inference that it resulted from careless driving. Thus, in *Rabjohns v Burgar* [1971] RTR 234, the defendant's car collided with the wall of a bridge, leaving skid marks on the road. The weather was fine and the road dry. There was no evidence of the involvement of any other vehicle, and no witnesses. The defendant did not give evidence or put forward any explanation. The Divisional Court held that the only conclusion possible on this evidence was that the defendant had driven carelessly.

Where the defendant does put forward an exculpatory explanation, however, it is incumbent on the prosecution to disprove it, provided that it is not fanciful. For example, in *Butty* v *Davey* [1972] RTR 75, rain had made the road unexpectedly slippery. The defendant's car slid to the wrong side of the road and hit another vehicle. The magistrates found that this did not constitute driving without due care and attention, and their decision was upheld. Similarly, in *Lodwick* v *Jones* [1983] RTR 273, the defendant put forward the existence of an unexpected icy patch as an explanation for skidding. Again, this was accepted by the justices and it was held that they were entitled to do so.

10.3.1 PROCEDURAL MATTERS

By s. 24 of the RTOA 1988, a verdict of careless driving is an alternative where dangerous driving is charged (see **10.2.3**). Careless driving is one of those specified offences for which a notice of intended prosecution is usually necessary (see **10.2.2**). But note that by s. 2(4) of the RTOA 1988, a failure to warn a suspect of an intended prosecution does not act as a bar to conviction of one of the alternative offences specified in s. 24, i.e., provided that notice has been given in relation to the original offence, the defendant can be convicted of one of the alternatives.

10.3.2 PUNISHMENT

Careless driving is a summary offence, punishable by a fine of up to £2,500, with discretionary disqualification. Endorsement is obligatory (3 to 9 points), except where there are special reasons.

10.4 Failing to Stop/Failing to Report

This offence is created by s. 170 of the RTA 1988:

170.—*(1)   This section applies in a case where, owing to the presence of a mechanically propelled vehicle on a road, an accident occurs by which—*
(a)   personal injury is caused to a person other than the driver of that mechanically propelled vehicle, or
(b)   damage is caused—
(i)   to a vehicle other than that mechanically propelled vehicle or a trailer drawn by that mechanically propelled vehicle, or
(ii)   to an animal other than an animal in or on that mechanically propelled vehicle or a trailer drawn by that mechanically propelled vehicle, or
(iii)   to any other property constructed on, fixed to, growing in or otherwise forming part of the land on which the road in question is situated or land adjacent to such land.
(2)   The driver of the mechanically propelled vehicle must stop and, if required to do so by any person having reasonable grounds for so requiring, give his name and address and also the name and address of the owner and the identification marks of the vehicle.
(3)   If for any reason the driver of the mechanically propelled vehicle does not give his name and address under subsection (2) above, he must report the accident.
(4)   A person who fails to comply with subsection (2) or (3) above is guilty of an offence.
(5)   If, in a case where this section applies by virtue of subsection (1)(a) above, the driver of a motor vehicle does not at the time of the accident produce such a certificate of insurance or security, or other evidence, as is mentioned in section 165(2)(a) of this Act—
(a)   to a constable, or
(b)   to some person who, having reasonable grounds for so doing has required him to produce it, the driver must report the accident and produce such a certificate or other evidence.

This subsection does not apply to the driver of an invalid carriage.

(6)   To comply with a duty under this section to report an accident or to produce such a certificate of insurance or security, or other evidence, as is mentioned in section 165(2)(a) of this Act, the driver—

(a)   must do so at a police station or to a constable, and

(b)   must do so as soon as is reasonably practicable and, in any case, within twenty-four hours of the occurrence of the accident.

(7)   A person who fails to comply with a duty under subsection (5) above is guilty of an offence, but he shall not be convicted by reason only of a failure to produce a certificate or other evidence if, within [seven] days after the occurrence of the accident, the certificate or other evidence is produced at a police station that was specified by him at the time when the accident was reported.

(8)   In this section 'animal' means horse, cattle, ass, mule, sheep, pig, goat or dog.

By s. 170(2), then, the driver of a vehicle involved in an accident which falls within the definition laid down in s. 170(1), must stop and, if reasonably required to do so, give appropriate details. If the driver does not give his or her name and address, then he or she must report the accident to the police as soon as possible and, in any event, within 24 hours of the accident (s. 170(3)).

A contravention of s. 170 is a summary offence, punishable by up to six months' imprisonment or a fine of £5,000 or both. It carries discretionary disqualification, and obligatory endorsement (5 to 10 points), subject to special reasons (see **12.4**).

ELEVEN

DRINK DRIVING OFFENCES

11.1   Introduction

Alcohol is a major cause of road accidents. One in five drivers killed in road accidents have levels of alcohol which are over the legal limit. The seriousness with which the problem of drink driving is viewed is reflected not only by the range of offences created in the Road Traffic Acts (driving with excess alcohol, failure to provide a specimen for analysis etc.) but also by the very severe penalties imposed for those offences (see **Chapter 12**).

11.2   Prescribed Limits and Specimen Tests

Under the drink driving provisions, drink means an alcoholic drink and drugs can refer to medicines as well as prohibited drugs and substances which affect the control of the body (e.g., *Bradford* v *Wilson* [1993] Crim LR 482, toluene inhaled when glue sniffing). The prescribed limits are 35 microgrammes (µg) of alcohol in 100 ml of breath, or 80 mg of alcohol in 100 ml of blood or 107 mg of alcohol in 100 ml of urine. This level can be achieved by a man drinking about 3½ to 5 units within an hour and a woman drinking about 2½ to 4 units within an hour. (A unit of alcohol is approximately equal to a half pint of ordinary beer, lager or cider, or a single measure of spirits (whisky, vodka, gin, bacardi, etc.) or a glass of wine or small glass of sherry.) There is no sure way of telling how much an individual can drink before reaching this limit. It varies with each person depending on weight, age, sex, whether the person has just eaten and the sort of drinks which have been consumed. These factors may also affect the rate of absorption of alcohol into the blood. Most of the alcohol drunk is rapidly absorbed into the bloodstream. Nearly all the alcohol has to be burnt up by the liver, the rest is disposed of either in sweat or urine. Only time can remove the alcohol from the bloodstream. In an average sized man it may be broken down at the rate of about one unit per hour.

There are three ways of providing a specimen for analysis: breath, blood or urine. The roadside breath test is really a preliminary test on an approved device where the driver inflates a small bag by blowing into it. The bag has to be inflated by a single breath and there should be no smoking immediately before or during the test as this may affect the result. In addition, 20 minutes ought to have elapsed between the last drink of alcohol and the use of the device. This also relates to other aromatic drinks and mouth sprays. In *DPP* v *Kay* (1999) RTR 109, the Divisional Court held that the failure of officers to ask questions such as when the defendant had last drank or smoked did not invalidate the roadside breath test or the subsequent arrest. The Home Office has warned that the operation of breath test devices may be affected by police radio equipment operating within inches of the devices. Where the police require the breath sample to be analysed the driver has to attend the police station and provide a sample of breath on an approved device, either the Lion Intoximeter or Camic Breath Analyser. These two machines analyse the alcohol level in breath and produce a print-out of two samples of breath taken within a short time. The lower of the two readings is the one that the prosecution will rely on in determining whether a prosecution can be founded. The machines also operate a self-check system to indicate that they are operating accurately. The driver is given a copy of the print-out. The print-out forms part of the admissible evidence against the defendant. In *DPP* v *Spurrier, The Times*, 12 August 1999, the Divisional Court held that it was not always necessary for magistrates to hear expert evidence to rebut the presumption of reliability of a Lion Intoximeter when the defendant's evidence of consumption was contradicted by the device. The defendant had not driven erratically, was not unsteady on her feet and her eyes were not glazed but she produced a reading of 143 mg (four times over the limit). She claimed to have consumed two cans of lager and a significant proportion of a bottle of whisky, 12 hours previously. Accepting her evidence the justices concluded that the Lion Intoximeter could not have been reliable and that there was no need to call evidence on that point.

Where the machine is broken or unavailable or the suspected offence may be due to a drug rather than alcohol, or there are medical reasons for not requiring a sample of breath the police constable will offer the driver the chance to provide a blood specimen (for which a doctor will be called) or a urine sample (which does not need to be taken by a doctor). The choice of whether to provide a blood or urine sample is that of the police officer and not the driver (s. 7(4)).

11.3 Driving, Attempting to Drive or Being in Charge of a Vehicle when Unfit

Under RTA 1988, s. 4 it is an offence to drive, to attempt to drive, or to be in charge of a mechanically propelled vehicle on a road or other public place when under the influence of drink or drugs. The relevant parts read as follows:

4.—(1) A person who, when driving or attempting to drive a [mechanically propelled vehicle] on a road or other public place, is unfit to drive through drink or drugs is guilty of an offence.

(2) Without prejudice to subsection (1) above, a person who, when in charge of a [mechanically propelled vehicle] which is on a road or other public place, is unfit to drive through drink or drugs is guilty of an offence.

(3) For the purposes of subsection (2) above, a person shall be deemed not to have been in charge of a [mechanically propelled vehicle] if he proves that at the material time the circumstances were such that there was no likelihood of his driving it so long as he remained unfit to drive through drink or drugs.

(4) The court may, in determining whether there was such a likelihood as is mentioned in subsection (3) above, disregard any injury to him and any damage to the vehicle.

(5) For the purposes of this section, a person shall be taken to be unfit to drive if his ability to drive properly is for the time being impaired.

(6) A constable may arrest a person without warrant if he has reasonable cause to suspect that person is or has been committing an offence under this section.

(7) For the purpose of arresting a person under the power conferred by subsection (6) above, a constable may enter (if need be by force) any place where that person is or where the constable, with reasonable cause, suspects him to be.

The essence of driving is the use of the driver's controls to direct the movement of the vehicle (*McDonagh* [1974] QB 48). Being in charge is a wide concept, see *DPP* v *Watkins* [1989] QB 821. The owner or a person who has recently driven the vehicle would be in charge unless he or she has put the vehicle in someone else's charge or unless there was no realistic possibility of resuming control of the vehicle. It is a question of fact and degree if someone is in charge, see *DPP* v *Watkins* [1989] QB 821.

'Road' is defined in s. 192 as 'any highway and any other road to which the public has access'. The other public place need not be a road but must be a place to which the public has access e.g. a car park.

Evidence of unfitness may be provided by specimen sample of blood/breath/urine. Opinion evidence may also be received of the defendant's state (e.g. eyes glazed, speech slurred, unsteady on feet, etc.) but not of whether or not the defendant was fit to drive (*Davies* [1962] 3 All ER 97). In *Leethams* v *DPP* (1999) RTR 29 officers gave evidence that the defendant's eyes were red, his speech slurred and slow. He admitted smoking a cannabis cigarette some hours earlier. The blood sample showed no alcohol but cannabis consumption some time before the sample. (The effect of cannabis begins immediately after use, rises to a maximum after 20 minutes and disperses after two to four hours.) The Divisional Court held that despite lack of evidence from a doctor the officers had proved the case by the evidence of the appellant's driving, his appearance, behaviour and admission.

The offence under s. 4(1) is punishable with six months' imprisonment or a £5,000 fine, or both, and obligatory disqualification. Where penalty points are endorsed the range is 3 to 11 points. The offence under s. 4(2) is punishable with three months' imprisonment or a £2,500 fine, or both, and discretionary disqualification. Endorsement carries 10 penalty points.

11.4 Driving or Being in Charge above the Prescribed Limit

The offence of driving, attempting to drive or being in charge when over the prescribed limit is dealt with in s. 5:

> **5.**—*(1) If a person—*
> *(a) drives or attempts to drive a motor vehicle on a road or other public place, or*
> *(b) is in charge of a motor vehicle on a road or other public place,*
> *after consuming so much alcohol that the proportion of it in his breath, blood or urine exceeds the prescribed limit he is guilty of an offence.*
>
> *(2) It is a defence for a person charged with an offence under subsection (1)(b) above to prove that at the time he is alleged to have committed the offence the circumstances were such that there was no likelihood of his driving the vehicle whilst the proportion of alcohol in his breath, blood or urine remained likely to exceed the prescribed limit.*
>
> *(3) The court may, in determining whether there was such a likelihood as is mentioned in subsection (2) above, disregard any injury to him and any damage to the vehicle.*

In *DPP* v *H* [1998] RTR 200 it was affirmed that driving with excess alcohol was an offence of strict liability, so that *mens rea* was not an issue and the defence of insanity was not available.

The prosecution are entitled to do a back-calculation to show that at the time of driving, attempting to drive or being in charge, the alcohol in the driver's breath was in excess of the prescribed amount. In *Gumbley* v *Cunningham* [1988] QB 170, the appellant was involved in a fatal accident before midnight. He gave a specimen of blood with a reading of 59 µg at 3.35 a.m. the following morning. The prosecution adduced evidence of a calculation showing that a person with the appellant's age and physical characteristics would eliminate blood alcohol at the rate of 10 to 25 µg per hour and therefore his blood alcohol level at the time of the accident would have been between 120 and 130 Bg of alcohol per 100 ml of blood. This means that where a specimen contains less than the legal limit, but it can be shown by back calculation that the driver had excess alcohol at the time of the offence then a conviction will follow. Mann J said, 'those who drive whilst above the prescribed limits cannot necessarily escape punishment because of the lapse of time'. He further stressed that:

> the prosecution should not seek to rely on evidence of back-calculation save where that evidence is easily understood and clearly persuasive of the presence of excess alcohol at the time when a defendant was driving. Moreover, justices must be very careful especially where there is conflicting evidence not to convict unless, upon the scientific and other evidence which they find it safe to rely on, they are sure an excess of alcohol was in the defendant's body when he was actually driving as charged.

11.4.1 THE HIP-FLASK DEFENCE

Where the defendant wishes to claim that a post-driving drink took him over the limit (the hip-flask defence) the burden of proof lies on him to show that on a balance of probabilities. The court is entitled to assume that the alcohol level at the time of driving was not less than that at the time of the test (RTOA 1988, s. 15(2)). This statutory assumption will not be made if the defendant proves that he consumed alcohol after he stopped driving, attempting to drive or being in charge and before he provided a specimen, and that had he not done so the proportion of alcohol in his breath/blood/urine would not have exceeded the prescribed limit. See *DPP* v *Williams* [1989] Crim LR 382.

11.4.2 NO LIKELIHOOD OF DRIVING

Under s. 5(2), it is a defence for a person charged with driving or being in charge with excess alcohol to prove that there was no likelihood of his or her driving the vehicle whilst the proportion of alcohol in his or her breath/blood/urine remained likely to exceed the prescribed limit. Under s. 4(3) the accused has to show that there was no likelihood of driving while unfit. In both cases the burden of proof is on the defendant; the standard is the balance of probabilities. The fact that the defendant was too drunk to drive would probably not satisfy the test as it would need to be shown that the alcohol level exceeded the limit, in other words that the defendant would not simply have driven when the worst effects had worn off (see *Northfield* v *Pinder* [1968] 3 All ER 854). Expert medical or scientific evidence may need to be called in respect of s. 5(2).

11.4.3 LACED DRINKS

It is not a defence to the charge but the fact that drinks may have been laced may be put forward as a reason for not disqualifying. The defendant would have to show that he or she had been misled by a third party and would be expected to have made some enquiry about what he or she was drinking. The person lacing the drinks may be convicted of procuring a person to commit an offence under RTA 1988, s. 5. See *Attorney-General's Reference (No. 1 of 1975)* [1975] QB 773.

The offence under s. 5(1)(a) is punishable with six months' imprisonment or a £5,000 fine, or both, and obligatory disqualification. Where penalty points are endorsed the range is 3 to 11 points. The offence under s. 5(1)(b) is punishable with three months' imprisonment or a £2,500 fine, or both, and discretionary disqualification. Endorsement carries 10 penalty points.

11.5 Failure to Provide a Specimen

11.5.1 BREATH TESTS

Under RTA 1988, s. 6(4) (the roadside breath test), failure without reasonable excuse to provide a specimen of breath for a breath test when required to do so by a police constable in uniform is an offence. The section reads as follows:

6.—(1)   Where a constable in uniform has reasonable cause to suspect—
(a)   that a person driving or attempting to drive or in charge of a motor vehicle on a road or other public place has alcohol in his body or has committed a traffic offence whilst the vehicle was in motion, or
(b)   that a person has been driving or attempting to drive or been in charge of a motor vehicle on a road or other public place with alcohol in his body and that that person still has alcohol in his body, or
(c)   that a person has been driving or attempting to drive or been in charge of a motor vehicle on a road or other public place and has committed a traffic offence whilst the vehicle was in motion,

he may, subject to section 9 of this Act, require him to provide a specimen of breath for a breath test.

(2) If an accident occurs owing to the presence of a motor vehicle on a road or other public place, a constable may, subject to section 9 of this Act, require any person who he has reasonable cause to believe was driving or attempting to drive or in charge of the vehicle at the time of the accident to provide a specimen of breath for a breath test.

(3) A person may be required under subsection (1) or subsection (2) above to provide a specimen either at or near the place where the requirement is made or, if the requirement is made under subsection (2) above and the constable making the requirement thinks fit, at a police station specified by the constable.

(4) A person who, without reasonable excuse, fails to provide a specimen of breath when required to do so in pursuance of this section is guilty of an offence.

(5) A constable may arrest a person without warrant if—

(a) as a result of a breath test he has reasonable cause to suspect that the proportion of alcohol in that person's breath or blood exceeds the prescribed limit, or

(b) that person has failed to provide a specimen of breath for a breath test when required to do so in pursuance of this section and the constable has reasonable cause to suspect that he has alcohol in his body,

but a person shall not be arrested by virtue of this subsection when he is at a hospital as a patient.

(6) A constable may, for the purpose of requiring a person to provide a specimen of breath under subsection (2) above in a case where he has reasonable cause to suspect that the accident involved injury to another person or of arresting him in such a case under subsection (5) above, enter (if need be by force) any place where that person is or where the constable, with reasonable cause, suspects him to be.

Evidence has to be adduced to establish a reasonable cause to suspect the presence of alcohol. A court cannot infer reasonable cause from the mere fact of asking for a breath test (*Siddiqui* v *Swain* [1979] RTR 454). There is no restriction on random stopping of motorists but a subsequent request for a breath test can be made only if the constable has reasonable cause to suspect alcohol has been taken (*Chief Constable of Gwent* v *Dash* [1986] RTR 41). The constable's suspicions may arise after the defendant has been stopped. Although the absence of a reasonable cause may invalidate an arrest it will not invalidate the subsequent procedure (*DPP* v *Godwin* [1991] RTR 303). The court may always, of course, exercise its discretion to exclude the evidence under PACE 1984, s. 78.

The offence is punishable with a fine of £1,000, discretionary disqualification and endorsement of 4 penalty points.

11.5.2 SPECIMENS FOR ANALYSIS

Section 7 of the 1988 Act deals with provision of a specimen for analysis:

(1) In the course of an investigation into whether a person has committed an offence under [section 3A, 4] or 5 of this Act a constable may, subject to the following provisions of this section and section 9 of this Act, require him—

(a) to provide two specimens of breath for analysis by means of a device of a type approved by the Secretary of State, or

(b) to provide a specimen of blood or urine for a laboratory test.

(2) A requirement under this section to provide specimens of breath can only be made at a police station.

(3) A requirement under this section to provide a specimen of blood or urine can only be made at a police station or at a hospital; and it cannot be made at a police station unless—

(a) the constable making the requirement has reasonable cause to believe that for medical reasons a specimen of breath cannot be provided or should not be required, or

(b) at the time the requirement is made a device or a reliable device of the type mentioned in subsection (1)(a) above is not available at the police station or it is then for any other reason not practicable to use such a device there, or

(c) the suspected offence is one under [section 3A, 4] of this Act and the constable making the requirement has been advised by a medical practitioner that the condition of the person required to provide the specimen might be due to some drug; but may then be made notwithstanding that the person required to provide the specimen has already provided or been required to provide two specimens of breath.

(4) If the provision of a specimen other than a specimen of breath may be required in pursuance of this section the question whether it is to be a specimen of blood or a specimen of urine shall be decided by the constable making the requirement, but if a medical practitioner is of the opinion that for medical reasons a specimen of blood cannot or should not be taken the specimen shall be a specimen of urine.

(5) A specimen of urine shall be provided within one hour of the requirement for its provision being made and after the provision of a previous specimen of urine.

(6) A person who, without reasonable excuse, fails to provide a specimen when required to do so in pursuance of this section is guilty of an offence.

(7) A constable must, on requiring any person to provide a specimen in pursuance of this section, warn him that a failure to provide it may render him liable to prosecution.

The section requires two specimens of breath for analysis and the prosecution rely on the lower reading for their case. Where the lower reading is not more than 50 μg of alcohol in 100 ml of breath, the person providing the sample may request that it should be replaced by a blood or urine sample (s. 8(2)). Although the accused can express a preference for a particular sample, the choice will be made by the officer (see *DPP* v *Warren* [1993] RTR 58). The only right of the defendant to object to giving blood and to give urine instead will be for medical reasons to be determined by the medical practitioner. In *Epping Justices, ex parte Quy* [1998] RTR 158 the Divisional Court held that a fear of needles was capable of being a medical reason. In that case the officer should have asked further questions and/or called a medical practitioner. A specimen of blood must be taken with the accused's consent and by a medical practitioner. The officer must warn the accused that failure to provide the specimen of breath, blood or urine is an offence that may render the accused liable to prosecution and also carries the penalty of disqualification (s. 7(7)). Failure to give the warning renders the results of the test inadmissible (*Murray* v *DPP* [1993] Crim LR 968).

Guidance and clarification as to the procedures to be followed by the police under s. 7(3) or s. 8(2) following *DPP* v *Warren*, was set out by the House of Lords in *DPP* v *Jackson; Stanley* v *DPP* [1998] 3 All ER 769. It was held *inter alia*, that (i) it was for the police officer to decide whether the specimen was to be of blood or urine (s. 7(4)); (ii) the specimen of blood was to be taken by a doctor (s. 11(4)). In addition, the right of the police officer to choose whether the specimen was to be of blood or urine was subject to the qualification that if a medical reason was raised why a specimen of blood could not or should not be taken, the issue was to be decided by a doctor and not by the police officer; (iii) an offence under s. 7(6) for failure to provide a specimen of blood or urine or an offence under s. 5(1), proved by a specimen of breath where the driver had not claimed under s. 8(2) to replace it with a specimen of blood or urine was an unusual offence in that the driver had the choice to make, in the police station prior to the charge being made; (iv) it was not a mandatory requirement but a driver should be aware, whether in a s. 7(3) case or a s. 8(2) case of the role of a doctor in the taking of a specimen of blood and in determining any medical objections which he might raise to the giving of such a specimen. The mandatory requirements were: (a) in a s. 7(3) case the warning as to the risk of prosecution required by s. 7(7); (b) in a s. 7(3) case the statement of the reason under the subsection why breath specimens could not be taken or used; and (c) in a s. 8(2) case the statement that the specimen of breath which the driver had given containing the lower proportion of alcohol did not exceed 50 μg of alcohol in 100 ml of breath.

11.5.3   FAILURE

What constitutes failure is a question of fact. Failure includes a refusal and also includes a conditional agreement (e.g. only allowing blood to be taken from an inappropriate part of the body, *Solesbury* v *Pugh* [1969] 2 All ER 1171). A refusal may be implied from conduct. In *Smyth* v *DPP, The Times*, 21 June 1995, the defendant said 'no' when asked to provide a specimen, but within five seconds said that he wanted to change his mind. He was convicted by the magistrates. The Queen's Bench Division, allowing his appeal and concluding he had not refused to provide a specimen, said that the tribunal should have had regard to all the defendant's words and conduct.

11.5.4   REASONABLE EXCUSE

The issue of reasonable excuse has to be raised by the defendant; the burden is on the prosecution to disprove it beyond reasonable doubt. A physical inability to provide a specimen may amount to a reasonable excuse.

No fear short of a phobia recognised by medical science to be as strong and inhibiting as, for instance, claustrophobia can be allowed to excuse failure to provide a specimen for a laboratory test, and in most if not all cases where the fear of providing it is claimed to be invincible the claim will have to be supported by medical evidence (per Lord Widgery CJ in *Harding* [1974] RTR 325).

An inability to understand what is being said due to a limited grasp of English may also be a reasonable excuse (*Chief Constable of Avon and Somerset* v *Singh* [1988] RTR 107). In *Harling* [1970] RTR 441, a reasonable excuse was said to exist where the defendant lost confidence in the doctor's ability after the doctor had made three unsuccessful attempts to take blood.

Cases in which the defence of reasonable excuse have failed are *Sykes* v *White* [1983] RTR 419 (dislike of blood not amounting to a phobia); *DPP* v *Fountain* [1988] Crim LR 123 (fear of contracting AIDS through the use of needles, but compare *DeFreitas* v *DPP* [1992] Crim LR 894, a genuine but unreasonable phobia of contracting AIDS was found to be a reasonable excuse); *Woolman* v *Lenton* [1985] Crim LR 516 (difficulty in blowing through the nose); (*Daniels* v *DPP* [1992] RTR 140 (a belief that no offence had been committed); *DPP* v *Coyle, The Times*, 20 July 1995 (motorist not told of necessity to provide required specimen within a total of three minutes, see also *Cosgrove* v *DPP, The Times*, 29 March 1996); *Thomas* v *DPP* [1991] RTR 292 (a previous unlawful arrest was not relevant to the subsequent procedures and could not amount to a reasonable excuse, see also *Matto* v *Wolverhampton Crown Court* [1987] RTR 337).

In *DPP* v *Varley* [1999] Crim LR 753, the defendant asked for legal advice before he would agree to the breath test procedure. The sergeant said that he was not prepared to wait for the duty solicitor. The magistrates concluded that the defendant had a reasonable excuse and acquitted him. The Divisional Court held that those facts were not capable of amounting to a reasonable excuse; generally a reasonable excuse existed when a defendant was mentally or physically unable to provide a specimen.

Where the specimen is required to ascertain ability to drive, or the proportion of alcohol at the time the accused was driving, or attempting to drive, the offence is punishable with six months' imprisonment or a £5,000 fine, or both, and obligatory disqualification. Endorsement carries 3 to 11 penalty points. In all other cases it is three months' imprisonment, discretionary disqualification or 10 penalty points.

11.5.5   PROTECTION FOR HOSPITAL PATIENTS

If the accused is in hospital as a patient there can be no requirement to provide a specimen unless the medical practitioner in charge of the case has been notified and the specimen is provided at the hospital. If the medical practitioner decides that the provision of a specimen or the warning required under s. 7(7) would be prejudicial to the proper care and treatment of the patient, then the requirement must not be made (s. 9).

11.6 Causing Death by Careless Driving when under the Influence of Drink or Drugs

The offence under RTA 1988, s. 3A is indictable only and reads as follows:

> *(1)   If a person causes the death of another person by driving a mechanically propelled vehicle on a road or other public place without due care and attention, or without reasonable consideration for other persons using the road or place, and—*
>
> > *(a)   he is, at the time when he is driving, unfit to drive through drink or drugs, or*
> >
> > *(b)   he has consumed so much alcohol that the proportion of it in his breath, blood or urine at that time exceeds the prescribed limit, or*
> >
> > *(c)   he is, within 18 hours after that time, required to provide a specimen in pursuance of section 7 of this Act, but without reasonable excuse fails to provide it,*
> >
> > *he is guilty of an offence.*
>
> *(2)   For the purposes of this section a person shall be taken to be unfit to drive at any time when his ability to drive properly is impaired.*
>
> *(3)   Subsection (1)(b) and (c) above shall not apply in relation to a person driving a mechanically propelled vehicle other than a motor vehicle.*

A jury acquitting a defendant of an offence under s. 3A may convict on an alternative offence under s. 3 (careless and inconsiderate driving), s. 4(1) (driving when unfit through drink or drugs), s. 5(1)(a) (driving with excess alcohol in breath, blood or urine), or s. 7(6) (failing to provide a specimen). Alternative verdicts are set out in RTOA 1988, s. 24; see **10.2.3**.

The s. 3A offence is punishable with 10 years' imprisonment or a fine, or both. Disqualification is obligatory.

11.7 Cycling when under the Influence of Drink or Drugs

Section 30 of the RTA 1988 states:

> *A person who, when riding a cycle on a road or other public place, is unfit through drink or drugs (that is to say, is under the influence of drink or a drug to such an extent as to be incapable of having proper control of the cycle) is guilty of an offence.*

The offence covers riding a bicycle, tricycle or other cycle having four or more wheels, but not being a motor vehicle, on a road. The offence is committed on public highways as well as footways. The police cannot require the cyclist to provide a specimen of breath, blood or urine but if one is provided it may be used in a prosecution.

The offence is summary only and punishable by a maximum fine of £1,000.

11.8 Procedure and Sentence

Most motoring offences are summary only offences and are brought to court by way of summons, but in most drink driving cases the motorist will have been charged at the police station. The defendant is generally bailed to appear at the magistrates' court. Advance disclosure is not available in summary only offences. As the drink driving offences carry punishment of disqualification, which cannot be ordered in the defendant's absence, the offences cannot be dealt with by way of postal written pleas of guilty.

Legal aid is rarely given in road traffic cases, but the criteria set out in Legal Aid Act 1988, s. 22, for considering the grant of legal aid may be satisfied in some drink driving cases.

For sentencing see **Chapter 12** generally. Driving with excess alcohol carries a maximum six months' imprisonment. The Magistrates' Association Guidelines state that those driving with more than 115mg in 100ml of breath (i.e., over three times the limit) should be considered for a custodial sentence; see also *Shoult* [1996] RTR 298. Aggravating features identified by the Magistrates' Association include; police chase, causing injury/fear/damage, carrying passengers for reward, large goods vehicle, nature of driving, high reading.

TWELVE

ROAD TRAFFIC OFFENCES: PENALTIES

12.1 Introduction

The distinctive penalties for road traffic offences are endorsement and disqualification from driving. It is common for the court to impose a fine for a driving offence, although in appropriate cases a custodial or community sentence might be imposed. This chapter concentrates on endorsement and disqualification.

12.2 Endorsement

An endorsement involves entering details of the conviction on the offender's driving licence. If the endorsement is obligatory, then the court must cause it to be carried out. It is 'part of the penalty'. The matters to be endorsed include the convicting court, the dates of offence, conviction and sentence, the particulars of offence and the sentence imposed. The court notifies the Driving and Vehicle Licensing Agency (DVLA) in Swansea, which carries out the endorsement.

12.2.1 EXPIRY OF THE ENDORSEMENT

The endorsement will remain on the defendant's licence until he or she can apply for a clean one, surrendering the one which has been endorsed and paying an administrative fee. Application for a clean licence can be made:

(a) after 11 years from the date of conviction for an excess alcohol offence;

(b) after four years from the date of conviction where the defendant was disqualified, or the offence is one of dangerous driving;

(c) after four years from the date of the offence in other cases.

12.2.2 PRODUCTION OF LICENCE

The defendant is under an obligation to produce a driving licence when convicted of an offence involving endorsement. It is an offence to fail to do so. If the defendant is unable to produce a licence, then the court will lack vital information in determining sentence. It may therefore decide to adjourn for the licence to be produced, or a printout of the defendant's driving record to be produced from DVLA, so as to establish any previous endorsements. When it does come to sentence the offender, the court may take into account any endorsements, including old ones which are no longer effective for 'totting up' purposes (see **12.3.1.2**).

12.2.3 PENALTY POINTS

The framework for the imposition of penalty points is set out in the Road Traffic Offenders Act (RTOA) 1988, s. 28:

28.—(1)   Where a person is convicted of an offence involving obligatory endorsement, then, subject to the following provisions of this section, the number of penalty points to be attributed to the offence is—

(a)   the number shown in relation to the offence in the last column of part I or part II of schedule 2 to this Act, or

(b)   where a range of numbers is shown, a number within that range.

(2)   Where a person is convicted of an offence committed by aiding, abetting, counselling or procuring, or inciting to the commission of, an offence involving obligatory disqualification, then, subject to the following provisions of this section, the number of penalty points to be attributed to the offence is 10.

(3)   Where both a range of numbers and a number followed by the words '(fixed penalty)' is shown in the last column of part I of schedule 2 to this Act in relation to an offence, that number is the number of penalty points to be attributed to the offence for the purposes of sections 57(5) and 77(5) of this Act; and, where only a range of numbers is shown there, the lowest number in the range is the number of penalty points to be attributed to the offence for those purposes.

(4)   Where a person is convicted (whether on the same occasion or not) of two or more offences committed on the same occasion and involving obligatory endorsement, the total number of penalty points to be attributed to them is the number or highest number that would be attributed on a conviction of one of them (so that if the convictions are on different occasions the number of penalty points to be attributed to the offences on the later occasion or occasions shall be restricted accordingly).

(5)   In a case where (apart from this subsection) subsection (4) above would apply to two or more offences, the court may if it thinks fit determine that that subsection shall not apply to the offences (or, where three or more offences are concerned, to any one or more of them).

(6)   Where a court makes such a determination it shall state its reasons in open court and, if it is a magistrates' court . . . shall cause them to be entered in the register . . . of its proceedings.

The penalty points applicable to those offences which carry them are set out in RTOA 1988, sch. 2, extracts from which are reprinted below.

ROAD TRAFFIC OFFENDERS ACT 1988 SCHEDULE 2 (EXTRACTS)
PROSECUTION AND PUNISHMENT OF OFFENCES
PART I
OFFENCES UNDER THE TRAFFIC ACTS

(1) Provision creating offence	(2) General nature of offence	(3) Mode of prosecution	(4) Punishment	(5) Disqualification	(6) Endorsement	(7) Penalty points
Offences under the Road Traffic Regulation Act 1984						
RTRA section 16(1)	Contravention of temporary prohibition or restriction.	Summarily.	Level 3 on the standard scale.	Discretionary if committed in respect of a speed restriction.	Obligatory if committed in respect of a speed restriction.	3–6 or 3 (fixed penalty).
RTRA section 17(4)	Use of special road contrary to scheme or regulations.	Summarily.	Level 4 on the standard scale.	Discretionary if committed in respect of a motor vehicle otherwise than by unlawfully stopping or allowing the vehicle to remain at rest on a part of a special road on which vehicles are in certain circumstances permitted to remain at rest.	Obligatory if committed as mentioned in the entry in column 5.	3–6 or 3 (fixed penalty) if committed in respect of a speed restriction, 3 in any other case.
RTRA section 25(5)	Contravention of pedestrian crossing regulations.	Summarily.	Level 3 on the standard scale.	Discretionary if committed in respect of a motor vehicle.	Obligatory if committed in respect of a motor vehicle.	3
RTRA section 28(3)	Not stopping at school crossing.	Summarily.	Level 3 on the standard scale.	Discretionary if committed in respect of a motor vehicle.	Obligatory if committed in respect of a motor vehicle.	3
RTRA section 29(3)	Contravention of order relating to street playground.	Summarily.	Level 3 on the standard scale	Discretionary if committed in respect of a motor vehicle.	Obligatory if committed in respect of a motor vehicle.	2
RTRA section 89(1)	Exceeding speed limit.	Summarily.	Level 3 on the standard scale.	Discretionary.	Obligatory.	3–6 or 3 (fixed penalty).
Offences under the Road Traffic Act 1988						
RTA section 1	Causing death by dangerous driving.	On indictment.	10 years.	Obligatory.	Obligatory.	3–11
RTA section 2	Dangerous Driving.	(a) Summarily. (b) On indictment.	(a) 6 months or the statutory maximum or both. (b) 2 years or a fine or both.	Obligatory.	Obligatory.	3–11
RTA section 3	Careless, and inconsiderate, driving.	Summarily.	Level 4 on the standard scale.	Discretionary.	Obligatory.	3–9
RTA section 3A	Causing death by careless driving when under influence of drink or drugs.	On indictment.	10 years or a fine or both.	Obligatory.	Obligatory.	3–11
RTA section 4(1)	Driving or attempting to drive when unfit to drive through drink or drugs.	Summarily.	6 months or level 5 on the standard scale or both.	Obligatory.	Obligatory.	3–11

(1) Provision creating offence	(2) General nature of offence	(3) Mode of prosecution	(4) Punishment	(5) Disqualification	(6) Endorsement	(7) Penalty points
RTA section 4(2)	Being in charge of a mechanically propelled vehicle when unfit to drive through drink or drugs.	Summarily.	3 months or level 4 on the scale or both.	Discretionary.	Obligatory.	10
RTA section 5(1)(a)	Driving or attempting to drive with with excess alcohol in breath, blood or urine.	Summarily.	6 months or level 5 on the standard scale or both.	Obligatory.	Obligatory.	3–11
RTA section 5(1)(b)	Being in charge of a mechanically propelled vehicle with excess alcohol in breath, blood or urine.	Summarily.	3 months or level 4 on the standard scale or both.	Discretionary.	Obligatory.	10
RTA section 6	Failing to provide a specimen of breath for a breath test.	Summarily.	Level 3 on the standard scale.	Discretionary.	Obligatory.	4
RTA section 7	Failing to provide specimen for analysis or laboratory test.	Summarily.	(a) Where the specimen was required to ascertain ability to drive or proportion of alcohol at the time offender was driving or attempting to drive, 6 months or level 5 on the standard scale or both. (b) In any other case, 3 months or level 4 on the standard scale or both.	(a) Obligatory in case mentioned in column 4(a). (b) Discretionary in any other case.	Obligatory.	(a) 3–11 in case mentioned in column 4(a). (b) 10 in any case.
RTA section 12	Motor racing and speed trials on public ways.	Summarily.	Level 4 on the standard scale.	Obligatory.	Obligatory.	3–11
RTA section 22	Leaving vehicles in dangerous positions.	Summarily.	Level 3 on the standard scale.	Discretionary if committed in respect of a motor vehicle.	Obligatory if committed in respect of a motor vehicle.	3
RTA section 22A	Causing danger to road users.	(a) Summarily. (b) On indictment.	(a) 6 months or the statutory maximum or both. (b) 7 years or a fine or both.			
RTA section 23	Carrying passenger on motor-cycle contrary to section 23.	Summarily.	Level 3 on the standard scale.	Discretionary.	Obligatory.	3
RTA section 35	Failing to comply with traffic directions.	Summarily.	Level 3 on the standard scale.	Discretionary, if committed in respect of a motor vehicle by failure to comply with a direction of a constable or traffic warden.	Obligatory if committed as described in column 5.	3

(1) Provision creating offence	(2) General nature of offence	(3) Mode of prosecution	(4) Punishment	(5) Disqualification	(6) Endorsement	(7) Penalty points
RTA section 36	Failing to comply with traffic signs.	Summarily.	Level 3 on the standard scale.	Discretionary, if committed in respect of a motor vehicle by failure to comply with an indication given by a sign specified for the purposes of this paragraph in regulations under RTA section 36.	Obligatory if committed as described in column 5.	3
RTA section 40A	Using vehicle in dangerous condition etc.	Summarily.	(a) Level 5 on the standard scale if committed in respect of a goods vehicle or a vehicle adapted to carry more than eight passengers. (b) Level 4 on the standard scale in any other case.	Discretionary.	Obligatory.	3
RTA section 41A	Breach of requirement as to brakes, steering-gear or tyres.	Summarily.	(a) Level 5 on the standard scale if committed in respect of a goods vehicle or a vehicle adapted to carry more than eight passengers. (b) Level 4 on the standard scale in any other case.	Discretionary.	Obligatory.	3
RTA section 87(1)	Driving otherwise than in accordance with a licence.	Summarily.	Level 3 on the standard scale.	Discretionary in a case where the offender's driving would not have been in accordance with any licence that could have been granted to him.	Obligatory in the case mentioned in column 5.	3–6
RTA section 92(10)	Driving after making false declaration as to physical fitness.	Summarily.	Level 4 on the standard scale.	Discretionary.	Obligatory.	3–6
RTA section 93(3)	Failure to deliver revoked licence and counterpart to Secretary of State.	Summarily.	Level 3 on the standard scale.			
RTA section 94(3)	Failure to notify Secretary of State of onset of, or deterioration in, relevant or prospective disability.	Summarily.	Level 3 on the standard scale.			
RTA section 94(3A)	Driving after such a failure.	Summarily.	Level 3 on the standard scale.	Discretionary.	Obligatory.	3–6
RTA section 94A	Driving after refusal of licence under section 92(3) or revocation under section 93.	Summarily.	6 months or level 5 on the standard scale or both.	Discretionary.	Obligatory.	3–6

(1) Provision creating offence	(2) General nature of offence	(3) Mode of prosecution	(4) Punishment	(5) Disqualification	(6) Endorsement	(7) Penalty points
RTA section 96	Driving with uncorrected defective eyesight, or refusing to submit to test of eyesight.	Summarily.	Level 3 on the standard scale.	Discretionary.	Obligatory.	3
RTA section 99(5)	Driving licence holder failing, when his licence is revoked, to surrender it and its counterpart or when his particulars become incorrect, to surrender licence and counterpart and give particulars.	Summarily.	Level 3 on the standard scale			
RTA section 103(1)(a)	Obtaining driving licence while disqualified.	Summarily.	Level 3 on the standard scale.			
RTA section 103(1)(b)	Driving while disqualified.	Summarily.	6 months or level 5 on the standard scale or both.	Discretionary.	Obligatory.	6
RTA section 143	Using motor vehicle while uninsured or unsecured against third party risks.	Summarily.	Level 5 on the standard scale.	Discretionary.	Obligatory.	6–8
RTA section 170(4)	Failing to stop after accident and give particulars or report accident.	Summarily.	6 months or level 5 on the standard scale or both.	Discretionary.	Obligatory.	5–10
RTA section 170(7)	Failure by driver, in case of accident involving injury to another, to produce evidence of insurance or security or to report accident.	Summarily.	Level 3 on the standard scale.			
RTA section 171	Failure by owner of motor vehicle to give police information for verifying compliance with requirement of compulsory insurance or security.	Summarily.	Level 4 on the standard scale.			
RTA section 172	Failure of person keeping vehicle and others to give police information as to identity of driver, etc., in the case of certain offences.	Summarily.	Level 3 on the standard scale.	Discretionary if committed otherwise than by virtue of subsection (5) or (11).	Obligatory if committed otherwise than by virtue of subsection (5) or (11).	3

For most offences carrying penalty points, the number of points is fixed, e.g., 3 points for failing to comply with a traffic sign (by jumping a red light, for instance). Other offences have a range, from which the sentencer can select the most appropriate, e.g., 3 to 6 points for speeding.

What if the defendant is convicted of two or more offences on the same occasion, and both carry penalty points? Say, for example, that the defendant is convicted of careless driving (for which a range of 3 to 9 points is laid down) and driving without insurance

(6 to 8 points). Assume further that the episode of careless driving took place while the defendant was uninsured. The situation used to be that the court had to decide which of the offences committed on the same occasion was the more serious, and fix the appropriate number of points for that offence. It could not then impose any extra points for the other offence(s) (*Johnson* v *Finbow* [1983] 1 WLR 879).

The position is now governed by RTOA 1988, s. 28(5). The court can now, if it thinks fit, impose penalty points for more than one offence committed on the same occasion. In the example given above, that would mean that the court could, for example, impose 9 points for the careless driving, and an additional 6 points for the driving without insurance, thus triggering off a penalty points disqualification (see **12.3.1.2**). The normal practice, however, is still to impose penalty points only for the most serious offence. If the court wishes to exercise its powers under s. 28(5), it must state its reasons in open court and they must be put on the register.

12.3 Disqualification

All orders of disqualification from driving run from the moment they are pronounced (*Meese* [1973] 1 WLR 675 (CA)). In that case, the trial judge ordered that the two periods of disqualification which he was imposing should run consecutively. The Court of Appeal held that such a sentence was unlawful, since the start of the second period would be postponed. They must run concurrently.

Disqualification can be for any period — even life. But a life disqualification is extremely rare. The danger which the appellate courts have seen with very long periods of disqualification (e.g., 10 years) is that they may shut the defendant out of a substantial number of jobs, and create an incentive to disregard the law.

12.3.1 CATEGORIES OF DISQUALIFICATION

There are three categories of disqualification: obligatory; penalty points; and discretionary. The succeeding paragraphs deal with each in turn.

12.3.1.1 Obligatory

Where an offence carries obligatory disqualification, there must be an order of disqualification unless there are special reasons (see **12.4**).

As far as the minimum period for which the court must disqualify is concerned:

(a) The minimum is usually 12 months.

(b) For certain of the most serious offences (manslaughter, causing death by dangerous driving, and causing death by careless driving while under the influence of drink or drugs) there is a longer minimum of two years.

(c) A minimum of two years must be imposed when the defendant has been disqualified for 56 days or more at least twice in the three years preceding the commission of the offence in question.

(d) There is a special minimum sentence of three years disqualification under RTOA 1988, s. 34(3) where the defendant is convicted of an alcohol-related offence which was committed within 10 years of the date of conviction of an earlier alcohol-related offence.

12.3.1.2 Penalty points

This applies where the defendant 'tots up' 12 or more points within three years (RTOA 1988, s. 29). Such a 'totter' is then disqualified for a minimum of six months, in the absence of clearly defined 'mitigating grounds'.

The penalty points to be taken into account are:

(a) any for the offence(s) of which the defendant is now convicted (disregarding any for which the court disqualifies);

(b) any ordered to be endorsed on a previous occasion for an offence *committed* in the preceding three years (by RTOA 1988, s. 35, 'if any of the offences was committed more than three years before another, the points in respect of that offence are not to be added to those in respect of the other').

The law used to be that, if the defendant was disqualified, the slate was wiped clean and he or she started again to tot up towards 12. Now, there is no general rule that the slate will be wiped clean once there is disqualification. The rule is that all penalty points remain until there is a penalty points disqualification, whereupon they are wiped off.

The court may decide not to impose a penalty points disqualification (or impose a shorter one than six months) if there are mitigating grounds. When the term is applied to a 'totter', then it has a restricted meaning. Certain factors may not be mitigating grounds by virtue of RTOA 1988, s. 35(4), i.e.:

(a) any circumstances that are alleged to make the offence(s) not a serious one;

(b) hardship, other than exceptional hardship;

(c) any circumstances taken into account as mitigating grounds in the preceding three years.

Frequently, 'exceptional hardship' is argued in relation to the offender's employment. The court might take into account the following factors, together with any others which appear from the facts:

(a) whether the offender requires a licence to drive as a necessary part of the job;

(b) whether he or she needs to drive in order to get to work;

(c) the distances to be travelled to work;

(d) the availability of public transport;

(e) the hours required by the job (e.g., are they at a time when public transport is available);

(f) the offender's age and health;

(g) any other means of transport available;

(h) any particular hardship caused to the offender's family by the loss of the job or reduced wages;

(i) any employees dependent on the offender's ability to drive.

12.3.1.3 Discretionary
The court can disqualify for a specific offence where it imposes less than 12 points.

12.3.1.4 Probationary period
Every driver who qualified on or after 1 June 1997 is subject to a probationary period of two years, beginning with the day on which he or she qualified (Road Traffic (New Drivers) Act 1995). A driver who acquires six or more penalty points during that probationary period, will have his or her licence revoked and must undergo retesting before a full driving licence can once again be issued.

12.3.2 ENDING DISQUALIFICATION

In the normal course of events, the disqualification will end once the period laid down by the court expires. Prior to that, the offender can apply for his or her licence back before the period of disqualification ends, provided that a certain period of time has elapsed. That period is:

(a) at least two years in any event;

(b) half the period of disqualification if the period ordered is between four and ten years;

(c) five years if the disqualification is for ten years or more.

12.3.3 ORDER FOR RETEST

There is, however, provision for the sentencing court to lay down that the offender must pass a driving test before the disqualification comes to an end. Whilst such an order is within the court's discretion, it should not be imposed on a punitive basis, but in order to protect the safety of other road users, e.g., because of the age, infirmity or lack of experience of the offender, or the nature of the offence (*Guilfoyle* [1973] 2 All ER 844). Retests are now compulsory when the court disqualifies for manslaughter or for dangerous driving (whether it causes death or not): RTOA 1988, s. 36.

12.4 Special Reasons

As mentioned above, where disqualification is obligatory, the court must disqualify unless there are 'special reasons'. A similar rule applies where endorsement is obligatory.

Where special reasons are necessary, these must relate to the offence, and not the circumstances of the offender. As it was put in *Whittal* v *Kirby* [1947] KB 194:

A 'special reason' within the exception is one which is special to the facts of the particular case, that is, special to the facts which constitute the offence. It is, in other words, a mitigating or extenuating circumstance, not amounting in law to a defence to the charge, yet directly connected with the commission of the offence, and one which the court ought properly to take into consideration when imposing punishment. A circumstance peculiar to the offender as distinguished from the offence is not a 'special reason' within the exception.

Frequently, special reasons are put forward where the defendant alleges that his or her drink was laced. Guidance has now been laid down in *DPP* v *O'Connor* [1992] RTR 66 as to what constitutes special reasons in these circumstances. The defence must show on the balance of probabilities:

(a) that the defendant's drink had been laced;

(b) that the defendant did not know or suspect that it had been laced;

(c) that, if the defendant had not taken the laced drink, his or her alcohol level would not have exceeded the prescribed limit.

Another series of cases relates to drink driving in an emergency. In *Chatters* v *Burke* [1986] 1 WLR 1321, the court laid down seven matters which the justices ought to take into account in such cases:

First of all they should consider how far the vehicle was in fact driven; secondly, in what manner it was driven; thirdly, what was the state of the vehicle; fourthly, whether it was the intention of the driver to drive any further; fifthly, the prevailing conditions with regard to the road and the traffic upon it; sixthly, whether there was any possibility of danger by contact with other road users; and finally, what was the reason for the vehicle being driven at all.

The argument that there are special reasons is not, however, confined to drink driving cases. For example, it also has application to a speeding case (*Police Prosecutor* v *Humphreys* [1970] Crim LR 234).

Further, the defendant can argue that there are special reasons not to impose penalty points.

THIRTEEN

REGULATORY LAW

This chapter discusses, with specific reference to food safety, some of the principles relating to prosecutions of individuals, firms and companies by regulatory authorities for breach of regulations and offences under legislation such as the Health and Safety at Work etc. Act 1974, the Consumer Protection Act 1987, the Food Safety Act 1990 (FSA 1990), the Environmental Protection Act 1990 and the Water Resources Act 1991.

The plethora of legislation in the area of regulatory law is based on increasing concern for the protection of the community. The principle applied is that the polluter pays, and offences are of strict liability.

13.1 The Basic Provisions of the Food Safety Act 1990

The food safety legislation provides a useful guide to the nature of regulatory law and to the types of breaches which give rise to prosecutions.

The definitions of 'food' and other basic expressions are provided in s. 1 of the FSA 1990:

> *1.—(1) In this Act 'food' includes—*
>   *(a)   drink;*
>   *(b)   articles and substances of no nutritional value which are used for human consumption;*
>   *(c)   chewing gum and other products of a like nature and use; and*
>   *(d)   articles and substances used as ingredients in the preparation of food or anything falling within this subsection.*
>   *(2)   In this Act 'food' does not include—*
>   *(a)   live animals or birds, or live fish which are not used for human consumption while they are alive;*
>   *(b)   fodder or feeding stuffs for animals, birds or fish;*
>   *(c)   controlled drugs within the meaning of the Misuse of Drugs Act 1971; or*
>   *(d)   subject to such exceptions as may be specified in an order made by the Ministers—*
>   *(i)   medicinal products within the meaning of the Medicines Act 1968 in respect of which product licences within the meaning of that Act are for the time being in force; or*
>   *(ii)   other articles or substances in respect of which such licences are for the time being in force in pursuance of orders under section 104 or 105 of that Act (application of Act to other articles and substances).*
>   *(3)   In this Act, unless the context otherwise requires—*
>   *'business' includes the undertaking of a canteen, club, school, hospital or institution, whether carried on for profit or not, and any undertaking or activity carried on by a public or local authority;*
>   *'commercial operation', in relation to any food or contact material, means any of the following, namely—*
>   *(a)   selling, possessing for sale and offering, exposing or advertising for sale;*

>   (b)   consigning, delivering or serving by way of sale;
>   (c)   preparing for sale or presenting, labelling or wrapping for the purpose of sale;
>   (d)   storing or transporting for the purpose of sale;
>   (e)   importing and exporting;
> and, in relation to any food source, means deriving food from it for the purpose of sale or for purposes connected with sale;
>   'contact material' means any article or substance which is intended to come into contact with food;
>   'food business' means any business in the course of which commercial operations with respect to food or food sources are carried out;
>   'food premises' means any premises used for the purposes of a food business;
>   'food source' means any growing crop or live animal, bird or fish from which food is intended to be derived (whether by harvesting, slaughtering, milking, collecting eggs or otherwise);
>   'premises' includes any place, any vehicle, stall or moveable structure and, for such purposes as may be specified in an order made by the Ministers, any ship or aircraft of a description so specified.
>   (4)   The reference in subsection (3) above to preparing for sale shall be construed, in relation to any contact material, as a reference to manufacturing or producing for the purpose of sale.

The extended meaning of 'sale' etc. is provided in s. 2 of the FSA 1990:

> **2.**—(1)   For the purposes of this Act—
>   (a)   the supply of food, otherwise than on sale, in the course of a business; and
>   (b)   any other thing which is done with respect to food and is specified in an order made by the Ministers,
> shall be deemed to be a sale of the food, and references to purchasers and purchasing shall be construed accordingly.
>   (2)   This Act shall apply—
>   (a)   in relation to any food which is offered as a prize or reward or given away in connection with any entertainment to which the public are admitted, whether on payment of money or not, as if the food were, or had been, exposed for sale by each person concerned in the organisation of the entertainment;
>   (b)   in relation to any food which, for the purpose of advertisement or in further- ance of any trade or business is offered as a prize or reward or given away, as if the food were, or had been, exposed for sale by the person offering or giving away the food; and
>   (c)   in relation to any food which is exposed or deposited in any premises for the purpose of being so offered or given away as mentioned in paragraph (a) or (b) above, as if the food were, or had been, exposed for sale by the occupier of the premises;
> and in this subsection 'entertainment' includes any social gathering, amusement, exhibition, performance, game, sport or trial of skill.

The presumptions that food is intended for human consumption are provided for in s. 3 of the FSA 1990:

> **3.**—(1)   The following provisions shall apply for the purposes of this Act.
>   (2)   Any food commonly used for human consumption shall, if sold or offered, exposed or kept for sale, be presumed, until the contrary is proved, to have been sold or, as the case may be, to have been or to be intended for sale for human consumption.
>   (3)   The following, namely—
>   (a)   any food commonly used for human consumption which is found on premises used for the preparation, storage, or sale of that food; and
>   (b)   any article or substance commonly used in the manufacture of food for human consumption which is found on premises used for the preparation, storage or sale of that food,
> shall be presumed, until the contrary is proved, to be intended for sale, or for manufacturing food for sale, for human consumption.
>   (4)   Any article or substance capable of being used in the composition or prepara- tion of any food commonly used for human consumption which is found on premises

on which that food is prepared shall, until the contrary is proved, be presumed to be intended for such use.

The definitions of 'minister(s)' having functions under the Act are provided in s. 4 of the FSA 1990:

4.—*(1)   In this Act—*
'the Minister' means, subject to subsection (2) below—
(a)   in relation to England and Wales, the Minister of Agriculture, Fisheries and Food or the Secretary of State;
(b)   in relation to Scotland, the Secretary of State subject to subsection (3)(a) below, the food authorities in Scotland are the islands or district councils;
'the Ministers' means—
(a)   in relation to England and Wales, the following Ministers acting jointly, namely, the Minister of Agriculture, Fisheries and Food and the Secretaries of State respectively concerned with health in England and food and health in Wales;
(b)   in relation to Scotland, the Secretary of State subject to subsection (3)(a) below, the food authorities in Scotland are the islands or district councils.
(2)   In this Act, in its application to emergency control orders, 'the Minister' means the Minister of Agriculture, Fisheries and Food or the Secretary of State.

The food authorities and authorised officers are set out in s. 5 of the FSA 1990:

5.—*(1)   Subject to subsections (3) and (4) below, the food authorities in England are—*
(a)   as respects each London borough, district or non-metropolitan county, the council of that borough, district or county;
(b)   as respects the City of London (including the Temples), the Common Council;
(c)   as respects the Inner Temple or the Middle Temple, the appropriate Treasurer.
(1A)   Subject to subsection (3)(a) and (b) below, the food authorities in Wales are, as respects each county or county borough, the council of that county or county borough.
(2)   in relation to Scotland, the Secretary of State subject to subsection (3)((a) below, the food authorities in Scotland are the islands or district councils.
(3)   Where any functions under this Act are assigned—
(a)   by an order under section 2 or 7 of the Public Health (Control of Disease) Act 1984, to a port health authority or, by an order under section 172 of the Public Health (Scotland) Act 1897, to a port local authority;
(b)   by an order under section 6 of the Public Health Act 1936, to a joint board for a united district; or
(c)   by an order under paragraph 15(6) of Schedule 8 to the Local Government Act 1985, to a single authority for a metropolitan county,
any reference in this Act to a food authority shall be construed, so far as relating to those functions, as a reference to the authority to whom they are so assigned.
(4)   The Ministers may by order provide, either generally or in relation to cases of a particular description, that any functions under this Act which are exercisable concurrently—
(a)   as respects a non-metropolitan district, by the council of that district and the council of the non-metropolitan county;
(b)   as respects the Inner Temple or the Middle Temple, by the appropriate Treasurer and the Common Council,
shall be exercisable solely by such one of those authorities as may be specified in the order.
(5)   In this section—
'the appropriate Treasurer' means the Sub-Treasurer in relation to the Inner Temple and the Under Treasurer in relation to the Middle Temple;
'the Common Council' means the Common Council of the City of London;
'port local authority' includes a joint port local authority.
(6)   In this Act 'authorised officer', in relation to a food authority, means any person (whether or not an officer of the authority) who is authorised by them in writing, either generally or specially, to act in matters arising under this Act; but if regulations made by the Ministers so provide, no person shall be so authorised unless he has such qualifications as may be prescribed by the regulations.

The definition of 'the enforcement authority' and provisions relating to enforcement are contained in s. 6 of the FSA 1990:

6.—*(1) In this Act 'the enforcement authority', in relation to any provisions of this Act or any regulations or orders made under it, means the authority by whom they are to be enforced and executed.*

(2) Every food authority shall enforce and execute within their area the provisions of this Act with respect to which the duty is not imposed expressly or by necessary implication on some other authority.

(3) The Ministers may direct, in relation to cases of a particular description or a particular case, that any duty imposed on food authorities by subsection (2) above shall be discharged by the Ministers or the Minister and not by those authorities.

(4) Regulations or orders under this Act shall specify which of the following authorities are to enforce and execute them, either generally or in relation to cases of a particular description or a particular area, namely—

(a) the Ministers, the Minister of Agriculture, Fisheries and Food, the Secretary of State, food authorities and such other authorities as are mentioned in section 5(3) above; and

(b) in the case of regulations, the Commissioners of Customs and Excise;

and any such regulations or orders may provide for the giving of assistance and information, by any authority concerned in the administration of the regulations or orders, or of any provisions of this Act, to any other authority so concerned, for the purposes of their respective duties under them.

(5) An enforcement authority in England and Wales may institute proceedings under any provisions of this Act or any regulations or orders made under it and, in the case of the Ministers or the Minister, may take over the conduct of any such proceedings which have been instituted by some other person.

Rendering food injurious to health constitutes an offence under s. 7 of the FSA 1990:

7.—*(1) Any person who renders any food injurious to health by means of any of the following operations, namely—*

(a) adding any article or substance to the food;

(b) using any article or substance as an ingredient in the preparation of the food;

(c) abstracting any constituent from the food; and

(d) subjecting the food to any other process or treatment,

with intent that it shall be sold for human consumption, shall be guilty of an offence.

(2) In determining for the purposes of this section and section 8(2) below whether any food is injurious to health, regard shall be had—

(a) not only to the probable effect of that food on the health of a person consuming it; but

(b) also to the probable cumulative effect of food of substantially the same composition on the health of a person consuming it in ordinary quantities.

(3) In this Part 'injury', in relation to health, includes any impairment, whether permanent or temporary, and 'injurious to health' shall be construed accordingly.

Selling food not complying with food safety requirements constitutes an offence under s. 8 of the FSA 1990:

8.—*(1) Any person who—*

(a) sells for human consumption, or offers, exposes or advertises for sale for such consumption, or has in his possession for the purpose of such sale or of preparation for such sale; or

(b) deposits with, or consigns to, any other person for the purpose of such sale or of preparation for such sale,

any food which fails to comply with food safety requirements shall be guilty of an offence.

(2) For the purposes of this Part food fails to comply with food safety requirements if—

(a) it has been rendered injurious to health by means of any of the operations mentioned in section 7(1) above;

(b)   it is unfit for human consumption; or

(c)   it is so contaminated (whether by extraneous matter or otherwise) that it would not be reasonable to expect it to be used for human consumption in that state; and references to such requirements or to food complying with such requirements shall be construed accordingly.

(3)   Where any food which fails to comply with food safety requirements is part of a batch, lot or consignment of food of the same class or description, it shall be presumed for the purposes of this section and section 9 below, until the contrary is proved, that all of the food in that batch, lot or consignment fails to comply with those requirements.

(4)   For the purposes of this Part, any part of, or product derived wholly or partly from, an animal—

(a)   which has been slaughtered in a knacker's yard, or of which the carcase has been brought into a knacker's yard; or

(b)   in Scotland, which has been slaughtered otherwise than in a slaughterhouse, shall be deemed to be unfit for human consumption.

(5)   In subsection (4) above, in its application to Scotland, 'animal' means any description of cattle, sheep, goat, swine, horse, ass or mule; and paragraph (b) of that subsection shall not apply where accident, illness or emergency affecting the animal in question required it to be slaughtered as mentioned in that paragraph.

Manufacturers of food or confectionery must be vigilant to take all precautions to ensure that offences are not committed under this provision. In *F & M Dobson Ltd, The Times*, 8 March 1995, the defendants, confectionery manufacturers, were prosecuted under s. 8(1)(a) and s. 8(2)(c) of the FSA 1990 for selling a nut brittle sweet which contained a blade of a Stanley knife which cut the consumer's tongue, drawing blood and causing soreness which lasted for two days. They were convicted by the Crown Court, fined £25,000 and ordered to pay £7,834 costs. The Court of Appeal reduced the fine to £7,000 and stated that although culpability was an important factor, deterrence was also a major factor. In the case of manufacturers of food or confectionery likely to be put in the consumer's mouth without close inspection and in confidence that what was being consumed was wholesome, there was a very high duty on the company to do all that they could to see that no foreign bodies, particularly those as dangerous as Stanley knife blades, got into their products. The defendants had no metal detector attached at the end of the production line, but had installed one after the complaint was made. The costs order stood, however, as the defendants had brought this on themselves by electing jury trial.

Provisions for the inspection and seizure of suspected food are contained in s. 9 of the FSA 1990:

9.—*(1)   An authorised officer of a food authority may at all reasonable times inspect any food intended for human consumption which—*

(a)   has been sold or is offered or exposed for sale; or

(b)   is in the possession of, or has been deposited with or consigned to, any person for the purpose of sale or of preparation for sale;

and subsections (3) to (9) below shall apply where, on such an inspection, it appears to the authorised officer that any food fails to comply with food safety requirements.

(2)   The following provisions shall also apply where, otherwise than on such an inspection, it appears to an authorised officer of a food authority that any food is likely to cause food poisoning or any disease communicable to human beings.

(3)   The authorised officer may either—

(a)   give notice to the person in charge of the food that, until the notice is withdrawn, the food or any specified portion of it—

(i)   is not to be used for human consumption; and

(ii)   either is not to be removed or is not to be removed except to some place specified in the notice; or

(b)   seize the food and remove it in order to have it dealt with by a justice of the peace;

and any person who knowingly contravenes the requirements of a notice under paragraph (a) above shall be guilty of an offence.

(4)   Where the authorised officer exercises the powers conferred by subsection (3)(a) above, he shall, as soon as is reasonably practicable and in any event within 21 days, determine whether or not he is satisfied that the food complies with food safety requirements and—

(a)   if he is so satisfied, shall forthwith withdraw the notice;

(b)   if he is not so satisfied, shall seize the food and remove it in order to have it dealt with by a justice of the peace.

(5)   Where an authorised officer exercises the powers conferred by subsection (3)(b) or (4)(b) above, he shall inform the person in charge of the food of his intention to have it dealt with by a justice of the peace and—

(a)   any person who under section 7 or 8 above might be liable to a prosecution in respect of the food shall, if he attends before the justice of the peace by whom the food falls to be dealt with, be entitled to be heard and to call witnesses; and

(b)   that justice or the peace may, but need not, be a member of the court before which any person is charged with an offence under that section in relation to that food.

(6)   If it appears to a justice of the peace, on the basis of such evidence as he considers appropriate in the circumstances, that any food falling to be dealt with by him under this section fails to comply with food safety requirements, he shall condemn the food and order—

(a)   the food to be destroyed or to be disposed of as to prevent it from being used for human consumption; and

(b)   any expenses reasonably incurred in connection with the destruction or disposal to be defrayed by the owner of the food.

(7)   If a notice under subsection (3)(a) above is withdrawn, or the justice of the peace by whom any food falls to be dealt with under this section refuses to condemn it, the food authority shall compensate the owner of the food for any depreciation in its value resulting from the action taken by the authorised officer.

(8)   Any disputed question as to the right to or the amount of any compensation payable under subsection (7) above shall be determined by arbitration.

(9)   In the application of this section to Scotland—

(a)   any reference to a justice of the peace includes a reference to the sheriff and to a magistrate;

(b)   paragraph (b) of subsection (5) above shall not apply;

(c)   any order made under subsection (6) above shall be sufficient evidence in any proceedings under this Act of the failure of the food in question to comply with food safety requirements; and

(d)   the reference in subsection (8) above to determination by arbitration shall be construed as a reference to determination by a single arbiter appointed, failing agreement between the parties, by the sheriff.

Provisions relating to the sevice of and compliance with improvement notices are contained in s. 10 of the FSA 1990:

10.—*(1)   If an authorised officer of an enforcement authority has reasonable grounds for believing that the proprietor of a food business is failing to comply with any regulations to which this section applies, he may, by a notice served on that proprietor (in this Act referred to as an 'improvement notice')—*

(a)   state the officer's grounds for believing that the proprietor is failing to comply with the regulations;

(b)   specify the matters which constitute the proprietor's failure so to comply;

(c)   specify the measures which, in the officer's opinion, the proprietor must take in order to secure compliance; and

(d)   require the proprietor to take those measures, or measures which are at least equivalent to them, within such period (not being less than 14 days) as may be specified in the notice.

(2)   Any person who fails to comply with an improvement notice shall be guilty of an offence.

(3)   This section and section 11 below apply to any regulations under this part which make provision—

(a) for requiring, prohibiting or regulating the use of any process or treatment in the preparation of food; or

(b) for securing the observance of hygienic conditions and practices in connection with the carrying out of commercial operations with respect to food or food sources.

13.2 Orders and Notices under the Food Safety Act 1990

Provisions for the making of prohibition orders are contained in s. 11 of the FSA 1990:

11.—*(1) If—*

(a) the proprietor of a food business is convicted of an offence under any regulations to which this section applies; and

(b) the court by or before which he is so convicted is satisfied that the health risk condition is fulfilled with respect to that business,

the court shall by an order impose the appropriate prohibition.

(2) The health risk condition is fulfilled with respect to any food business if any of the following involves risk of injury to health, namely—

(a) the use for the purposes of the business of any process or treatment;

(b) the construction of any premises used for the purposes of the business, or the use for those purposes of any equipment; and

(c) the state or condition of any premises or equipment used for the purposes of the business.

(3) The appropriate prohibition is—

(a) in a case falling within paragraph (a) of subsection (2) above, a prohibition on the use of the process or treatment for the purposes of the business;

(b) in a case falling within paragraph (b) of that subsection, a prohibition on the use of the premises or equipment for the purposes of the business or any other food business of the same class or description;

(c) in a case falling within paragraph (c) of that subsection, a prohibition on the use of the premises or equipment for the purposes of any food business.

(4) If—

(a) the proprietor of a food business is convicted of an offence under any regulations to which this section applies by virtue of section 10(3)(b) above; and

(b) the court by or before which he is so convicted thinks it proper to do so in all the circumstances of the case,

the court may, by an order, impose a prohibition on the proprietor participating in the management of any food business, or any food business of a class or description specified in the order.

(5) As soon as practicable after the making of an order under subsection (1) or (4) above (in this Act referred to as a 'prohibition order'), the enforcement authority shall—

(a) serve a copy of the order on the proprietor of the business; and

(b) in the case of an order under subsection (1) above, affix a copy of the order in a conspicuous position on such premises used for the purposes of the business as they consider appropriate;

and any person who knowingly contravenes such an order shall be guilty of an offence.

(6) A prohibition order shall cease to have effect—

(a) in the case of an order under subsection (1) above, on the issue by the enforcement authority of a certificate to the effect that they are satisfied that the proprietor has taken sufficient measures to secure that the health risk condition is no longer fulfilled with respect to the business;

(b) in the case of an order under subsection (4) above, on the giving by the court of a direction to that effect.

(7) The enforcement authority shall issue a certificate under paragraph (a) of subsection (6) above within three days of their being satisfied as mentioned in that paragraph; and on an application by the proprietor for such a certificate, the authority shall—

(a) determine, as soon as is reasonably practicable and in any event within 14 days, whether or not they are so satisfied; and

(b) if they determine that they are not so satisfied, give notice to the proprietor of the reasons for that determination.

(8) The court shall give a direction under subsection (6)(b) above if, on an application by the proprietor, the court thinks it proper to do so having regard to all the circumstances of the case, including in particular the conduct of the proprietor since the making of the order; but no such application shall be entertained if it is made—

(a) within six months after the making of the prohibition order; or

(b) within three months after the making by the proprietor of a previous application for such a direction.

(9) Where a magistrates' court or, in Scotland, the sheriff makes an order under section 12(2) below with respect to any food business, subsection (1) above shall apply as if the proprietor of the business had been convicted by the court or sheriff of an offence under regulations to which this section applies.

(10) Subsection (4) above shall apply in relation to a manager of a food business as it applies in relation to the proprietor of such a business; and any reference in subsection (5) or (8) above to the proprietor of the business, or to the proprietor, shall be construed accordingly.

(11) In subsection (10) above 'manager', in relation to a food business, means any person who is entrusted by the proprietor with the day to day running of the business, or any part of the business.

Provisions relating to emergency prohibition notices and orders are contained in s. 12 of the FSA 1990:

12.—(1) If an authorised officer of an enforcement authority is satisfied that the health risk condition is fulfilled with respect to any food business, he may, by a notice served on the proprietor of the business (in this Act referred to as an 'emergency prohibition notice'), impose the appropriate prohibition.

(2) If a magistrates' court or, in Scotland, the sheriff is satisfied, on the application of such an officer, that the health risk condition is fulfilled with respect to any food business, the court or sheriff shall, by an order (in this Act referred to as an 'emergency prohibition order'), impose the appropriate prohibition.

(3) Such an officer shall not apply for an emergency prohibition order unless, at least one day before the date of the application, he has served notice on the proprietor of the business of his intention to apply for the order.

(4) Subsections (2) and (3) of section 11 above shall apply for the purpose of this section as they apply for the purposes of that section, but as if the reference in subsection (2) to risk of injury to health were a reference to imminent risk of such injury.

(5) As soon as practicable after the service of an emergency prohibition notice, the enforcement authority shall affix a copy of the notice in a conspicuous position on such premises used for the purposes of the business as they consider appropriate; and any person who knowingly contravenes such a notice shall be guilty of an offence.

(6) As soon as practicable after the making of an emergency prohibition order, the enforcement authority shall—

(a) serve a copy of the order on the proprietor of the business; and

(b) Affix a copy of the order in a conspicuous position on such premises used for the purposes of that business as they consider appropriate;

and any person who knowingly contravenes such an order shall be guilty of an offence.

(7) An emergency prohibition notice shall cease to have effect—

(a) if no application for an emergency prohibition order is made within the period of three days beginning with the service of the notice, at the end of that period;

(b) if such an application is so made, on the determination or abandonment of the application.

(8) An emergency prohibition notice or emergency prohibition order shall cease to have effect on the issue by the enforcement authority of a certificate to the effect that they are satisfied that the proprietor has taken sufficient measures to secure that the health risk condition is no longer fulfilled with respect to the business.

(9) The enforcement authority shall issue a certificate under subsection (8) above within three days of their being satisfied as mentioned in that subsection; and on an application by the proprietor for such a certificate, the authority shall—

(a) determine, as soon as is reasonably practicable and in any event within 14 days, whether or not they are so satisfied; and

(b) if they determine that they are not so satisfied, give notice to the proprietor of the reasons for that determination.

(10) Where an emergency prohibition notice is served on the proprietor of a business, the enforcement authority shall compensate him in respect of any loss suffered by reason of his complying with the notice unless—

(a) an application for an emergency prohibition order is made within the period of three days beginning with the service of the notice; and

(b) the court declares itself satisfied, on the hearing of the application, that the health risk condition was fulfilled with respect to the business at the time when the notice was served;

and any disputed question as to the right to or the amount of any compensation payable under this subsection shall be determined by arbitration or, in Scotland, by a single arbiter appointed, failing agreement between the parties, by the sheriff.

Provisions relating to making of emergency control orders are contained in s. 13 of the FSA 1990:

13.—(1) If it appears to the Minister that the carrying out of commercial operations with respect to food, food sources or contact materials of any class or description involves or may involve imminent risk of injury to health, he may, by an order (in this Act referred to as an 'emergency order'), prohibit the carrying out of such operations with respect to food, food sources or contact materials of that class or description.

(2) Any person who knowingly contravenes an emergency control order shall be guilty of an offence.

(3) The Minister may consent, either unconditionally or subject to any condition that he considers appropriate, to the doing in a particular case of anything prohibited by an emergency control order.

(4) It shalll be a defence for a person charged with an offence under subsection (2) above to show—

(a) that consent had been given under subsection (3) above to the contravention of the emergency control order; and

(b) that any condition subject to which that consent was given was complied with.

(5) The Minister—

(a) may give such directions as appear to him to be necessary or expedient for the purpose of preventing the carrying out of commercial operations with respect to any food, food sources or contact materials which he believes, on reasonable grounds, to be food, food sources or contact materials to which an emergency control order applies; and

(b) may do anything which appears to him to be necessary or expedient for that purpose.

(6) Any person who fails to comply with a direction under this section shall be guilty of an offence.

(7) If the Minister does anything by virtue of this section in consequence of any person failing to comply with an emergency control order or a direction under this section, the Minister may recover from that person any expenses reasonably incurred by him under this section.

13.3 Nature or Substance or Quality

The sale of food not of the nature or substance or quality demanded constitutes an offence under s. 14 of the FSA 1990:

14.—(1) Any person who sells to the purchaser's prejudice any food which is not of the nature or substance or quality demanded by the purchaser shall be guilty of an offence.

(2) In subsection (1) above the reference to sale shall be construed as a reference to sale for human consumption; and in proceedings under that subsection it shall not

be a defence that the purchaser was not prejudiced because he bought for analysis or examination.

Although a foreign body in food may amount to prima facie evidence of an offence under s. 14 of the FSA 1990, it does not rule out the possibility of a due diligence defence under s. 21. In *Bow Street Magistrates' Court, ex parte Cow and Gate Nutrition plc.* (1995) 159 JP 120, complaint was made of a piece of bone found in a jar of baby food manufactured by the defendants who were prosecuted under s. 14 for selling food not of the nature or substance or quality demanded. The magistrate held that the mere fact that the bone was present was enough to enable the court to convict and refused to state a case. The Divisional Court granted judicial review and held that the mere fact that the bone was present did not rule out the possibility of a due diligence defence.

13.4   Defences under the Food Safety Act 1990

Offences due to the fault of another party may be prosecuted under s. 20 of the FSA 1990:

20. *Where the commission by any person of an offence under any of the preceding provisions of this Part is due to an act or default of some other person, that other person shall be guilty of the offence; and a person may be charged with and convicted of the offence by virtue of this section whether or not proceedings are taken against the first-mentioned person.*

A defence of due diligence is provided by s. 21 of the FSA 1990:

21.—*(1) In any proceedings for an offence under any of the preceding provisions of this Part (in this section referred to as 'the relevant provision'), it shall, subject to subsection (5) below, be a defence for the person charged to prove that he took all reasonable precautions and exercised all due diligence to avoid the commission of the offence by himself or by a person under his control.*

(2) Without prejudice to the generality of subsection (1) above, a person charged with an offence under section 8, 14 or 15 above who neither—

(a) prepared the food in respect of which the offence is alleged to have been committed; nor

(b) imported it into Great Britain,

shall be taken to have established the defence provided by that subsection if he satisfies the requirements of subsection (3) or (4) below.

(3) A person satisfies the requirements of this subsection if he proves—

(a) that the commission of the offence was due to an act or default of another person who was not under his control, or to reliance on information supplied by such a person;

(b) that he carried out all such checks of the food in question as were reasonable in all the circumstances, or that it was reasonable in all the circumstances for him to rely on checks carried out by the person who supplied the food to him; and

(c) that he did not know and had no reason to suspect at the time of the commission of the alleged offence that his act or omission would amount to an offence under the relevant provision.

(4) A person satisfies the requirements of this subsection if he proves—

(a) that the commission of the offence was due to an act or default of another person who was not under his control, or to reliance on information supplied by such a person;

(b) that the sale or intended sale of which the alleged offence consisted was not a sale or intended sale under his name or mark; and

(c) that he did not know, and could not reasonably have been expected to know, at the time of the commission of the alleged offence that his act or omission would amount to an offence under the relevant provision.

(5) If in any case the defence provided by subsection (1) above involves the allegation that the commission of the offence was due to an act or default of another person, or to reliance on information supplied by another person, the person charged shall not, without leave of the court, be entitled to rely on that defence unless—

(a) at least seven clear days before the hearing; and
(b) where he has previously appeared before a court in connection with the alleged offence, within one month of his first such appearance,
he has served on the prosecutor a notice in writing giving such information identifying or assisting in the identification of that other person as was then in his possession.
(6) In subsection (5) above any reference to appearing before a court shall be construed as including a reference to being brought before a court.

An example of where a defence of due diligence is made out is where it is considered reasonable for a defendant to place reliance on a local authority inspector's certificate that food supplied is fit for human consumption. In *Carrick District Council* v *Taunton Vale Meat Traders Ltd* (1994) 158 JP 347, the company had supplied to meat processors a carcass of beef which had been stamped in error by an authorised meat inspector as being fit for human consumption. The company was charged under s. 8(1) of the FSA 1990 with consigning for sale, beef unfit for human consumption. The company was convicted on summary trial, but was acquitted by the Crown Court on appeal. The prosecutor's appeal by way of case stated to the Divisional Court was dismissed, for the court considered that the company had been reasonable to place reliance on the meat inspector's certificate, and the defence of due diligence had been made out. Smith J, delivering the judgment of the court, stated the reasoning of the court as follows:

There is nothing in the words of section 21(1) which prevents a defendant from relying upon the action of a third party in his attempt to show that he has taken all reasonable precautions and exercised all due diligence. The precautions which he takes, and the diligence which he exercises, may sometimes entail reliance, if appropriate, on a third party. . . .

If, in the particular circumstances of a case, the court considers that it was reasonable for a defendant to place reliance upon a certificate of examination provided by another, I can see no reason, as a matter of law, why the court should not be free to permit such reliance and declare itself satisfied, if it sees fit, that the defence of due diligence has been made out.

It may be that such cases will be rare. Indeed, it should not be thought that this case will amount to authority for the proposition that all that any slaughterer need do to comply with his duties under the Food Safety Act 1990 is to rely on the meat inspector's certificate. I say only that if the court considers that in the particular case it is reasonable for the defendant to rely on the inspector's certificate, it must be free to come to that conclusion.

. . . The company could satisfy the defence pursuant to section 21(1) of the Food Safety Act 1990 by relying on the certificate of inspection of the local meat inspector. No further system of inspection set up by the company involving a further check on the meat inspector is necessary before the defendants can rely on the defence. . . .

See also *Walkers Snack Foods Ltd* v *Coventry City Council* [1998] 3 All ER 163 (piece of plastic in packet of crisps).

13.5   Procedure, Penalties and Definitions

The time limit for prosecutions is set out in s. 34 of the FSA 1990:

34. *No prosecution for an offence under this Act which is punishable under section 35(2) below shall be begun after the expiry of—*
(a) three years from the commission of the offence; or
(b) one year from its discovery by the prosecutor,
whichever is the earlier.

Penalties for offences under the FSA 1990 are set out in s. 35:

35.—(1) A person guilty of an offence under section 33(1) above shall be liable on summary conviction to a fine not exceeding level 5 on the standard scale or to imprisonment for a term not exceeding three months or to both.

(2) A person guilty of any other offence under this Act shall be liable—

(a) on conviction on indictment, to a fine or to imprisonment for a term not exceeding two years or to both;

(b) on summary conviction, to a fine not exceeding the relevant amount or to imprisonment for a term not exceeding six months or to both.

(3) In subsection (2) above 'the relevant amount' means—

(a) in the case of an offence under section 7, 8 or 14 above, £20,000;

(b) in any other case, the statutory maximum.

(4) If a person who is—

(a) licensed under section 1 of the Slaughterhouses Act 1974 to keep a slaughterhouse or knacker's yard;

(b) registered under section 4 of the Slaughter of Animals (Scotland) Act 1980 in respect of any premises for use as a slaughterhouse; or

(c) licensed under section 6 of that Act to use any premises as a knacker's yard, is convicted of an offence under Part II of this Act, the court may, in addition to any other punishment, cancel his licence or registration.

Provisions relating to offences by bodies corporate are contained in s. 36 of the FSA 1990:

36.—(1) Where an offence under this Act which has been committed by a body corporate is proved to have been committed with the consent or connivance of, or to be attributable to any neglect on the part of—

(a) any director, manager, secretary or other similar officer of the body corporate; or

(b) any person who was purporting to act in any such capacity, he as well as the body corporate shall be deemed to be guilty of that offence and shall be liable to be proceeded against and punished accordingly.

(2) In subsection (1) above 'director', in relation to any body corporate established by or under any enactment for the purpose of carrying on under national ownership any industry or part of an industry or undertaking, being a body corporate whose affairs are managed by its members, means a member of that body corporate.

Provisions regarding the general interpretation and definition of terms used in the Act are contained in s. 53 of the FSA 1990:

53.—(1) In this Act, unless the context otherwise requires—

'the 1984 Act' means the Food Act 1984;

'the 1956 Act' means the Food and Drugs (Scotland) Act 1956;

'advertisement' includes any notice, circular, label, wrapper, invoice or other document, and any public announcement made orally or by any means of producing or transmitting light or sound, and 'advertise' shall be construed accordingly;

'analysis' includes microbiological assay and any technique for establishing the composition of food, and 'analyse' shall be construed accordingly;

'animal' means any creature other than a bird or fish;

'article' does not include a live animal or bird, or a live fish which is not used for human consumption while it is alive;

'container' includes any basket, pail, tray, package or receptacle of any kind, whether open or closed;

'contravention', in relation to any provision, includes any failure to comply with that provision;

'cream' means that part of milk rich in fat which has been separated by skimming or otherwise;

'equipment' includes any apparatus;

'exportation' and 'importation' have the same meanings as they have for the purposes of the Customs and Excise Management Act 1979, and 'export' and 'import' shall be construed accordingly;

'fish' includes crustaceans and molluscs;

'functions' includes powers and duties;

'human consumption' includes use in the preparation of food for human consumption;

'knacker's yard' means any premises used in connection with the business of slaughtering, flaying or cutting up animals the flesh of which is not intended for human consumption;

'milk' includes cream and skimmed or separated milk;

'occupier', in relation to any ship or aircraft of a description specified in an order made under section 1(3) above or any vehicle, stall or place, means the master, commander or other person in charge of the ship, aircraft, vehicle, stall or place;

'officer' includes servant;

'preparation', in relation to food, includes manufacture and any form of processing or treatment, and 'preparation for sale' includes packaging, and 'prepare for sale' shall be construed accordingly;

'presentation', in relation to food, includes the shape, appearance and packaging of the food, the way in which the food is arranged when it is exposed for sale and the setting in which the food is displayed with a view to sale, but does not include any form of labelling or advertising, and 'present' shall be construed accordingly;

'proprietor', in relation to a food business, means the person by whom that business is carried on;

'ship' includes any vessel, boat or craft, and a hovercraft within the meaning of the Hovercraft Act 1968, and 'master' shall be construed accordingly;

'slaughterhouse' means a place for slaughtering animals, the flesh of which is intended for sale for human consumption, and includes any place available in connection with such a place for the confinement of animals while awaiting slaughter there or for keeping, or subjecting to any treatment or process, products of the slaughtering of animals there;

'substance' includes any natural or artificial substance or other matter, whether it is in solid or liquid form or in the form of a gas or vapour;

'treatment', in relation to any food, includes subjecting it to heat or cold.

(2) The following Table shows provisions defining or otherwise explaining expressions used in this Act (other than provisions defining or explaining an expression used only in the same section)—

authorised officer of a food authority	section 5(6)
business	section 1(3)
commercial operation	section 1(3) and (4)
contact material	section 1(3)
emergency control order	section 13(1)
emergency prohibition notice	section 12(1)
emergency prohibition order	section 12(2)
enforcement authority	section 6(1)
examination and examine	section 28(2)
food	section 1(1), (2) and (4)
food authority	section 5
food business	section 1(3)
food premises	section 1(3)
food safety requirements and related expressions	section 8(2)
food source	section 1(3)
improvement notice	section 10(1)
injury to health and injurious to health	section 7(3)
the Minister	section 4(1) and (2)
the Ministers	section 4(1)
premises	section 1(3)
prohibition order	section 11(5)
public analyst	section 27(1)
sale and related expressions	section 2
unfit for human consumption	section 8(4)

(3) Any reference in this Act to regulations or orders made under it shall be construed as a reference to regulations or orders made under this Act by the Ministers or the Minister.

(4) For the purposes of this Act, any class or description may be framed by reference to any matters or circumstances whatever, including in particular, in the case of a description of food, the brand name under which it is commonly sold.

(5)   Where, apart from this subsection, any period of less than seven days which is specified in this Act would include any day which is—
    (a)   a Saturday, a Sunday, Christmas Day or Good Friday; or
    (b)   a day which is a bank holiday under the Banking and Financial Dealings Act 1971 in the part of Great Britain concerned,
that day shall be excluded from that period.

13.6   Food Hygiene Regulations

Food hygiene regulations are set out in the Food Safety (General Food Hygiene) Regulations 1995 as follows:

2.   Interpretation
(1)   In these Regulations, unless the context otherwise requires—
'the Act' means the Food Safety Act 1990;
'the Directive' means Council Directive 93/43/EEC of 14th June 1993 on the hygiene of foodstuffs;
'food authority' does not include—
    (a)   the council of a non-metropolitan county in England or Wales, unless that council is a unitary authority; or
    (b)   as respects the Inner Temple or the Middle Temple, the appropriate Treasurer;
'food business' means any undertaking, whether carried on for profit or not and whether public or private, carrying out any or all of the following operations, namely, preparation, processing, manufacturing, packaging, storing, transportation, handling or offering for sale or supply, of food;
'hygiene' means all measures necessary to ensure the safety and wholsomeness of food during preparation, processing, manufacturing, packaging, storing, transportation, distribution, handling and offering for sale or supply to the consumer, and 'hygienic' shall be construed accordingly;
'potable water' means water which at the time of supply is or was not likely in a given case to affect adversely the wholesomeness of a particular foodstuff in its finished form, and which is or was either—
    (a)   of the quality demanded in order for it to be regarded as wholesome for the purposes of—
        (i)   Part VIA of the Water (Scotland) Act 1980, or
        (ii)   Chapter III of Part III of the Water Industry Act 1991; or
    (b)   not of that quality, but the water is or was derived—
        (i)   from a public supply in Scotland and the Secretary of State is not required, by virtue of section 76E of the Water (Scotland) Act 1980, to make an order under section 11(2) of the Water (Scotland) Act 1980 in relation to the authority supplying that water,
        (ii)   from a public supply in England or Wales and the Secretary of State is not required to make or confirm (with or without modifications) an enforcement order under section 18 of the Water Industry Act 1991 in relation to the company supplying that water, or
        (iii)   from a private supply in relation to which a private supply notice has been served or the option of a private supply notice has been considered and rejected by the local authority with remedial powers in relation to that private supply,
unless since the time of supply the quality of the water has deteriorated in a way which, in a given case, has adversely affected or is likely to affect adversely the wholesomeness of a particular foodstuff in its finished form.
'primary production' includes harvesting, slaughter and milking;
'private supply' has—
    (a)   in Scotland, the same meaning as in section 76L(1) of the Water (Scotland) Act 1980;
    (b)   in England and Wales, the same meaning as in section 93(1) of the Water Industry Act 1991;
'private supply notice' means—
    (a)   in Scotland, a notice under section 76G of the Water (Scotland) Act 1980;
    (b)   in England and Wales, a notice under section 80 of the Water Industry Act 1991;

'public supply' means a supply of water which is not a private supply;

'unitary authority' means—

(a) in England, any authority which is the sole principal council for its local government area;

(b) in Wales, a county or county borough council established under the Local Government (Wales) Act 1994;

'water' includes water in any form, but does not include water which is—

(a) recognised as a natural mineral water under the Natural Mineral Water Regulations 1985;

(b) a medicinal product within the meaning of the Medicines Act 1968 ('the 1968 Act') or is a product in respect of which any provision of the 1968 Act has effect in relation to it as if it were a medicinal product within the meaning of the 1968 Act; or

(c) drinking water within the meaning of the Drinking Water in Containers Regulations 1994;

'wholesomeness' means, in relation to food, its fitness for human consumption so far as hygiene is concerned,

and any other words and expressions used both in these Regulations and in the Directive shall bear the same meaning in these Regulations as they have in the Directive.

(2) In determining for the purposes of these Regulations whether any matter involves a risk to food safety or wholesomeness, regard shall be had to the nature of the food, the manner in which it is handled and packed, any process to which the food is subjected before supply to the consumer, and the conditions under which it is displayed or stored.

(3) In Schedule 1, 'where appropriate' and 'where necessary' mean where appropriate and where necessary respectively for the purposes of ensuring the safety and wholesomeness of food.

(4) In these Regulations, unless the context otherwise requires, a reference—

(a) to a numbered regulation or Schedule is to the regulation in or Schedule to these Regulations bearing that number;

(b) in a regulation or Schedule to a numbered paragraph is to the paragraph of that regulation or Schedule bearing that number; and

(c) in a paragraph to a numbered or lettered sub-paragraph is to the sub-paragraph in that paragraph bearing that number or letter.

3. Application of provisions of these Regulations

(1) Subject to paragraphs (3) to (5), regulations 4 and 5 shall apply to neither—

(a) primary production; nor

(b) a person carrying on any activity which is regulated by or under any of the Regulations listed in paragraph (2), but only with respect to the carrying on of that activity.

(2) The Regulations referred to in paragraph (1)(b) are—

(a)–(e) (revoked)

(f) the Egg Products Regulations 1993;

(g) the Meat Products (Hygiene) Regulations 1994;

(h) the Fresh Meat (Hygiene and Inspection) Regulations 1995;

(i) the Poultry Meat, Farmed Game Bird Meat and Rabbit Meat (Hygiene and Inspection) Regulations 1995;

(j) the Dairy Products (Hygiene) Regulations 1995;

(k) the Dairy Products (Hygiene) (Scotland) Regulations 1995;

(l) the Wild Game Meat (Hygiene and Inspection) Regulations 1995;

(m) the Minced Meat and Meat Preparations (Hygiene) Regulations 1995;

(n) the Food Safety (Fishery Products and Live Shellfish) (Hygiene) Regulations 1998.

(3) Notwithstanding paragraph (1)(b), the provisions of paragraph 1 of Chapter VII of Schedule 1 and of regulation 4(2)(d) in so far as it relates to that paragraph of that Chapter shall apply to a proprietor of a food business, unless—

(a) he is carrying on an activity which relates to a particular stage in the production of a product and a provision in any of the Regulations listed in paragraph (2) imposes a further or alternative requirement in relation to the supply and use of potable water in connection with that stage in the production of that product; or

(b)   he is carrying out commercial operations on board a fishing vessel.

(4)   Notwithstanding paragraph (1)(b), the provisions of Chapter X of Schedule 1 and of regulation 4(2)(d) in so far as it relates to that Chapter shall apply to a proprietor of a food business, unless a provision in any of the Regulations listed in paragraph (2) imposes a further or alternative requirement in relation to the instruction or training of food handlers.

4.   Obligations upon proprietors of food businesses

(1)   A proprietor of a food business shall ensure that any of the following operations, namely, the preparation, processing, manufacturing, packaging, storing, transportation, distribution, handling and offering for sale or supply, of food are carried out in a hygienic way.

(2)   A proprietor of a food business shall ensure that—

(a)   the requirements set out in Chapter I of Schedule 1 are complied with as respects any food premises used for the purposes of that business;

(b)   the requirements set out in Chapter II of Schedule 1 are complied with as respects any room where food is prepared, treated or processed in the course of the activities of that business, other than dining areas and premises covered by Chapter III of Schedule 1;

(c)   the requirements set out in Chapter III of Schedule 1 are complied with as respects any of the following used for the purposes of that business—

(i)   movable or temporary premises (such as marquees, market stalls and mobile sales vehicles),

(ii)   premises used primarily as a private dwelling house,

(iii)   premises used occasionally for catering purposes, and

(iv)   vending machines; and

(d)   the requirements set out in Chapters IV to X of Schedule 1 are complied with as respects that business.

(3)   A proprietor of a food business shall identify any step in the activities of the food business which is critical ensuring food safety and ensure that adequate safety procedures are identified, implemented, maintained and reviewed on the basis of the following principles—

(a)   analysis of the potential food hazards in a food business operation;

(b)   identification of the points in those operations where food hazards may occur;

(c)   deciding which of the points identified are critical to ensuring food safety ('critical points');

(d)   identification and implementation of effective control and monitoring procedures at those critical points; and

(e)   review of the analysis of food hazards, the critical points and the control and monitoring procedures periodically, and whenever the food business's operations change.

5.   Persons suffering from certain medical conditions

(1)   Subject to paragraph (2), a person working in a food handling area who—

(a)   knows or suspects that he is suffering from or that he is a carrier of a disease likely to be transmitted through food; or

(b)   is afflicted with an infected wound, a skin infection, sores, diarrhoea or with any analoguous medical condition,

in circumstances where there is any likelihood of him directly or indirectly contaminating any food with pathogenic micro-organisms, shall report that knowledge, suspicion or affliction to the proprietor of the food business at which he is working.

(2)   This regulation shall not apply to a person unless he is working in a food handling area in which a food business proprietor, seeking to comply with regulation 4(2)(d) and paragraph 2 of Chapter VIII of Schedule 1, may be required to refuse him permission to work.

6.   Offences and penalties

(1)   If any person contravenes regulation 4 (including any provision of Schedule 1) or 5, he shall be guilty of an offence against these Regulations.

(2)   Any person guilty of an offence against these Regulations shall be liable—

(a)   on summary conviction, to a fine not exceeding the statutory maximum;

(b)   on conviction on indictment, to a fine or imprisonment for a term not exceeding two years or both.

7.   Application of provisions of the Act
The following provisions of the Act shall apply for the purposes of these Regulations as they apply for the purposes of sections 8, 14 and 15 of the Act, and unless the context otherwise requires, a reference in them to the Act shall for the puposes of these Regulations be construed as a reference to these Regulations—
(a)   section 2 (extended meaning of 'sale' etc.);
(b)   section 3 (presumptions that food intended for human consumption);
(c)   section 20 (offences due to fault of another person);
(d)   section 21 (defence of due diligence);
(e)   section 30(8) (which relates to documentary evidence);
(f)   section 33 (obstruction etc. of officers);
(g)   section 34 (time limit for prosecutions);
(h)   section 36 (offences by bodies corporate), subject to the following modifications—
(i)   after the words 'body corporate', at the three places where they occur in section 36(1) of the Act, there shall be inserted the words 'or Scottish partnership', and
(ii)   for the word 'secretary' there shall be substituted the words 'secretary, partner';
(i)   section 44 (protection of officers acting in good faith).

8.   Enforcement and execution
(1)   Each food authority shall enforce and execute these Regulations within its area.
(2)   In executing and enforcing these Regulations, a food authority shall—
(a)   ensure that—
(i)   food premises are inspected with a frequency which has regard to the risk associated with those premises, and
(ii)   inspections include a general assessment of the potential food safety hazards associated with the food business being inspected;
(b)   pay particular attention to the critical control points identified by food businesses to assess whether the necessary monitoring and verification controls are being operated;
(c)   give due consideration to whether the proprietor of a food business has acted in accordance with any relevant guide to good hygiene practice which has been—
(i)   forwarded by the Secretary of State to the Commission pursuant to article 5.5 of the Directive, unless the Secretary of State has announced that it no longer complies with article 3 of the Directive, or
(ii)   developed in accordance with articles 5.6 and 7 of the Directive and published in accordance with article 5.8 of the Directive.

SCHEDULE 1
RULES OF HYGIENE

CHAPTER I   GENERAL REQUIREMENTS FOR FOOD PREMISES
(OTHER THAN THOSE SPECIFIED IN CHAPTER III)
1.   Food premises must be kept clean and maintained in good repair and condition.
2.   The layout, design, construction and size of food premises shall—
(a)   permit adequate cleaning and/or disinfection;
(b)   be such as to protect against the accumulation of dirt, contact with toxic materials, the shedding of particles into food and the formation of condensation or undesirable mould on surfaces;
(c)   permit good food hygiene practices, including protection against cross contamination between and during operations, by foodstuffs, equipment, materials, water, air supply or personnel and external sources of contamination such as pests; and
(d)   provide, where necessary, suitable temperature conditions for the hygienic processing and storage of products.

3. *An adequate number of washbasins must be available, suitably located and designated for cleaning hands. An adequate number of flush lavatories must be available and connected to an effective drainage system. Lavatories must not lead directly into rooms in which food is handled.*

4. *Washbasins for cleaning hands must be provided with hot and cold (or appropriately mixed) running water, materials for cleaning hands and for hygienic drying. Where necessary, the provisions for washing food must be separate from the hand-washing facility.*

5. *There must be suitable and sufficient means of natural or mechanical ventilation. Mechanical air flow from a contaminated area to a clean area must be avoided. Ventilation systems must be so constructed as to enable filters and other parts requiring cleaning or replacement to be readily accessible.*

6. *All sanitary conveniences within food premises shall be provided with adequate natural or mechanical ventilation.*

7. *Food premises must have adequate natural and/or artificial lighting.*

8. *Drainage facilities must be adequate for the purpose intended; they must be designed and constructed to avoid the risk of contamination of foodstuffs.*

9. *Adequate changing facilities for personnel must be provided where necessary.*

CHAPTER II
SPECIFIC REQUIREMENTS IN ROOMS WHERE FOODSTUFFS ARE PREPARED, TREATED OR PROCESSED (EXCLUDING DINING AREAS AND THOSE PREMISES SPECIFIED IN CHAPTER III)

1. *In rooms where food is prepared, treated or processed (excluding dining areas)—*

(a) floor surfaces must be maintained in a sound condition and they must be easy to clean and, where necessary, disinfect. This will require the use of impervious, non-absorbent, washable and non-toxic materials, unless the proprietor of the food business can satisfy the food authority that other materials used are appropriate. Where appropriate, floors must allow adequate surface drainage;

(b) wall surfaces must be maintained in a sound condition and they must be easy to clean and, where necessary, disinfect. This will require the use of impervious, non-absorbent, washable and non-toxic materials and require a smooth surface up to a height appropriate for the operations, unless the proprietor of the food business can satisfy the food authority that other materials are appropriate;

(c) ceilings and overhead fixtures must be designed, constructed and finished to prevent the accumulation of dirt and reduce condensation, the growth of undesirable moulds and the shedding of particles;

(d) windows and other openings must be constructed to prevent the accumulation of dirt. Those which can be opened to the outside environment must where necessary be fitted with insect-proof screens which can be easily removed for cleaning. Where open windows would result in contamination of foodstuffs, windows must remain closed and fixed during production;

(e) doors must be easy to clean and, where necessary, disinfect. This will require the use of smooth and non-absorbent surfaces, unless the proprietor of the food business can satisfy the food authority that other materials used are appropriate;

(f) surfaces (including surfaces of equipment) in contact with food must be maintained in a sound condition and be easy to clean and, where necessary, disinfect. This will require the use of smooth, washable and non-toxic materials, unless the proprietor of the food business can satisfy the food authority that other materials used are appropriate.

2. *Where necessary, adequate facilities must be provided for the cleaning and disinfecting of work tools and equipment. These facilities must be constructed of materials resistant to corrosion and must be easy to clean and have an adequate supply of hot and cold water.*

3. *Where appropriate, adequate provision must be made for any necessary washing of the food. Every sink or other such facility provided for the washing of food must have an adequate supply of hot and/or cold potable water as required, and be kept clean.*

CHAPTER III REQUIREMENTS FOR MOVABLE AND/OR TEMPORARY PREMISES (SUCH AS MARQUEES, MARKET STALLS, MOBILE SALES VEHICLES) PREMISES USED PRIMARILY AS A PRIVATE DWELLING HOUSE, PREMISES USED OCCASIONALLY FOR CATERING PURPOSES AND VENDING MACHINES

1. Premises and vending machines shall be so sited, designed, constructed, and kept clean and maintained in good repair and condition, as to avoid the risk of contaminating foodstuffs and harbouring pests, so far as is reasonably practicable.

2. In particular and where necessary—

(a) appropriate facilities must be available to maintain adequate personal hygiene (including facilities for the hygienic washing and drying of hands, hygienic sanitary arrangements and changing facilities);

(b) surfaces in contact with food must be in a sound condition and be easy to clean and, where necessary, disinfect. This will require the use of smooth, washable, non-toxic materials, unless the proprietor of the food business can satisfy the food authority that other materials used are appropriate;

(c) adequate provision must be made for the cleaning and, where necessary, disinfecting of work utensils and equipment;

(d) adequate provision must be made for the cleaning of foodstuffs;

(e) an adequate supply of hot and/or cold potable water must be available;

(f) adequate arrangements and/or facilities for the hygienic storage and disposal of hazardous and/or inedible substances and waste (whether liquid or solid) must be available;

(g) adequate facilities and/or arrangements for maintaining and monitoring suitable food temperature conditions must be available;

(h) foodstuffs must be so placed as to avoid, so far as is reasonably practicable, the risk of contamination.

CHAPTER IV TRANSPORT

1. Conveyances and/or containers used for transporting foodstuffs must be kept clean and maintained in good repair and condition in order to protect foodstuffs from contamination, and must, where necessary, be designed and constructed to permit adequate cleaning and/or disinfection.

2.—(1) Receptacles in vehicles and/or containers must not be used for transporting anything other than foodstuffs where this may result in contamination of foodstuffs.

(2) Bulk foodstuffs in liquid, granular or powder form must be transported in receptacles and/or containers/tankers reserved for the transport of foodstuffs if otherwise there is a risk of contamination. Such containers must be marked in a clearly visible and indelible fashion, in one or more Community languages, to show that they are used for the transport of foodstuffs, or must be marked 'for foodstuffs only'.

3. Where conveyances and/or containers are used for transporting anything in addition to foodstuffs or for transporting different foodstuffs at the same time, there must be effective separation of products, where necessary, to protect against the risk of contamination.

4. Where conveyances and/or containers have been used for transporting anything other than foodstuffs or for transporting different foodstuffs, there must be effective cleaning between loads to avoid the risk of contamination.

5. Foodstuffs in conveyances and/or containers must be so placed and protected as to minimize the risk of contamination.

6. Where necessary, conveyances and/or containers used for transporting foodstuffs, must be capable of maintaining foodstuffs at appropriate temperatures and, where necessary, designed to allow those temperatures to be monitored.

CHAPTER V EQUIPMENT REQUIREMENTS

1. All articles, fittings and equipment with which food comes into contact shall be kept clean and—

(a) be so constructed, be of such materials, and be kept in such good order, repair and condition, as to minimize any risk of contamination of the food;

(b) with the exception of non-returnable containers and packaging, be so constructed, be of such materials and be kept in such good order, repair and condition, as to enable them to be kept thoroughly cleaned and, where necessary, disinfected, sufficient for the purposes intended;

(c) be installed in such a manner as to allow adequate cleaning of the surrounding area.

CHAPTER VI   FOOD WASTE

1. Food waste and other refuse must not be allowed to accumulate in food rooms, except so far as is unavoidable for the proper functioning of the business.

2. Food waste and other refuse must be deposited in closable containers unless the proprietor of the food business can satisfy the food authority that other types of containers used are appropriate. These containers must be of an appropriate construction, kept in sound condition, and where necessary be easy to clean and disinfect.

3. Adequate provision must be made for the removal and storage of food waste and other refuse. Refuse stores must be designed and managed in such a way as to enable them to be kept clean, and to protect against access by pests, and against contamination food, drinking water, equipment or premises.

CHAPTER VII   WATER SUPPLY

1. There must be an adequate supply of potable water. This potable water must be used whenever necessary to ensure foodstuffs are not contaminated.

2. Where appropriate, ice must be made from potable water. This ice must be used whenever necessary to ensure foodstuffs are not contaminated. It must be made, handled and stored under conditions which protect it from all contamination.

3. Steam used directly in contact with food must not contain any substance which presents a hazard to health, or is likely to contaminate the product.

4. Water unfit for drinking used for the generation of steam, refrigeration, fire control and other similar purposes not relating to food, must be conducted in separate systems, readily indentifiable and having no connection with, nor any possibility of reflux into, the potable water systems.

CHAPTER VIII   PERSONAL HYGIENE

1. Every person working in a food handling area shall maintain a high degree of personal cleanliness and shall wear suitable, clean and, where appropriate, protective clothing.

2. No person, known or suspected to be suffering from, or to be a carrier of, a disease likely to be transmitted through food or while afflicted, for example with infected wounds, skin infections, sores or with diarrhoea, shall be permitted to work in any food handling area in any capacity in which there is any likelihood of directly or indirectly contaminating food with pathogenic micro-organisms.

CHAPTER IX   PROVISIONS APPLICABLE TO FOODSTUFFS

1. No raw materials or ingredients shall be accepted by a food business if they are known to be, or might reasonably be expected to be, so contaminated with parasites, pathogenic micro-organisms, or toxic, decomposed or foreign substances, that after normal sorting and/or preparatory or processing procedures hygienically applied by food businesses, they would still be unfit for human consumption.

2. Raw materials and ingredients stored in the establishment shall be kept in appropriate conditions designed to prevent harmful deterioration and to protect them from contamination.

3. All food which is handled, stored, packaged, displayed and transported, shall be protected against any contamination likely to render the food unfit for human consumption, injurious to health or contamination in such a way that it would be unreasonable to expect it to be consumed in that state. In particular, food must be so placed and/or protected as to minimise any risk of contamination. Adequate procedures must be in place to ensure pests are controlled.

4. Hazardous and/or inedible substances, including animal feedstuffs, shall be adequately labelled and stored in separate and secure containers.

CHAPTER X   TRAINING

1. The proprietor of a food business shall ensure that food handlers engaged in the food business are supervised and instructed and/or trained in food hygiene matters commensurate with their work activities.

Useful articles on aspects of prosecutions for regulatory offences are: Samuels, A., 'Punishment for Environmental Crime', *Journal of Planning and Environmental Law*, May 1994, p. 412; Jackson, R., 'Planning and Environmental Law Offences' (1994) 158 JPN 784; and Parry, D. L., 'Judicial Approaches to Due Diligence' [1995] Crim LR 695.

PART III
A CASE TO PREPARE

FOURTEEN

INTRODUCTION TO THE SAMPLE BRIEF

This chapter introduces the papers for a criminal case (reproduced in **Chapter 16**) which are intended to provide you with the opportunity to make use of some of the skills which are required of a barrister in criminal practice. The issues which are involved are ones which ought to be familiar by the time you have reached this part of the manual. From time to time, however, you will find it helpful to make reference to some of the other manuals in this series, e.g., the **Opinion Writing Manual**, the **Advocacy Manual** and the **Conference Skills Manual**.

The case is one where there are a number of co-defendants, who are charged with offences of violence and offences against public order. There may be a conflict of interest between the two defendants whom you are initially instructed to advise, so you must consider whether there should be separate representation for those two defendants — a point on which the barrister in criminal practice is frequently asked to advise. There are also issues relating to identification, alibi, severance of the indictment, admissibility and the overall strengths and weaknesses of the prosecution case. You need to address the question of advising on plea and on sentence. The set of papers includes a questionnaire which has to be filled in before the Plea and Directions Hearing, so that you have to consider whether it can be filled in on the information which you have to hand, or whether more details are needed (e.g. from the client in conference) before you are able to do so. The consideration of the questionnaire will give you the opportunity to become familiar with a document which the barrister in criminal practice frequently has to consider. In addition, the papers include a copy of a custody record, which is a fertile source of information for both sides in a criminal trial, and needs careful consideration as you advise and prepare for trial. There are copies of other documents in common use, such as crime complaint forms.

In making use of this set of papers, it is suggested that you should proceed as follows:

(a) use the papers as an exercise in writing an Advice on Evidence;

(b) then use them to prepare for a conference with the client;

(c) finally, use them to prepare for the advocacy tasks involved in a trial.

Each of these suggestions is considered in more detail in the succeeding sections.

14.1 Advice on Evidence

The papers take the form of a brief received by counsel, with instructions to provide an Advice on Evidence for the defendants Nicholas Spring and John Hanson (or Hanson only if there is a conflict of interest between them). Your initial use of the papers ought therefore to be as an exercise in writing an Opinion — an Advice on Evidence in a criminal case. Prior to doing so, you should read through **Chapter 14** of the **Opinion**

Writing Manual, which deals with this task. You may also find it helpful to take a look at **Chapter 17** in the *Case Preparation Manual*. *(You should avoid looking at the sample Advice which is printed at the end of this manual. If you do so, it will obviously destroy much of the value in doing the Advice as an exercise.)*

Once you have refreshed your memory as to the steps involved in writing an Advice on Evidence in a criminal case, you should be ready to start. In order to make sure that you manage your time effectively, and to ensure that you do not become too remote from the situation in practice, it is suggested that you work against the clock, and that you do not allow yourself more than six hours to produce the Advice, including any legal research which you need to do.

Having started the clock, you might read through the papers once, quickly, in order to get the general sense. Second and third readings are then likely to be necessary in order to be able to analyse the evidence and form an initial judgment on the points which need to be dealt with in the Advice. As you read the papers for the second or third time, you might compile a chronology, a list of issues, a schedule of the various descriptions of the defendants in whom you are particularly interested. You should also begin to make a list of the points on which your instructing solicitors need to take action, the documents which you need to see and the missing pieces of information.

Having gone through the papers several times in this way, you are in a position to make a plan of your Advice. Consider how the various points which you need to cover should be dealt with and the logical order in which you should present them. You can then write your Advice, keeping an eye on the clock so that you do not produce something which is unrealistic in terms of length and degree of detail.

Once your Advice is completed, and you have taken a pause in order to recover, look at the sample Advice, which is printed in **Chapter 16**. *(This should be the first time that you have glanced at it!)*

Consider your Advice against the sample. Bear in mind that it is a sample and not a model. Your version may be superior, at least in certain respects, to what is printed. But wherever you reach a different conclusion from the sample, you should consider which is preferable, and why. Think also about the form in which the sample is written and compare it with yours in order to gain some constructive feedback.

14.2   Preparing for Conference

The next task which you might undertake with the *Hanson* papers is preparation for conference. It is not giving away any deep secret to suggest that part of the advice which you are likely to provide is that there should be a conference with the client. In preparing for this task, you may work in parallel with a friend or colleague, with each of you working separately, and then comparing your conclusions.

In any event, you will find it helpful before using the papers in this way to read the relevant sections of the *Conference Manual* — in particular **Chapter 5**. You will need to consider, among other matters, the information which you need to obtain from your client(s), and how best to obtain it; and the advice which needs to be given, for example on plea and likely sentence if convicted. Having prepared and produced a working plan for the conference, compare notes with the friend or colleague who has been performing the same task.

14.3   Preparing for Trial

The papers can be used again to prepare for trial. Again you might wish to work in parallel with someone on this task. It would be sensible if the two of you worked out the answers which you have been given in the imaginary conference referred to in **14.2**. This will then give you a basis for preparation for trial, i.e. you prepare on the assumption that the client has given you certain answers to the questions which you asked in conference.

As to the areas which need preparation, it is suggested that you deal with each of the areas described in the following paragraphs.

14.3.1   CLOSING SPEECH

It actually makes a lot of sense to prepare your closing speech before preparing the matters which you have to deal with during the course of the trial.

Your closing speech ought to be your interpretation of the points which arise in trial. If you are able to make certain realistic assumptions about what is likely to emerge during the trial, preparing your closing speech first gives the rest of your preparation a clear focus. Obviously, if the trial actually took place, the speech would need to be rewritten at intervals during its course, in order to ensure that it was based, not on assumptions, but on the evidence which in fact emerged.

14.3.2   SUBMISSIONS

From the time that you prepared to write your Advice on Evidence, it will have been apparent that there would be disputes about the admissibility of certain pieces of evidence. You need to consider how you will present the argument in relation to these points of admissibility. In doing so, you are likely to find **Chapter 20** of the *Advocacy Manual* of assistance. Similarly, you should consider whether you are at all likely to be making a submission of no case to answer on behalf of your client(s). If so, prepare a framework, using **Chapter 21** of the *Advocacy Manual* to remind yourself of the process involved.

14.3.3   CROSS-EXAMINATION

There are two areas of cross-examination which you must prepare. First, there are the prosecution witnesses, both police and civilian. The themes and arguments which you intend to develop in your closing speech will determine the course of cross-examination here to some extent. Your cross-examination will also be affected by the instructions which you have received in the brief and those which are obtained in conference.

Consider whether there any co-defendants who stand trial with your client. If they appear on the indictment before your client, you will have to cross-examine them before your client gives evidence. It is worth reminding yourself of the special evidential considerations which apply to co-defendants, which are dealt with in **Chapter 4** of this manual. In addition, consider the points to keep in mind in preparing any cross-examination (see **Chapter 18** of the *Advocacy Manual*).

14.3.4   EXAMINATION IN CHIEF

One of the most important tasks in preparing for trial as defence counsel is to consider the impression your client would make as a witness. Will it be necessary for your client to give evidence? If it is, then prepare to examine him in chief, using **Chapter 17** of the *Advocacy Manual* as a reminder of the steps you need to take.

14.3.5   COMPARING NOTES

Once you have dealt with each of the advocacy tasks which you are likely to face, discuss your approach with your friend or colleague and compare notes.

14.4   The Papers in *R v Nicholas Spring, John Hanson and Others*

You can now read the brief contained in **Chapter 15**, and start preparing the Advice on Evidence. (*Remember not to look at the sample Advice in **Chapter 16** until you have finished.*)

FIFTEEN

R v SPRING, HANSON AND OTHERS

Contents

<u>IN THE OXTON CROWN COURT</u>
<u>T980155</u>

BETWEEN:

R

–and–

NICHOLAS SPRING
JOHN HANSON & Others

INSTRUCTIONS TO COUNSEL

Messrs. Archer & Balcombe
Centenary House,
Bray Street,
Oxton. OT5 16MM

<u>Solicitors for the Defendants</u>

IN THE OXTON CROWN COURT

T980155

BETWEEN:

R

–v–

NICHOLAS SPRING
and JOHN HANSON and Others

INSTRUCTIONS TO COUNSEL

Counsel has herewith:

1. Copy Indictment.
2. Statements of prosecution witnesses.
3. Interviews of Mr Spring & Mr Hanson.
4. Custody records.
5. Unused material.
6. Previous convictions of the Defendants.
7. Proof of Evidence of Mr Hanson.
8. Defence Statement of Mr Hanson.

Counsel is instructed on behalf of the Defendants, Nicholas Spring and John Hanson, who are charged with Violent Disorder, Causing Grievous Bodily Harm with intent to resist arrest of Nicholas Spring and on behalf of John Hanson who is charged, alone, with attempted robbery.

The facts of this case are set out in the various documents and Instructiong Solicitors do not intend to repeat them herein. All defendants were committed for trial on 17th January.

The other Defendants are represented by Messrs Glidewell and Speed. They have informed us that Sean Baker and Martin Thompson will plead guilty to Violent Disorder whilst Louis Bucknell, Simon Bratt and Anthony Mead will plead guilty to Affray. The CPS have indicated that these pleas are acceptable.

Instructing Solicitors feel that there may be a conflict of interest so that two counsel may be required and counsel is asked to advise on separate representation, generally on evidence, and any other matters arising plea and possible sentence if convicted. If counsel is of the view that there is a conflict of interest, then such advice is requested in respect of John Hanson.

Counsel is also requested to complete the questionnaire for the Plea and Directions Hearing, which is to be held on 12th February 2000 and to draft a defence case statement (draft enclosed).

21 January, 2000

Plea and Directions Hearing

Judge's Questionnaire

(In accordance with the practice rules issued by
the Lord Chief Justice)

*A copy of this questionnaire, completed as far as
possible with the agreement of both advocates,
is to be handed in to the court prior to the
commencement of the Plea and Directions
Hearing.*

The Crown Court at

Case No. T
PTI URN
R v

Date of PDH
Name of Prosecution Advocate at PDH

Name of Defence Advocate at PDH

1	a	Are the actual/proposed not guilty pleas definitely to be maintained through to a jury trial?	Yes ☐ No ☐
	b	Has the defence advocate advised his client of section 48 of CJPOA 1994? (*Reductions in sentence for guilty pleas*)	Yes ☐ No ☐
	c	Will the prosecution accept part guilty or alternative pleas?	Yes ☐ No ☐
2		How long is the trial likely to take?	
3		What are the issues in the case?	
4		Issues as to the mental or medical condition of any defendant or witness.	
5		Prosecution witnesses whose evidence will be given. Can any statement be read instead of calling the witnesses?	To be read (number) ☐ To be called (number) ☐ Names:

Form 5122   Plea and Directions Hearings in the Crown Court Practice Rules 1995

6	a	Number of Defence witnesses whose evidence will be placed before the Court.	Defendant + [ ]
	b	Any whose statements have been served which can be agreed and accepted in writing.	
7		Is the prosecution intending to serve any further evidence? If **Yes**, what area(s) will it cover? What are the witnesses' names?	Yes [ ] No [ ]
8		Facts which are admitted and can be reduced into writing. (s. 10(2)(b) CJA 1967)	
9		Exhibits and schedules which are to be admitted.	
10		Is the order and pagination of the prosecution papers agreed?	
11		Any alibi which should have been disclosed in accordance with CJA 1967?	Yes [ ] No [ ]
12	a	Any points of law likely to arise at trial?	
	b	Any questions of admissibility of evidence together with any authorities it is intended to rely upon.	
13	a	Has the defence notified the prosecution of any issue arising out of the record of interview? (*Practice Direction (Crime: Tape Recording of Police Interview)* [1989] 1 WLR 631)	Yes [ ] No [ ]
	b	What efforts have been made to agree verbatim records or summaries and have they been successful?	

Form 5122   *Plea and Directions Hearings in the Crown Court Practice Rules 1995*

14   Any applications granted/pending for:

    (i)   evidence to be given through live television links?   Yes ☐ No ☐

    (ii)   evidence to be given by pre-recorded video interviews with children?   Yes ☐ No ☐

    (iii) screens?   Yes ☐ No ☐

    (iv) the use of video equipment during the trial?   Yes ☐ No ☐

    (v)   use of tape playback equipment?   Yes ☐ No ☐

15   Any other significant matter which might affect the proper and convenient trial of the case? (e.g. expert witnesses or other cases outstanding against the defendant)

16   Any other work which needs to be done.

    Orders of the Court with time limits should be noted on page 4.

    Prosecution

    Defence

17   a   Witness availability and approximate length of witness evidence.

    Prosecution

    Defence

    b   Can any witness attendance be staggered?   Yes ☐ No ☐

    c   If Yes, have any arrangements been agreed?   Yes ☐ No ☐

18   Advocates' availability?

    Prosecution

    Defence

Form 5122   Plea and Directions Hearings in the Crown Court Practice Rules 1995

Case listing arrangements

Name of Trial Judge:

Custody Cases *Fixed or warned list within 16 weeks of committal*

Fixed for trial on

Place in a warned list for trial   for week beginning

Further directions fixed for

Not fixed or put in warned list within 16 weeks because:

Bail Cases

Further directions fixed for

Fixed for trial on

Fixed as a floater/backer on

Place in a reserve/warned list for trial   for week beginning

List officer to allocate   ☐ within ☐ days/weeks

     ☐ before

Sentence

Adjourned for sentence on

(to follow trial of R v

Other directions, orders, comments

Signed: *Judge*   Date:

Form 5122   Plea and Directions Hearings in the Crown Court Practice Rules 1995

INDICTMENT   No. T980155

THE CROWN COURT AT OXTON

THE QUEEN -v- NICHOLAS SPRING, JOHN HANSON, MARTIN THOMPSON, SEAN BAKER, LOUIS BUCKNELL, SIMON BRATT and ANTHONY MEAD

are charged as follows:

Count 1

STATEMENT OF OFFENCE

VIOLENT DISORDER, Contrary to Section 2(1) of the Public Order Act 1986.

PARTICULARS OF OFFENCE

NICHOLAS SPRING, JOHN HANSON, MARTIN THOMPSON, SEAN BAKER, LOUIS BUCKNELL, SIMON BRATT and ANTHONY MEAD on the 11th day of July 1999, being present together with each other and with other persons unknown used or threatened unlawful violence and their conduct (taken together) was such as would cause a person of reasonable firmness present at the scene to fear for his personal safety.

Count 2

STATEMENT OF OFFENCE

CAUSING GRIEVOUS BODILY HARM WITH INTENT, Contrary to Section 18 of the Offences Against the Person Act 1861.

PARTICULARS OF OFFENCE

NICHOLAS SPRING, JOHN HANSON, MARTIN THOMPSON, SEAN BAKER, LOUIS BUCKNELL, SIMON BRATT and ANTHONY MEAD on the 11th day of July 1999 unlawfully caused grievous bodily harm to Martin Kemp with intent to resist or prevent the lawful apprehension or detainer of the said Nicholas Spring.

Count 3

STATEMENT OF OFFENCE

ATTEMPTED ROBBERY, Contrary to Section 1(1) of the Criminal Attempts Act 1981.

PARTICULARS OF OFFENCE

JOHN HANSON, on the 11th day of July 1999 at Kelly's Off-Licence, Crewkerne Street, Upton attempted to rob Michael Kelly of the contents of a cash till.

OFFENCES ADDED UNDER SECTION 40 of the CRIMINAL JUSTICE ACT 1988

STATEMENT OF OFFENCE

DRIVING WHILST UNFIT THROUGH DRINK OR DRUGS, Contrary to Section 4(1) of the Road Traffic Act 1988.

PARTICULARS OF OFFENCE

JOHN HANSON, on 11th day of July 1999 at Upton in the county of Downshire drove a motor vehicle on a road or other public place, namely the junction of Upton Road and Lymehurst Road, whilst unfit through drink or drugs.

<u>WITNESS STATEMENT</u>

Statement of   Stephen Jordan PC 303 ....

Age if under 21   ....

This statement (consisting of 1 pages each signed by me) is true to the best of my knowledge and belief and I make it knowing that, if it is tendered in evidence, I shall be liable to prosecution if I have wilfully stated in it anything which I know to be false or do not believe to be true.

Dated the 13th day of July   19 99

Signature: ....S. Jordan..

I am a PC in the Downshire Constabulary currently stationed at Upton. I am currently assigned to 'Homebeat' duties on the Abbey Estate. On the 11th July 1999 I went with other officers to an incident on the Abbey Estate.

We arrived at about 3.35 p.m. On arrival I saw that PC 37 was being led to a vehicle by PC 211. Both of them appeared to be dishevilled and PC 37 was bleeding profusely from the nose area. A number of youths appeared to be dispersing from the area, some of them were being chased by other officers. As I am familiar with the estate and the people living there I was able to identify 2 men, who got into a blue Vauxhall parked at the rear of Fountains House, as Tony Mead and Simon Bratt. Tony Mead was wearing blue jeans and a yellow shirt. I was able to identify him easily as he has a shaved head and is 6′ 3″. I only saw the back of Simon Bratt but I have arrested him on a number of occasions and he is well known to me. He was wearing a denim jacket and jeans. There were other people in the car but I was unable to identify any of them. I am unable to say who was driving the car. I then assisted other officers in dispersing the crowd and removing prisoners to Upton police station.

On the 12th July at 6.15 a.m. with other officers I went to 27 Fountains House where I arrested Simon Bratt for an offence of violent disorder. He was cautioned at 6.20 a.m. and made no reply. Also at 27 Fountains House were Kieran Bratt, Tony Mead and Louis Bucknell. They were also arrested for Violent Disorder and taken to Upton police station.

Signed: S. Jordan

Signature witnessed by: R. Parry.

<u>WITNESS STATEMENT</u>

Statement of   Raymond Parry PC 211 ....
Age if under 21   ....

This statement (consisting of 1 pages each signed by me) is true to the best of my knowledge and belief and I make it knowing that, if it is tendered in evidence, I shall be liable to prosecution if I have wilfully stated in it anything which I know to be false or do not believe to be true.

Dated the   13th   day of   July   19 99
Signature: ......*R. Parry*..

I am a PC in the Downshire Constabulary currently stationed at Upton. On the 11th July 1999 I was operating a single manned mobile unit when I was called to an incident on the Abbey Estate at about 3.20 p.m.

When I arrived I saw PC 37 struggling with a youth I now know to be Nick Spring. Spring was behaving in a very aggressive and violent manner and PC 37 was acting merely to restrain him. Gathered around them was a group of about 15 youths. There were also a number of bystanders, some with children. The children, in particular, appeared to be scared about what was going on. I parked my vehicle some 30 yards away and immediately radioed for back-up and then got out of my vehicle to assist PC 37. When I got to the edge of the group I shouted out for them to stop and attempted to force my way through to assist PC 37. At this I was immediately set on by a number of youths including one whom I know as Sean Baker. These youths started to punch and kick me. I resisted and attempted to arrest the group but as I was about to tell them they were under arrest I was pulled to the ground and pinioned. One of them, who I now know to be Kieran Bratt spat at me and said 'shut up copper or we'll kick the shit out of you'. At that stage the largest of the youths who were attacking me sat on my legs and groin whilst Bratt with another youth called Louis Bucknell knelt on my shoulders and pinioned my arms. I was extremely frightened at this stage and fearful for my life and safety.

I had been on the ground for a minute or two and was attempting to get up when I heard the sound of police sirens. The youths then let go. I got to my feet and went to see if PC 37 was alright. He was covered with blood which seemed to come from his nose area. I assisted him to his feet and to waiting police transport.

Of the youths I remember Bucknell was wearing a purple tie-dye T shirt with white trousers and black trainers. Baker was wearing a brown bomber type jacket with black jeans and trainers and a baseball cap. Bratt, who was about 5' 9" with collar length hair and bad acne was wearing a denim jacket and jeans with white trainers and a white T shirt.

Signed: *R. Parry.*

Signature witnessed by: S. Jordan

<u>WITNESS STATEMENT</u>

Statement of	Martin Kemp PC 37 ....
Age if under 21	....

This statement (consisting of 2 pages each signed by me) is true to the best of my knowledge and belief and I make it knowing that, if it is tendered in evidence, I shall be liable to prosecution if I have wilfully stated in it anything which I know to be false or do not believe to be true.

Dated the 14th day of July   1999

Signature: ....M Kemp..

I am a Police Officer. On 11th July 1999 I commenced duty at 8 a.m. as a car response driver. At about 3.20 p.m. I was called to a domestic incident at Augustinian Close on the Abbey Estate, Upton. I was single manned at this time. On arriving at Augustinian Close a member of the public directed me to the rear of Fountains House where I saw a man I know to be Nicholas Spring. He was speaking to a girl with long fair hair who he identified as his girlfriend. He was shouting at her that she was not having her car keys because she had been drinking. It was obvious to me that they had both been drinking. I asked where she had to go and she said that she lived in Lymehurst. I stated that was not a problem and if she went to my police car I would ensure that she got home and could collect her car and keys when she was sober.

During this conversation Spring was joined by 3 other males, one of whom I knew as Sean Baker. The other two were not known to me. All 4 men were white. Of the 2 others the first who I shall call (1) was about 6 foot tall with a blue denim jacket, blue shirt, blue jeans and white trainers. He had dark cropped hair and tattoos on his wrists. The other man (2) was 5′ 10″, also with dark cropped hair. He was wearing a brown jacket with black jeans and white trainers. He had a light coloured shirt on but I do not recall if it was white or grey. Both men appeared to be in their early twenties.

Spring didn't say much at this stage and after I had arranged transport for the girl everyone seemed happy. I then walked the girl across to my police car. The four men had walked in the direction of the phone box at the far end of the Close. I reached the police vehicle and as I did I heard a loud bang. I turned to see Spring and the others and could clearly hear Spring shouting that his girl was 'going off with a fucking pig'. I walked towards them and they walked towards me. As I got close to them Spring raised his fists and pushed them towards my face in a 'boxer like' pose. I pushed his hands away and he called me a 'fucking wanker'. I then decided to arrest him for an offence under section 4 of the Public Order Act 1986. I put my left hand on his right shoulder and said 'you are under arrest'. At this point Spring threw a punch at my head with his left fist. The punch missed but he then threw further punches at me which connected with my upper body. I then grabbed hold of him and wrestled him to the ground. In doing so I lost the grip on my radio which fell a few feet away. Whilst I was wrestling with Spring I attempted to reach my radio to call for assistance but he shouted out 'don't let him get it' and man 2 kicked it away so that I could not possibly reach it. We continued to struggle with Spring throwing punches. By this stage the original group had been joined by a number of others from Fountains House who formed a ring about me. At this stage I was on top of Spring. Man 1 then came up and with his right foot and kicked me on the left thigh. Spring shouted 'get the bastard off me'. I shouted back 'anyone who tries will get nicked'.

Spring continued to struggle and shout. My watch had come off my wrist and there was some money on the floor. The money was not mine. Male 2 then picked up the money whilst another youth took the watch. I was restraining Spring and had my hands on his shoulders whilst I was attempting to restrain him from kicking me by holding his legs with my knees. At this stage Spring shouted at the group and in particular at man 2 'Get him off me, kick the bastard in the face or you're out of my house and back on the fucking street'. Man 2 appeared to do nothing and Spring shouted out again 'you're a fucking wanker'. Spring then managed to get his arms free again and punched out hitting me in the chest, body, back and head. I pinned his arms with my hands and told him he was lucky that I wasn't going to hit him back. At this point I looked up and man 2 was standing right in front of me and kicked me in the face. It was a quite a deliberate kick as I am sure that he paused before doing it. I lost my grip on Spring and felt a rain of kicks from a number of quarters. One of those kicking me was Sean Baker and man 1. I was pushed off Spring by the force of the blows.

At this point Spring managed to get free and I then heard a police siren and the group began to scatter. Other officers then arrived. I saw Spring, Baker and man 1, who I now know as Martin Thompson, being arrested as were a number of others. However I did not see man 2.

I sustained injuries to my face and body and was admitted to Upton District Hospital where they diagnosed a broken nose and fairly extensive bruising.

Signed: *M Kemp*

Signature witnessed by:

G.G. Hartley

WITNESS STATEMENT

Statement of   Charlotte Robinson WPC 7 ....

Age if under 21   ....

This statement (consisting of 1 pages each signed by me) is true to the best of my knowledge and belief and I make it knowing that, if it is tendered in evidence, I shall be liable to prosecution if I have wilfully stated in it anything which I know to be false or do not believe to be true.

Dated the   14th   day of   July   1999

Signature: ...... *C Robinson* ....

I am WPC 7 of the Downshire Constabulary currently stationed at Upton. At 15.43 hrs on 11th July 1999 I was on duty in full police uniform in a marked police vehicle in company with police sergeant Church when as a result of information received we attended Augustinian Close on the Abbey Estate.

On arrival I saw a number of youths dispersing from outside Fountains House with PC 37 Kemp lying in the road. About 20 feet away from him PC 211 was getting up from the ground. I stopped the vehicle and ran up to PC Kemp. As I did so he shouted 'get the one in the brown jacket he's just kicked me'. I saw a male running up the slope by the side of Fountains House about 30 yards away. He was with but slightly ahead of a youth I know as Sean Baker. At this stage PC Kemp shouted out 'Get Baker as well he kicked me too'. I gave chase and managed to catch Baker but the man in the brown jacket had run to a blue Cavalier parked at the rear of Fountains House. He got into the driver's door and 2 others got in the car and it drove away. I was able to see the number plate and remember the first part of the registration as CLP but as I was in the process of arresting Sean Baker I was unable to make a full mental note of the number of the car.

I managed to restrain Baker who was struggling and then arrested him for assault on PC Kemp. I handcuffed him and cautioned him and he replied 'Drop dead fuck features I can't hear you'. I then placed him in the rear of a marked police van and he was subsequently conveyed to Upton police station arriving at 16.07 hours when he was taken in front of the custody sergeant.

Signed: *C Robinson*

Signature witnessed by:

       G.G. Hartley

<u>WITNESS STATEMENT</u>

Statement of   Ronald Keith PC 375 ....
Age if under 21   ....

This statement (consisting of <u>1</u> pages each signed by me) is true to the best of my knowledge and belief and I make it knowing that, if it is tendered in evidence, I shall be liable to prosecution if I have wilfully stated in it anything which I know to be false or do not believe to be true.

Dated the *12th* day of *July*   *1999*

Signature: ....*RKeith*..

On the 11th July 1999 I was on duty with PC 63 Raymond Tarry in a marked police vehicle. At about 19.30 hours we were outside Tesco's on the Upton Road when I noticed a metallic blue Vauxhall Cavalier registration number CLY 853X. This vehicle was being driven by a single white male and was driving very slowly and in an erratic manner. As a result of information that we had received earlier and because of the way that the vehicle was being driven I decided to stop the vehicle. This we did about 300 yards past Tesco's at the junction of the Upton and Lymehurst roads.

I approached the vehicle and spoke to the driver who I know as John Hanson. I leant in to the open window of the car, seized the keys and asked him to get out. He was very unsteady on his feet and disorientated. After he got out he collapsed on to the ground. I then arrested him on suspicion of driving a motor vehicle whilst under the influence of drugs and on suspicion of attempted robbery and cautioned him. I do not think that he understood the caution. Together with PC Tarry I then handcuffed him and called for police transport. He was then conveyed to Upton police station where the facts were related to the custody sergeant.

At the time of his arrest he was wearing a brown sports coat, black trousers and trainers.

Signed: *RKeith*

Signature witnessed by: *BBlake.*

WITNESS STATEMENT

Statement of   P. Waller PS 8 ....
Age if under 21   ....

This statement (consisting of 1 pages each signed by me) is true to the best of my knowledge and belief and I make it knowing that, if it is tendered in evidence, I shall be liable to prosecution if I have wilfully stated in it anything which I know to be false or do not believe to be true.

Dated the   12th   day of   July   1999

Signature: .....*P.Waller*..

On the 11th July 1999 at 19.45 hours I was the custody sergeant at Upton Police Station. At that time PC 375 and PC 63 brought a John Hanson into the custody area. I then opened a custody record on the CJS computer and the number 5OBC/00317/99 was allocated to the record.

Mr Hanson was unable to stand properly and was obviously disorientated. His eyes were glazed and his breath smelt of intoxicating liquor. I formed the view that he was intoxicated. PC 375 related the facts to me and as a result of what had happened during the the afternoon on the 11th July, the facts of which were known to me, I then arrested him on suspicion of an offence of violent disorder and told him that he was being detained for the breathalyser procedure to be conducted and that in addition he was under arrest on suspicion of robbery. I cautioned him to which he then replied 'I only tried to rob the place'. This was contemporaneously recorded on form 439M and 441N and attached to the custody record.

I then commenced the breathalyser procedure but after a short period it was apparent that Mr Hanson was unable to understand what was going on and I then had him placed in cell 11 and the FME was called. At this stage I was unable to give him his rights as he was intoxicated. On her arrival at 21.13 a specimen of blood was taken from Mr Hanson. The FME, Dr Craig also carried out a number of tests on Mr Hanson in my presense in the detention room. I then arrested Mr Hanson for an offence of driving a motor vehicle on a road whilst unfit to drive through drink or drugs and further cautioned him to which he made no reply.

I produce the custody record, marked as exhibit PW/1.

Signed: *P.Waller*

Signature witnessed by: *R.Keith*

<u>WITNESS STATEMENT</u>

Statement of   Nuala Carroll ....
Age if under 21   19...

This statement (consisting of | pages each signed by me) is true to the best of my knowledge and belief and I make it knowing that, if it is tendered in evidence, I shall be liable to prosecution if I have wilfully stated in it anything which I know to be false or do not believe to be true.

Dated the   14th   day of   July   1999

Signature: ......Nuala Carroll...

I am the above named. I live with my sister, Michelle Davison in Jervaulx House on the Abbey Estate in Upton. I have just finished studying for my 'A' levels at Upton College and hope to go on to a degree course in Portsmouth in September.

On 11th July 1999 I was at home when my sister came in and asked me to telephone the police. Before I did this I looked out of the window of the flat and saw Nick Spring and his girlfriend arguing, it looked to me as if Nick had hit her as she was clutching her face and crying hysterically. I telephoned the police and a car arrived about 5 minutes later with one police officer in it. I could see that Nick was with a number of other men. I didn't recognise any of them except that I remember one was wearing a brown type bomber jacket. When the policeman arrived there was a bit of noise and then it seemed to go quiet and I went to make some tea in the kitchen which overlooks the other side of Jervaulx House.

A few minutes after I heard a loud bang. I carried on making the tea but then after a few more minutes I heard shouting and screaming. I went to the window and saw 2 police officers being set on by a number of men. Some of them I recognised as coming from Fountains House opposite. The first police officer to arrive, who was a very large man appeared to be sitting on Nick, I heard him shouting out 'get the fuck off me' and 'you're strangling me'. The second officer to arrive, who was much smaller than the first officer and was quite slight, was being held back and hit by 3 men from Fountains House, including one I recognised as Sean Baker. I also think I recognised John Hanson in the crowd that had gathered around. I can't remember what he was wearing. He just seemed to be on the edge of the fight. I know John from the pub in Upton where I used to work as a part-time bar maid, he has only just come out of prison.

The fight seemed to go on for ages and while it was going on a number of people seemed to get involved and there were a number of people watching. I kept on watching but it was difficult to see all the time although I could hear a lot of threats and swearing. Towards the end of the incident, just before more police officers arrived I saw a man come out of the crowd and deliberately kick the first officer in the face. It made a sickening dull thud and must have been very painful. Then others started to kick and push him and Nick got free, stood up and went to talk with his girlfriend who was standing close by. At this stage a number of other policemen arrived and everybody scattered. I saw Sean Baker being arrested and Martin Thompson and Nick Spring. I don't really recall what clothes were worn by whom or what their footwear was.

I am willing to attend court and give evidence.

Signed: Nuala Carroll

Signature witnessed by: C Robinson

<u>WITNESS STATEMENT</u>

Statement of   Paula Anne Ryan ....
Age if under 21   ....

This statement (consisting of 2 pages each signed by me) is true to the best of my knowledge and belief and I make it knowing that, if it is tendered in evidence, I shall be liable to prosecution if I have wilfully stated in it anything which I know to be false or do not believe to be true.

Dated the   14th day of   July   19 99

Signature: ...D.A.Ryan...

I am Paula Anne Ryan and I live on the Abbey Estate, Upton at an address known to police.

At about 3.40 p.m. on the 11th July 1999 I was walking along Augustian Close coming from Bishop Montford School. I had my 5-year-old son, Thomas, with me and I was pushing my daughter Siobhan in a push chair.

As I came round the corner from the road which leads to the school I heard loud shouts from several male voices. I could see 2 men lying on the road just outside Fountains House. I immediately saw that one of the men was a police officer who was restraining a man on the tarmac. The man was lying on his back and the police officer was holding his arms and lying half across the man's chest.

I recognised the man as Nick Spring who I have known for 4 years or so, but only on a casual basis. He was shouting very loudly things like 'get off me', 'bastard, get off you bastard' and a barrage of foul language like that. I did not hear the police officer say anything. Nick was kicking violently with his legs and struggling to escape from the officer.

At that time I saw a number of men immediately next to the policeman and Nick. A handful of onlookers had gathered, including a number of youths from Fountains House. There were 2 men in particular close to the policeman, one was Sean Baker, the other was a man I have seen before but not recently. He was wearing a short jacket, I can't remember the colour. He had his hair short cropped and had dark trousers and white trainers on. I'm not sure that I would recognise the man again. Sean was wearing white trainers as well.

Nick was struggling very violently. I saw him break free a couple of times and the officer would grab him. Each time Nick would lash out at him, punching out with clenched fists and kicking out in a crazed and determined manner, trying with all his effort to punch the policeman in the head and face as hard as he could. The police officer's face was red where he had been punched, although I could see no blood. As Nick was flailing away the police officer bent foward to duck the punches and at the same time grabbed Nick around the waist and pushed him to the ground. Nick landed on his back and the policeman landed squarely on Nick's front. Sean and the other man carried on standing next to the policeman. They were swearing and saying things like 'get off him or you're dead' and other threats. The crowd was also noisy. During the fight another officer arrived. I don't know where he came from but some of the youths were struggling with him to prevent him from assisting his colleague. I then saw a girl come up to where Nick and the policeman were and tried to pull Nick off the policeman. Nick shrugged the girl off and continued to kick and punch in a violent manner. It was obvious nothing was going to stop him.

At that stage a whole load of other police officers arrived and a number of the crowd, including Nick and Sean were arrested. I did not see the man in the dark jacket again but I lost sight of a lot of what was going on because of the number of police and onlookers although I did have a clear and uninterrupted view of the incident which lasted for at least 5 to 10 minutes. I have a clear recollection of how red the police officer's face had turned from being repeatedly punched by Nick Spring.

I am willing to attend court and give evidence.

Signed: *P A Ryan*

Signature witnessed by: *C Robinson*

WITNESS STATEMENT

Statement of   Michele Martine Davison ....
Age if under 21   ....

This statement (consisting of **1** pages each signed by me) is true to the best of my knowledge and belief and I make it knowing that, if it is tendered in evidence, I shall be liable to prosecution if I have wilfully stated in it anything which I know to be false or do not believe to be true.

Dated the   14th   day of   July   19 99

Signature: .... *Michele Davison* ....

I live with my husband, 11-month-old son and sister Nuala in Jervaulx House on Abbey Estate in Upton.

At about 3.15 p.m. on 11th July 1999 I noticed an incident outside Fountains House, which is opposite Jervaulx House, involving Nick Spring and his girlfriend. Because I was concerned I asked Nuala to telephone the police when I got back to my flat. After a while a police car arrived and later I saw Nick's girlfriend go with the police officer to his car. At the same time Nick and a number of other men walked down to the phone kiosk at the bottom of the close. Nick was with Sean Baker and Martin Thompson and another man who I don't know. I can't really remember what they were wearing but Martin had a dark jacket on and the other man was wearing white trainers. As they got to the kiosk I saw Nick kick the glass in the kiosk and there was a loud bang as if it had smashed.

The policeman left Nick's girlfriend and walked towards the kiosk. Nick walked towards him with his friends just behind. I then heard Nick say 'he pushed me' pointing behind him with his thumb. At that stage Nick began to turn as if to walk away and the policeman took hold of his right arm. At that they began to struggle and were having a scuffle in the middle of the road. They both fell to the ground, the officer managing to sit on top of Nick and pinning his arms to the ground. After a while a number of other youths came out of Fountains House and joined Nick's friends who were gathered round the officer. Nick was struggling violently and kicking and lashing out at the officer. At one stage I saw one of the group kick the officer's radio away and there was a lot of shouting and swearing and abuse but I couldn't understand what was being said.

After a while another police officer arrived and he was set on by some of the youths from Fountains House. They were trying to stop him interfering with Nick Spring. I saw the girl get out of the car and go up to the group. I then saw one of the group, I think it was the male with the white trainers, approach the policeman who was restraining Nick and with great force kicked the officer directly in the face. The blow was with such force that the policeman's head went back and he lost his grip on Nick. Then a number of the group started to punch and kick the officer. At that time the other officer was being restrained near the edge of the group. I can't be sure but I think he was on the ground, my main attention was directed towards the first officer who had arrived.

I had already phoned the police during the fight but I became so incensed at their behaviour that I left and phoned again. When I came back I saw that a number of other officers had arrived and the group had dispersed and were being chased by the police. A number of people were arrested and taken away by the police.

I am willing to attend court and give evidence.

Signed: *Michele Davison*

Signature witnessed by: C Robinson

<u>WITNESS STATEMENT</u>

Statement of   Robert Lloyd-Jones ....
Age if under 21   ....Occupation: Dental Practitioner

This statement (consisting of ⅄ pages each signed by me) is true to the best of my knowledge and belief and I make it knowing that, if it is tendered in evidence, I shall be liable to prosecution if I have wilfully stated in it anything which I know to be false or do not believe to be true.

Dated the   17ᵗʰ   day of   July   19 99

Signature: ....*R Lloyd-Jones*..

I am a registered Dental Practitioner and my qualifications are: BDS 1977.

On the 17th July 1999 I examined Martin Kemp and found him to be suffering from psychological trauma associated with dental trauma.

On examination the upper right first central incisor was fractured at its distar incisal edge. This has been repaired by an incisal alisecthed restoration but in the long term may become non vital and need further treatment.

There was a fractured filling at the lower right first permanent premolar which was repaired with a routine filling.

There was extensive bruising to the sockets of the upper right molar teeth which was eased and improved by reshaping the occular fillings.

1.   The injury to the upper right first central incisor was probably caused by minor trauma (physical force).

2.   The fractured filling and the bruising of the sockets of the upper molar teeth may have been caused by stress related to a traumatic incident.

Signed: *A Lloyd-Jones*

Signature witnessed by: *Gjordan.*

WITNESS STATEMENT

Statement of   Richard Purkiss BSc ....
Age if under 21   ....

This statement (consisting of **1** pages each signed by me) is true to the best of my knowledge and belief and I make it knowing that, if it is tendered in evidence, I shall be liable to prosecution if I have wilfully stated in it anything which I know to be false or do not believe to be true.

Dated the   10th   day of   August   19 99

Signature: ....*RPurkiss*..

I am a forensic scientist employed by the Downshire Constabulary. On the 2nd August 1999 I took receipt of exhibit CC/1 a blood specimen labelled John Hanson. I tested the specimen and found it to contain not less than 103 milligrams of alcohol per 100 millilitres of blood.

Signed: *RPurkiss*

Signature witnessed by:

S.T. Harcourt

WITNESS STATEMENT

Statement of   Charlotte Craig. Forensic Medical Examiner ....
Age if under 21   ....

This statement (consisting of **1** pages each signed by me) is true to the best of my knowledge and belief and I make it knowing that, if it is tendered in evidence, I shall be liable to prosecution if I have wilfully stated in it anything which I know to be false or do not believe to be true.

Dated the   11th   day of   July   19 99

Signature: *Charlotte Craig* ....

On the 11th July 1999 I was called to Upton Police Station arriving at 21.09 hours. I then examined a man identified to me as John Hanson. I conducted a number of tests on Mr Hanson and as a result of my examination I formed the view that he was drunk and unfit to drive a motor vehicle. He was then asked to provide a specimen of blood which I took from him. I then divided the specimen into two parts labelled CC/JH/1 (container no. 01765) and CC/JH/2 (01766). In my presence Mr Hanson was offered the second container which he refused.

Signed: *Charlotte Craig.*

Signature witnessed by: P C H Mansell

WITNESS STATEMENT

Statement of Michael Kelly ....
Age if under 21 ....

This statement (consisting of **1** pages each signed by me) is true to the best of my knowledge and belief and I make it knowing that, if it is tendered in evidence, I shall be liable to prosecution if I have wilfully stated in it anything which I know to be false or do not believe to be true.

Dated the 12th day of July   19 99

Signature: ...... *Michael Kelly* ....

I am the owner of Kelly's off-licence in Crewkerne Street, I live in a flat over the shop with my family. On 11th July 1999 at about 6.25 p.m. I was at the till when a man burst into the shop. He was white, about 25, 5′ 10″ and had close cropped dark hair. He was wearing a brown jacket, blue shirt, jeans and white trainers. When he came into the shop he was waving his arms around and shouting. As he came up to the till he pulled his jacket over his face and rushed around the side of the counter shouting 'This is a stick up. Get on the floor'. He didn't have any weapon. The shop is well lit having a large front window and the lights were on. I am certain I would be able to recognise him again.

I started to go down on the floor and he pushed me on the neck. As I got to the floor he shouted at me again to open the till. As I turned to open the till I intended to grab him around the waist or the legs but Francis came running across and pushed him over me and into a display by the front window. I got up and as Francis appeared to be dealing with matters I decided the best thing was to ring the police. The male was shouting all the time this was going on and thrashing around. I tried to keep an eye on what was going on. I saw the male strike Francis on the nose and he then got up charged at me and shouted 'Ring the fucking police and you're dead'. He pushed me over again and ran out of the shop. Francis chased after him and I carried on contacting the police.

I am willing to attend court.

Signed: *Michael Kelly*

Signature witnessed by: *R Keith*

WITNESS STATEMENT

Statement of   Francis Kelly ....
Age if under 21   ....

This statement (consisting of 1 pages each signed by me) is true to the best of my knowledge and belief and I make it knowing that, if it is tendered in evidence, I shall be liable to prosecution if I have wilfully stated in it anything which I know to be false or do not believe to be true.

Dated the   12th day of July   1999

Signature: Francis Kelly ....

I am the above named and live at the address overleaf. I am employed by my brother Michael at his off-licence in Crewkerne Street. On 11th July 1999 I was in the shop in the store room at the back of the shop when at about 6.25 p.m. I heard a man shouting at Michael to get on the floor. I went to the door of the stock room and saw a man about 25-30, 6' tall with a blue jacket, black jeans and trainers pushing Michael by the neck. The shop is well lit and the lights were on. I would recognise him again. As he was pushing Michael he also started to hit him and he was screaming at him to open the till. I couldn't see if he was armed or had a weapon but as he had his back to me I ran at him and pushed him over Michael into a display near the window.

After he had fallen into the display I leaped on him and we started to fight. He was obviously drunk and struggled very violently. The next thing I knew he had punched me in the face and caused me to loosen my grip on him. With that he got up and ran over to Michael who was at the telephone. He shouted out 'Call the police and you're fucking dead' and then ran out of the shop colliding with a customer who was coming through the door.

I was dazed but managed to run after him and chased him part of the way down the street to the junction with Crown Street. As I got to the corner I saw him getting into a metallic blue Vauxhall Cavalier which drove down Crown Street in the direction of the Old Market Place. I did not see any one else in the vehicle and I did not manage to take the registration number of the car although I think it was 'Y' registered.

I would be willing to attend court.

Signed: Francis Kelly
Signature witnessed by: A Keith

DOWNSHIRE CONSTABULARY   **Form MG15(T)**
RECORD OF TAPE RECORDED INTERVIEW

Person interviewed	Nicholas SPRING	Police Exhibit No TH1
Place of interview	UPTON POLICE STATION	Number of pages 3
Date of interview	11.07.99	
Time commenced	20.03	**Time concluded** 20.24
Duration of interview	21MINS	**Tape Reference no's** 101124
Interviewing Officer(s)	WPC 7 ROBINSON	
Other persons present	DC 431 COLE, Mr J ARCHER (SOLICITOR)	

Tape counter times	Person speaking	Text
001		INTRODUCTION TO INTERVIEW. CAUTIONED
054		WPC ROBINSON explained that SPRING had been arrested at 3.30 p.m. following an incident at the Abbey Estate involving SPRING and others.
0410		General discussion about the estate and who lived with SPRING including SEAN BAKER, MARTIN THOMPSON, ANTHONY MEAD AND JOHN HANSON.
0715	ROBINSON	Nick, why did you assault PC KEMP?
	SPRING	I didn't, he assaulted me. I went to speak to him after he shouted out to me, when Charlie was about to get in his car. We met in the road and he put his hand up and grabbed my arm . . .
	COLE	Which arm?
	SPRING	My right one. I pushed him away and he grabbed me round the neck and pulled me to the ground.
		WPC Robinson then reads the first half of PC Kemp's statement.
	ROBINSON	You were clearly told you were under arrest but you were looking for a fight as your girlfriend was going off with PC Kemp.
	SPRING	No. KEMP is enormous you'd have to be fucking mad to fight him . . .
1020	COLE	But you did Nick, didn't you.
	SPRING	No, I defended myself, he was strangling me.
	ROBINSON	Who else was there?
	SPRING	The BAKERS, LOUIS BUCKNALL, TONY, JOHN, . . .
	ROBINSON	JOHN who?
	SPRING	HANSON.
	ROBINSON	You said earlier that he was living with you
	SPRING	Yes
	ROBINSON	In the fight PC KEMP was kicked in the face. He is seriously injured. Who kicked him?
	SPRING	JOHN.
	ROBINSON	But you told him to.
	SPRING	Never. I'm asthmatic, KEMP was strangling me, I couldn't breathe and I just shouted to get off, to get him off . . .
1215	ROBINSON	Reads remainder of PC KEMP'S statement. You told HANSON to kick him in the face.

	SPRING	I didn't. HANSON kicked him in the face. He hates KEMP because he got him sent down last time. I just wanted KEMP to stop throttling me so I asked for help.
	ROBINSON	You threatened to put him out on the street.
1500	SPRING	That's rubbish, HANSON could always go and live in another squat or with his Mum or girlfriend, he didn't have to stay with me.

Further questions and discussion about the fight. SPRING stated that he was too pre-occupied with what was going on with PC KEMP to notice anything else. He agreed that HANSON had kicked the radio away. He also stated that a number of the others appeared to have kicked or punched PC KEMP but denied that he encouraged them in any way.

INTERVIEW CONCLUDES 20.24 HOURS.

DOWNSHIRE CONSTABULARY   Form MG15(T)

RECORD OF TAPE RECORDED INTERVIEW

Person interviewed	John HANSON	Police Exhibit No TH1
Place of interview	UPTON POLICE STATION	Number of pages 3
Date of interview	12.07.99	
Time commenced	12.07	**Time concluded** 12.45
Duration of interview	38 MINS	**Tape Reference no's** 101137
Interviewing Officer(s)	WPC 7 ROBINSON	
Other persons present	DC 431 COLE, Mr J ARCHER (SOLICITOR)	

Tape counter times	Person speaking	Text
001		INTRODUCTION TO INTERVIEW. CAUTIONED
024		WPC ROBINSON explained that HANSON had been arrested at 19.30 hours by police on suspicion of an assault at Kelly's off-licence.
0350		Discussion regarding what HANSON had been doing prior to the incident. He stated that he had been drinking throughout the day. He'd been to 3 pubs, the last being the Ratcatcher. He cannot remember anything after the Ratcatcher. He was drinking cider and might have had some lager and whisky. He cannot remember going into Kelly's and was not aware until told by an Inspector during his detention.
0900		WPC Robinson read excerpts from Mr F Kelly's statement but HANSON could still not remember. Discussion of injuries received, he stated he had a cut wrist and a sore neck and shoulder.
1100		Discussion regarding statement by Mr Kelly.
1415	WPC 7	So you can't remember any of that?
	HANSON	No, not at all, no.
1530		WPC Robinson showed HANSON the custody record where the Custody Sergeant had written his reply when being booked in. HANSON could not remember saying 'All I tried to do was rob the place'.
1640		Discussion regarding possession of cannabis.
		HANSON accepts the tin is his and the 2 pieces of greeny brown substance is cannabis belonging to him and that possession of cannabis is illegal.
1850		DC Cole asked HANSON to describe his clothing and self.
	HANSON	About 5' 11", dark hair.
	COLE	Brown wouldn't you say.
	HANSON	Brown, darkish anyway, I'm wearing a brown sports coat, blue denim shirt, black denim jeans, white trainers. Green brown eyes.
	COLE	Darkish skinned?
	HANSON	No.
	COLE	With cropped hair.
	HANSON	Close cut, not cropped.

	COLE	Well I'd say cropped.
	HANSON	That's for you.
2000	SOLICITOR	That can be determined, you've taken his photo.
	COLE	Yes. You know Nick Spring?
	HANSON	Yes.
	COLE	And you've been staying with him at Fountains House?
	HANSON	Yes, for about the last week.
	COLE	Since you were released from prison.
		Yesterday afternoon there was an incident on the Abbey Estate involving Spring. Where were you at 3.30 yesterday?
	HANSON	I think I was in the 'Coach' with VICKY BRYANT.
		Discussion regarding Vicky Bryant and where she lives.
2215	COLE	What about the car you were driving. Is that yours?
	HANSON	What car?
	COLE	Come off it John, the one you were driving when you were nicked.
	HANSON	I can't drive.
	COLE	That's what the arresting officer said.
	HANSON	No need to get snidey. I've had enough of this.
		Reminded of the caution/given special caution.
	ROBINSON	Whose car is it CLP 853Y a blue Cavalier.
	HANSON	It's not mine, I don't have a car.
	ROBINSON	You were driving it, whose is it?
	HANSON	I've had enough, I don't feel well.
	ROBINSON	You look fine to me. Whose is it?
	HANSON	No comment. I want to speak to Mr Archer.
	Tape off.	
2500	SOLICITOR	My client finds your manner aggressive. He is unwell and is currently being treated by his GP. On legal advice he does not wish to answer any further questions at this stage.
2515		Further matters put to HANSON who declines to comment.
2900		Interview terminated.

DOWNSHIRE CONSTABULARY

C.R. No. 7651/90

Division A   **Date** 3rd August 1999

Antecedents of: (full name) John Hanson

Committed from Upton   **Magistrates' Court on** 17th January 2000

For trial/sentence at Upton Crown   Court

for offence(s) of Grievous Bodily Harm with intent, Violent Disorder, Robbery

---

Date and place of birth: 12.04.75, Temple Newsome   **Age:** 24 years

Date of first entry into U.K.: n/a   **Nationality:** British

Date of arrest: 11.07.99, Remanded in custody   **In custody/on bail:** In custody

Education: 1986-1991   Bishop Cross School, Disbury Bridge.
1991-1992   Upton Technical College

Main employments since leaving school

1992-1995	Royal Artillery	Bombadier	
1995-1997	Unemployed		
1998	Sherratts Furniture	Labourer	Dismissed for theft
1999	Unemployed		

Present employment: (Show date of commencement, capacity in which employed, net salary/wage and employer's assessment).

Hanson is unemployed and in receipt of income support. Amount not disclosed.

At the time of his arrest he was a single man living with friends at 27 Fountains House, Abbot's Down, Abbey Estate, Upton, Downshire.

Hanson does not hold a firearms/shotgun certificate.

At time of the offence Hanson was on licence from Portsmouth Prison. He was released on 28.06.99 having served 2 months of a 4 month sentence for ABH, theft and kindred offences.

List of previous convictions attached:

Offences against the person:	1	Theft and kindred offences:	11
Offences against property:	3	Public Order offences:	2
Fraud and kindred offences:	0	Others:	0

If recently fined state whether paid or not: None traced

Date of last release from custodial sentence: 28.06.99

Names of co-prisoners (if dealt with elsewhere, give details):

173

<u>**DOWNSHIRE CONSTABULARY**</u>

PREVIOUS CONVICTIONS

Convictions recorded against: John Hanson   CRO No: 7651/90

Charged in name of: John Hanson   * Denotes spent conviction

Date	Court	Offence(s) (with details of any offence)	Sentence	Date of Release
12.05.95	Driffield Mags	Theft x 3	CSO 100 hours	
		Taking without consent	CSO 100 hours	
		Criminal Damage	£135.00 Compensation	
18.10.95	Alderley Mags	Theft x 2	6 months Young Offenders Institution	
		S. 4 Public Order Act	2 months Y.O.	
		Breach CSO	6 months Y.O. concurrent	18.01.96
11.6.96		Deception x 3	Probation 2 years	
31.08.98	Upton Crown Court	Aggravated vehicle taking	6 months' imprisonment L/E Disqualified 1 year	30.11.98
		Affray	4 months' imp concurrent	
		Making off without payment	2 months' imp concurrent	
29.04.99	Driffield Mags	Actual Bodily Harm	4 months' imprisonment	28.06.99

DOWNSHIRE CONSTABULARY

C.R. No. ___3741/95_____

Division ___A_____ **Date** ___3rd August 1999_____

Antecedents of: (full name) ___Nicholas Spring_____

Committed from __Upton____ **Magistrates' Court on** __17th January 2000____

For trial/sentence at __Upton Crown_____ Court

for offence(s) of __Grievous Bodily Harm with intent, Violent Disorder_____

Date and place of birth: 21.06.78, Driffield **Age:** 21 years

Date of first entry into U.K.: n/a **Nationality:** British

Date of arrest: 11.07.99, Remanded on bail **In custody/on bail:** on bail

Education: 1989-1994 Upton Comprehensive
1994-1995 Upton Technical College

Main employments since leaving school

1995-1998 Various periods of unemployment with casual labouring jobs
1998-1999 Floral Garden Centre.

Present employment: (Show date of commencement, capacity in which employed, net salary/wage and employer's assessment).

Spring works as a labourer at the Floral Garden Centre, Driffield, earning £160 a week gross, £133.95 net.

At the time of his arrest he was a single man living at 27 Fountains House, Abbot's Down, Abbey Estate, Upton, Downshire.

Spring does not hold a firearms/shotgun certificate.

List of previous convictions attached:

Offences against the person:	0	**Theft and kindred offences:**	2
Offences against property:	1	**Public Order offences:**	1
Fraud and kindred offences:	0	**Others:**	0

If recently fined state whether paid or not: None traced

Date of last release from custodial sentence: n/a

Names of co-prisoners (if dealt with elsewhere, give details):

DOWNSHIRE CONSTABULARY

PREVIOUS CONVICTIONS

Convictions recorded against: Nicholas Spring   **CRO No:** 3741/96

Charged in name of: Nicholas Spring   * Denotes spent conviction

Date	Court	Offence(s) (with details of any offence)	Sentence	Date of Release
15.06.96	Upton Mags	Theft	Conditional Discharge 12 months	
17.12.96		Taking vehicle without consent	CSO 60 hours	
		Criminal Damage	CSO 60 hours concurrent	
		Breach of Conditional Discharge	CSO 60 hours Concurrent	
31.08.98	Upton Crown Court	Affray	Probation 12 months	

STATEMENT OF JOHN HANSON

I, John Hanson, of HMP Ardington, will say as follows:

I am currently on remand at HMP Ardington and have been since the 11th July. I left full time education in 1992 when I was 17. I had 6 GCSE's and I decided because things were not good at home to join the army. I served in the army for 3 years including a period in the Gulf where I witnessed a number of very traumatic incidents including dogs eating Iraqi dead. As a result I have felt far from well since then and I believe this has led to my offending. In particular I had been prescribed Prozac from about May by the prison doctors. I am not sure if this led to my loss of memory on the 11th July. It may also explain why I behaved as I am alleged to have behaved in the off-licence. When I woke up in the police station I discovered that the bottle of Prozac which I had contained 4 less tablets than it should. I have never been warned against taking Prozac and alcohol together although I now understand that mixing the 2 can be dangerous.

On the 11th July I was living at 27 Fountains House on the Abbey estate in Upton. I had only been released from prison the week before from a sentence of 4 months' imprisonment imposed by Driffield Magistrates on the 29th April. I was living with Nick Spring at Fountains House but my girlfriend, Vicky Bryant had offered me a place at her house and I was due to move there on the 12th. I was also able to live with my Mother in Driffield but because of the events which led to my imprisonment in April I was not anxious to move there. I have known Nick since 1996 and we were co-defendants in the charge that led to me being imprisoned in August of 1996. I was at that time working for Sherratts furniture as a labourer but lost my job, not because of theft, but because I was imprisoned.

On the 11th July I received some money (£850) from an inheritance and I decided to celebrate. The Cavalier is Vicky Bryant's I had borrowed it the day before to get back from Vicky's place. I left Fountains House about 10 a.m. and collected the cheque from Chapmans (the solicitors in Upton) and then arranged to get some money from the bank. I had left the car and the keys at Fountains House. After I had got some money from the bank I went drinking. I was in the 3 Bells, then the Coach and Horses where I met Vicky and some other friends and later I went to the Ratcatcher. When I got to the Ratcatcher it was about 4 p.m. Tony a bloke who was also staying with Nick came in with Louis Bucknell, Simon Bratt, Kieran Bratt and a load of others. I could see that he had the keys to the Cavalier. They were all drunk or stoned. We had a row about him driving it and I took the keys back. They all then left. I was pretty drunk by this time and until I woke in the Police Station that is about all I can remember.

I have no recollection of going back to the Abbey Estate. I have spoken to Vicky and she is sure that I was with her at about 3 o'clock. I left her and went to the 'Rat' to meet a friend of mine called Frank. I owed him £50 and had arranged to pay him back. As far as I know I did but I haven't seen him since and although Vicky and some of my friends have been trying to find him it may not be easy as he is a 'Traveller'.

I do not dispute that I was in Kelly's off-licence and I understand that I am on the in-store video. I would like advice on my plea as I have, once again, no recollection of what took place there and no recollection of what I am alleged to have said to the custody sergeant at Upton Police station.

CUSTODY RECORD Police & Criminal Evidence Act 1984

Police Station   Force/Station reference

ARREST	DETAINEE
Comments made: YES/~~NO~~	Surname: Hanson
Where arrested: Upton Road jn Lymehurst Road	Forenames: John
Arrested by:	Address: 27 Fountains House Abbey Estate Upton
Name: keith	
Rank/No: 375 Station: Upton	
Time of arrest: 1932 Date: 11.7.99	Occupation: Unemployed
Time of arrival at Station: 1943 Date: 11.7.99	Age: 24 Date of Birth: 12.4.75

DETENTION AUTHORISED

Attempted robbery

To obtain evidence by questioning

Comments made: YES/~~NO~~
Name: P Waller   Rank/No: P58
Signature: P Waller   Time: Date: 11.7.99

DETAINEE (continued)

Place of Birth: Newton Abbot
Height: 5'11'   Sex: M
Ethnic Appearance: Caucasian
Nationality: British

Officer in case
        Name: Cole
        Rank/No: DC

Officer opening record
        Name: Waller
        Rank/No: P58
        Signature: P Waller

PRISONERS RIGHTS

1. A notice setting out my rights has been read to me and I have also been provided with a written notice setting out my entitlements whilst in custody.

    | John Hanson Signature | Time: 1945 Date: 11.7.99 |

    Notices of the detained persons rights and entitlements have been read to me and I have received a copy of each. I have been informed of the Grounds for the detention of the detained person.

    Appropriate Adult n/a   Signature   Time: Date:

2. I DO require somebody to be informed of my arrest.

    | John Hanson Signature | Time: 1945 Date: 11.7.99 |

    Nominated Person: v Bryant
    Address/Contact no:

3. I DO require a solicitor as soon as practicable.

    | John Hanson Signature | Time: 1945 Date: 11.7.99 |

    Nominated Solicitor: D. Sol.

    Appropriate Adult: n/a   Signature: Time: Date:

MEDICAL DETAILS

Are you currently:– Receiving medication
                   Suffering any illness/injury
                   Suffering any infirmity

Remarks:– Intoxicated

(FormCustody) 04/04/1995

CUSTODY RECORD (Property) Police & Criminal Evidence Act 1984

Police Station Upton   Force/Stn ref SOBE/00317/98 Date: 11.7.99

Detained Person Surname: Hanson

Forenames: John

Property retained by Police: re value, prevent harm/damage, interfere with evidence or effect an escape			
Description: Bottle Prozac tablets	Qty: 1	Value: N/K	Seal: 00356113
Description: Lighter	Qty: 1	Value:	Seal: 11
Description: Belt	Qty:	Value:	Seal: 11
Description: Wallet + various corresp	Qty:	Value:	Seal: 11
Description: £75 (7×10, 1×5) notes	Qty:	Value:	Seal: 11
Description: £4.36 (3×1, 2×50 + change)	Qty:	Value:	Seal: 11

Property retained by Person at own risk

Description: Qty: Value:

1 Packet B+H cigs

1 comb (plastic)

The above is a true record. Property retained by me is at my own risk.

Signature of detainee	Signature of Custody Officer (P.Waller)	Name: WALLER P Rank/No: 585
Refused to sign	Signature of Witness (K.Simpson)	Name: SIMPSON K Rank/No: PC 171

I have received all property listed above, subject to any variation shown in the custody record log.

Signature of person receiving	Signature of witness	Name: Rank/No:

Detainee searched by

Signature (K.Simpson)	Name: SIMPSON K Rank/No: PC 171

(FrmPtyCus1) Ver 1 Feb 95

RECORD OF PERSONAL PROPERTY

Sub-Divisional Custody No. ....SOBE/00317/99....

RECORD OF PERSONAL PROPERTY				RECORD OF PERSONAL PROPERTY CONTINUED	
Denominations of Notes	Cash Totals				
10×7 : 5×1	Notes £	75			
	£ Coin £	4			
	Silver £	20			
	Bronze	16			
	TOTAL £	79-36			
Item	Other Property			Searched by (sign) *Kfinger*	
1	Prozac tablets			Items ....3 + 6...............	
2	Lighter			I wish to retain the above items at my own risk	
3	Cigarettes			Signature ....Refused..........	
4	Wallet + coins			Seal No. 00356113	
5	Belt			Officer Sealing (sign) *Kfinger*	
6	Comb (plastic)			Witness (sign) *PWaller*	
				Property Locker No. 7	
				PROPERTY SUBJECT OF CHARGE	
				None	
				Property Seal No.	
				Officer Sealing (Sign)	
				Witness (Sign)	
				Special Property Reg. No.	

DOWNSHIRE CONSTABULARY

Detainee's Name: John Hanson

Any comments made after reasons for arrest given:

' I only tried to rob the place '

Any comments made after grounds for detention explained:

Any reasons given for not requiring legal advice:

Signed: P Uller   Rank/No: P 58

DOWNSHIRE CONSTABULARY

CONTINUATION OF CUSTODY RECORD

Page No.	5

Last review of detention conducted at ......1945......

....

Sub-Divisional Custody No. ....SOBC./..00317/..99.............

Name ......HANSON..

Date	Time	Full details of any action/occurrence involving detained person (include full particulars of all visitors/officers) Individual entries need not be restricted to one line All entries to be signed by the writer	Signature
11.7.98	1945	Fit + well. Detention authorised.	PS8
	1955	To cell (8). Check every 15 mins due to state of dg.	"
	2010	Checked in cell; asleep.	"
	2025	ditto	"
	2040	ditto	"
	2055	ditto	"
	2110	Checked in cell; asleep. Waken for ex by RME. Blood with consent. Concluded 2119. On arrest suspect stated in response to caution 'I only tried to rob the place'. PMculler	PS8
	2125	Awake. In cell. Refreshment + tea provided.	"
	2140	Awake drinking tea.	"
	2155	Asleep	"
	2210	ditto	"
	2225	Wakened to check alright	"
	2240	Asleep	
	2255	Asleep.	
	23:10	Asleep:- To be checked every 30 mins.	PS34.
	23:40	"	"
12/7/98	00:10	Asleep	"
	00:40	"	"
	01:10	"	"
	01:45	Further detention authorised to obtain evidence by questioning. Review at 07:45. Check every hour.	"

DOWNSHIRE CONSTABULARY

CONTINUATION OF CUSTODY RECORD

| | | | Page No. | 6 |

Last review of detention conducted at .....O.1.4.5....

....

Sub-Divisional Custody No. .....S.O.3.5. / .0.0.3.1.7. / .9.9.........

Name ....HANSON...

Date	Time	Full details of any action/occurrence involving detained person (include full particulars of all visitors/officers) Individual entries need not be restricted to one line All entries to be signed by the writer	Signature
12/7/98	02:45	Asleep	PS34
	03:45	Awake. Provided with tea + light.	PS34
	04.45	Asleep.	"
	05:45	Asleep.	"
	06:45	Asleep.	"
	0730	Review. Further detention authorised. Breakfast provided and light for cigs	PS15
	0845	Awake, wishes to see D/Solicitor	PS15
	0915	Duty Sol unavailable	PS15
	0935	D. Sol phoned. Unavailable until 1100 am	PS15
	0947	Phone enquiry from V Bryant. Access to DIP refused.	PS15
	1133	D/Sol (Mr Archer) arrives in custody area. DIP to solicitors for consultation.	PS15
	1145	Back to cell 5 pending interview.	PS15
	1200	Out of cell for interview.	PS15
	1257	Interview concluded, back to cell 7	PS15
	1310	Out of cell. Charged. Bail refused. To MC for 2 pm hearing	PS15

Custody Record No: SOBE/00317/99

Station: Upton

DOWNSHIRE POLICE
CHARGE SHEET

CUSTODY RECORD

PERSON CHARGED: John Hanson

ADDRESS 22 Fountain's House, Abbey Estate, Upton

PLACE/DATE OF BIRTH Newton Abbot / 12.4.75 OCCUPATION Unemployed

You are charged with the offence shown below.
You do not have to say anything. But it may harm your defence if you do not mention <u>now</u> something which you later rely on in court. Anything you do say may be given in evidence.

OF61019

1) On the 11th July being present with Nicholas Spring Martin Thompson, Sean Baker, Louis Bucknell, Simon Bratt and Anthony Mead used unlawful violence and this conduct (taken together) was such as would cause a person of reasonable firmness present at the scene to fear for his personal safety, contrary to section 2(1) of the Public Order Act 1986.

Reply: None

Officer in case: D.C. Cole
Station: Upton

Date Charged: 12th July 1999

Signature of person charging: Richard Cole

Signature of Officer accepting charge: Peter Maxwell.

Legal Aid forms served by:
Notices served:

Bail: Refused

DOWNSHIRE CONSTABULARY

Full Name John Hanson	Custody No SOBE / 00317 / 99

CONTINUATION OF CHARGES

You are charged with the offence(s) shown below. You do not have to say anything. But it may harm your defence if you do not mention now something which you later rely on in court. Anything you do say may be given in evidence.

2) On 11th July 1999 at Augustian Grove, Abbey Estate, Upton, unlawfully and maliciously caused grievous bodily harm to PC37 Martin Kemp with intent to cause grievous bodily harm, contrary to s. 18 of the Offences Against the Person Act 1861.

3) On the 11th July, attempted to rob Kelly's off-licence, contrary to s. 1(1) of the Criminal Attempts Act 1981.

4) On the 11th July 1999 at Upton Road junction with Lymehurst Road, drove a motor vehicle whilst unfit through drink and drugs, contrary to s. 4(1) of the Road Traffic Act 1988.

Continuation Sheet   Yes No

Reply (if any) ....

.... Time / Date.... 13 : 10/12 : 7 : 99 ..

Signed (Person reading charge) .... Richard Cole .... Rank / No.... DC 341 ....

Signed (Custody Officer) .... Peter Maxwell .... Rank / No.... DSIS ....

Officer in Case: Name .... R Cole ...... Rank/No .... DC 431 .... Station .... Upton ....

Custody Record copy

DOWNSHIRE CONSTABULARY
CRIME COMPLAINT/REPORT

M. F. No. ...1263.........

Area ..(Abbey Estate) Sub. Div .....6.............. Div.......F8...............

Upton

C. R. No. ....1054...........

(Where Committed)

SEE NOTES FOR GUIDANCE ON COVER

H.Q.'s USE ONLY	

CRIME COMPLAINT

1. OFFENCE AS REPORTED .....G.B.H........
2. REF. (TIME AND DATE REPORTED) ...1538......... TO WHOM REPORTED ....
3. NAME AND ADDRESS OF PERSON REPORTING ..Not given. Report.... from telephone box on Abbey Estate.... TEL. NO. —
4. ACTION TAKEN AND BY WHOM ...Vehicles despatched........

H.Q. use only
H.Q. Classification ....

CRIME REPORT

5. NAME/ADDRESS OF INJURED PERSON ..Martin Kemp PC37.... c/o Upton Police Station........... TEL. NO. — AGE ...29..
6. PLACE, TIME, DAY, DATE OF OFFENCE ....1530. Abbey Estate....... Augustian Close 11 July 1999...... MAP REF: ...C6......
7. INJURY TO VICTIM. FATAL ...... SERIOUS ✓. SLIGHT ...... THREATS .... NONE ...... TYPE OF WEAPON USED ....Foot........
8. TYPE OF PREMISES (NOTE 1) .....Abbey Estate........
9. METHOD (NOTE 2)
Police officer investigating report of fight (see CR1052) set upon by youths. Initial telephone report supplemented by officers who attended scene and victim who was attacked by N. Spring and then kicked in the face by suspect wearing blue jacket and jeans and white trainers
10. OFFENCE DETECTED YES/NO ....
11. DESCRIPTION OF SUSPECT OR VEHICLE USED ...Suspect decamped.... ...in blue Vauxhall.......

12. PROPERTY STOLEN/DAMAGED (NOTE 3)

.....1 police radio. Value.... ...not known..................

	STOLEN		RECOVERED	
	£	p	£	p

TOTAL

13. ENQUIRY TYPE

		NEIGH. WATCH AREA		PRIMARY INVESTIGATOR	
Child Abuse		Yes	✓	Uniform	✓
Domestic Violence		No		C.I.D.	
Other	✓				

R v John Hanson

Draft Defence Statement Issued Pursuant to Section 5 of the Criminal Procedure and Investigations Act 1996

John Hanson: alleged offences of assault and violent disorder

Mr Hanson was not present at the time of the alleged offences. He had drunk a considerable amount of alcohol and had taken Prozac tablets, but to the best of his recollection he was in either the Three Bells or the Coach and Horses public house at the time in question (both are in Bow Avenue, Upton). He was in the company of Miss Victoria Bryant of 13 Onyx Close, Upton.

John Hanson: alleged offence of attempted robbery

Mr Hanson has no recollection of the events constituting this alleged offence. Prior to the time in question he had drunk a considerable amount of alcohol, and had taken Prozac tablets. In the circumstances he was unable to form the intent necessary to commit the offence.

SIXTEEN

SAMPLE ADVICE IN *R v SPRING, HANSON AND OTHERS*

IN THE OXTON CROWN COURT

THE QUEEN

v

NICHOLAS SPRING, JOHN HANSON and OTHERS

ADVICE ON EVIDENCE

Introduction

1.   I am asked to advise John Hanson and (if there is no conflict of interest) Nicholas Spring on evidence, plea and possible sentence. Both are charged with violent disorder and causing grievous bodily harm with intent to resist the arrest of Mr Spring. Mr Hanson faces additional charges of attempted robbery and driving while unfit through drink or drugs.

The alleged offences

2.   The charges of violent disorder and assault arise from an incident on the Abbey Estate, in which a police officer, PC Kemp, sustained a number of quite serious injuries. The prosecution case is that after the officer had attempted to mediate between Mr Spring and his girlfriend, he was punched by Mr Spring. While he was in the process of arresting Mr Spring, PC Kemp was set upon by a group of young men and was repeatedly kicked by his assailants. The crowd dispersed when a number of other officers arrived and arrested several of the participants, including Mr Spring.

3.   As far as the charge of attempted robbery is concerned, this arises from an incident at an off-licence in which a man burst in, pulled his jacket over his face and demanded that the owner open the till and give him money. The would-be robber was frustrated by the entry of the owner's brother, whom he punched before escaping. No weapon was involved. Mr Hanson was arrested while he was in a car about an hour later, apparently on the basis that he and the car answered the description given by the witnesses at the off-licence.

Separate representation

4.   Those instructing me have asked whether there is a conflict of interest between Mr Spring and Mr Hanson, such that two counsel may be required. My view is that there is such a conflict of interest. In his interview, Mr Spring states that Mr Hanson was present during the Abbey Estate incident and played an active part in kicking PC Kemp, whereas Mr Hanson has no recollection of being there, and may in fact have an alibi. Accordingly, my advice is that separate representation is required, and in accordance with the wishes of those instructing me, the remainder of this advice relates to Mr Hanson alone.

Severance of the indictment

5.   I turn next to the indictment. It would seem to be in Mr Hanson's interests for the charges of attempted robbery and driving while unfit to be separated from those arising from the attack on PC Kemp. The counts in question do not appear to arise from the same facts, nor are they part of a series of offences of the same or similar character. They do not, therefore, meet the requirement of the Indictment Rules 1971, r. 9. I would advise that an application to sever Counts 3 and 4 from the indictment be made at the Plea and Directions Hearing.

The strength of the case: assault and violent disorder

6.   As far as the counts of violent disorder and causing grievous bodily harm are concerned, Mr Hanson's primary defence appears to be that of alibi. There is some doubt about this, in that his recollection of the events of the afternoon is unclear, and there is no statement as yet from Vicky Bryant or any of the others who may have been present in the various public houses in question that afternoon. It follows that those instructing me should as a matter of urgency take statements from these potential alibi witnesses. In doing so, of course, such times as the witnesses can recollect will be crucial, together with any reasons they might have for remembering dates and times.

7.   Mr Hanson's possible defence of alibi throws into question the strength of the prosecution's identifying evidence. The evidence as to Mr Hanson's presence depends largely on what PC Kemp says about 'Man 2', and the consistency between the description of that man and Mr Hanson on arrest. When PC Kemp's statement of the man who assaulted him is compared with those of PC Keith of Mr Hanson on arrest and Mr Hanson's description of himself in interview, it is apparent that there are a number of similar features, but also a number of discrepancies. To this should be added the statement of Nuala Carroll that 'I also think I recognised John Hanson in the crowd that had gathered round'. There is also the fact that the man in the brown jacket (who is apparently, on the prosecution's case, Mr Hanson) drove off in a blue Cavalier — the same colour and make of car as Mr Hanson was driving when he was arrested (see PC Keith's statement).

8.   Clearly a schedule of the various descriptions would be a useful working document for trial, but for the present suffice it to say that the identification of Mr Hanson as a participant in the assault is weak. In the light of this, it is astonishing that no identification parade was held, and the police failure to hold one can clearly be raised at trial in order to underline the weakness of the evidence of Mr Hanson's presence. Incidentally, it appears from Mr Spring's interview that PC Kemp knew Mr Hanson, and was responsible for his conviction on an earlier offence. The facts surrounding this allegation need to be ascertained from Mr Hanson. If it is true, it means that PC Kemp's failure to mention that he recognised 'Man 2' means that it is very unlikely that it was Mr Hanson.

9.   The effect of Mr Hanson's interview also needs to be considered. The fact that he refused to answer questions relating to the assault could potentially lead to inferences which might strengthen the case against him. In order to confirm this, it is necessary to know whether he was cautioned prior to interview about the effect of the refusal to mention matters which he might later wish to make use of in his defence. For this and other reasons, I need to listen to the tape of interview.

The strength of the case: attempted robbery

10.   As far as the attempted robbery is concerned, there are substantial gaps in the evidence which need to be filled before Mr Hanson can be properly advised. In particular, according to Mr Hanson's proof of evidence, there appears to be an in-store video on which he is alleged to have appeared. His further instructions on this point need to be obtained, so that I can assess its likely evidential weight. Again, there is the failure to hold an identification parade, which means that, in the absence of an admissible video, the prosecution will find it difficult to prove that it was Mr Hanson who attempted the robbery.

11. In addition, there is the question of the words which Mr Hanson is alleged to have uttered when arrested: 'I only tried to rob the place'. Its admissibility ought to be challenged, both under s. 76 of the Police and Criminal Evidence Act 1984 (reliability) and s. 78 (fairness). It is also remarkable that the custody record entry for 2110 hours states that these words were uttered on arrest. Yet Mr Hanson had been arrested shortly after 1930 hours by PC Keith; and was booked in by PS Waller at 1945 hours. This anomaly needs explanation at the least, and is likely to undermine the admission it contains, even if the judge rules that it is admissible.

12. Leaving aside the question of whether Mr Hanson was involved in the incident at the off-licence, there is the question of whether he had the capacity to form the necessary intent. In his proof of evidence, he raises points relating to his state of mind. In my view it is necessary to obtain expert evidence on the likely effect of the combination of Prozac and alcohol upon his mental state.

The driving charge

13. The driving charge is stated to have been added to the indictment under s. 40 of the Criminal Justice Act 1988. In fact, it cannot have been added under that provision, since 'driving while unfit through drink or drugs' is not one of the charges which appears in s. 40. That means that the charge can only be dealt with at the Crown Court if it was committed for plea under s. 41 of the 1988 Act by the magistrates. Sight of the committal papers will settle this question definitively. If the charge was committed by the magistrates under that provision, then it can only be dealt with if Mr Hanson pleads guilty to or is found guilty of one of the counts on the indictment, and then pleads guilty to the driving while unfit charge. If it was not committed by the magistrates, then it cannot in any event be dealt with.

Sentence

14. As far as sentence is concerned, if convicted Mr Hanson faces a custodial sentence on each of the violent disorder, assault and attempted robbery charges. It is likely that the first two would together attract a sentence of two to three years' imprisonment, given that serious injuries were caused to a policeman by kicking him while he was on the ground, and while the assailant was acting as part of a group. In coming to this conclusion, I have taken into account Mr Hanson's substantial record, which includes several offences of violence. As far as the attempted robbery is concerned, there is likely to be a consecutive sentence since the offence was entirely separate. Given the embryonic and disorganised nature of the offence, however, and the fact that no weapon was involved, the sentence may be no more than 18 months, despite the fact that one of the victims was punched. These estimates are based on conviction after trial. A substantial discount of perhaps as much as a third would be likely in the event of an early plea of guilty.

Action to be taken

15. It will be apparent from the points made above that there are a number of actions which I advise my instructing solicitors to take. In particular, I would ask that:

(a) statements be taken from Vicky Bryant and anyone else who may be able to establish Mr Hanson's presence in the various public houses in question on the afternoon in question;

(b) an early conference be arranged in order to obtain Mr Hanson's instructions on various of the matters canvassed above, and advise him more fully;

(c) the CPS be asked for the schedule of unused material, a copy of Mr Hanson's tape of interview, summaries of the interviews of the co-accused, copies of the criminal records of the co-accused and any witnesses, the crime report sheets and any relevant radio/telephone messages;

(d) a map of the estate be agreed;

(e) a schedule of the descriptions of the co-accused put forward by the various witnesses be prepared for use as a working document by the defence at trial;

(f)   expert evidence be sought as to the effect of combining Prozac and alcohol in the way in which Mr Hanson did.

16.   The case is not yet in a state where the Plea and Directions Hearing Questionnaire can be completed, but that position should be reached once a conference with Mr Hanson has been held. The arrangement of a conference is therefore a matter of urgency, given that the CPS must be notified of the prosecution witnesses whose presence will be required within the next few days. At the PDH, it will also be necessary for the defence to notify the points of law and admissibility canvassed above, and those relating to the defendant's state of mind.

Summary
17.   In summary, my advice is that there is a conflict of interest between Mr Hanson and Mr Spring, such that they should be represented by separate counsel at trial. As far as Mr Hanson is concerned, his instructions suggest a plea of not guilty on all counts. There are defects and discrepancies in the evidence against him, such that his chances of an acquittal on the violent disorder and assault charges are good. Until more information has been received regarding the attempted robbery, it is difficult to evaluate his chances on that count. There are a number of steps which need to be taken by instructing solicitors in the next few days to prepare for trial, and these are set out in paragraph 15.

CHARLES STRYVER

2 Atkin Building
London WC1

APPENDIX

CRIMINAL PROCEDURE AND INVESTIGATIONS ACT 1996: CODE OF PRACTICE UNDER PART II

Introduction

1.1 This code of practice is issued under Part II of the Criminal Procedure and Investigations Act 1996 ('the Act'). It applies in respect of criminal investigations conducted by police officers which begin on or after the day on which this code comes into effect. Persons other than police officers who are charged with the duty of conducting an investigation as defined in the Act are to have regard to the relevant provisions of the code, and should take these into account in applying their own operating procedures.

1.2 This code does not apply to persons who are not charged with the duty of conducting an investigation as defined in the Act.

1.3 Nothing in this code applies to material intercepted in obedience to a warrant issued under section 2 of the Interception of Communications Act 1985, or to any copy of that material as defined in section 10 of that Act.

1.4 This code extends only to England and Wales.

Definitions

2.1 In this code:

— a *criminal investigation* is an investigation conducted by police officers with a view to it being ascertained whether a person should be charged with an offence, or whether a person charged with an offence is guilty of it. This will include

— investigations into crimes that have been committed;

— investigations whose purpose is to ascertain whether a crime has been committed, with a view to the possible institution of criminal proceedings; and

— investigations which begin in the belief that a crime may be committed, for example when the police keep premises or individuals under observation for a period of time, with a view to the possible institution of criminal proceedings;

— charging a person with an offence includes prosecution by way of summons;

— an *investigator* is any police officer involved in the conduct of a criminal investigation. All investigators have a responsibility for carrying out the duties imposed on them under this code, including in particular recording information, and retaining records of information and other material;

— the *officer in charge of an investigation* is the police officer responsible for directing a criminal investigation. He is also responsible for ensuring that proper procedures are in place for recording information, and retaining records of information and other material, in the investigation;

— the *disclosure officer* is the person responsible for examining material retained by the police during the investigation; revealing material to the prosecutor during the investigation and any criminal proceedings resulting from it, and certifying that he has done this; and disclosing material to the accused at the request of the prosecutor;

— the *prosecutor* is the authority responsible for the conduct of criminal proceedings on behalf of the Crown. Particular duties may in practice fall to individuals acting on behalf of the prosecuting authority;

— *material* is material of any kind, including information and objects, which is obtained in the course of a criminal investigation and which may be relevant to the investigation;

— material may be *relevant to an investigation* if it appears to an investigator, or to the officer in charge of an investigation, or to the disclosure officer, that it has some bearing on any offence under investigation or any person being investigated, or on the surrounding circumstances of the case, unless it is incapable of having any impact on the case;

— *sensitive material* is material which the disclosure officer believes, after consulting the officer in charge of the investigation, it is not in the public interest to disclose;

— references to *primary prosecution disclosure* are to the duty of the prosecutor under section 3 of the Act to disclose material which is in his possession or which he has inspected in pursuance of this code, and which in his opinion might undermine the case against the accused;

— references to *secondary prosecution disclosure* are to the duty of the prosecutor under section 7 of the Act to disclose material which is in his possession or which he has inspected in pursuance of this code, and which might reasonably be expected to assist the defence disclosed by the accused in a defence statement given under the Act;

— references to the disclosure of material to a person accused of an offence include references to the disclosure of material to his legal representative;

— references to police officers and to the chief officer of police include those employed in a police force as defined in section 3(3) of the Prosecution of Offences Act 1985.

General responsibilities

3.1 The functions of the investigator, the officer in charge of an investigation and the disclosure officer are separate. Whether they are undertaken by one, two or more persons will depend on the complexity of the case and the administrative arrangements within each police force. Where they are undertaken by more than one person, close consultation between them is essential to the effective performance of the duties imposed by this code.

3.2   The chief officer of police for each police force is responsible for putting in place arrangements to ensure that in every investigation the identity of the officer in charge of an investigation and the disclosure officer is recorded.

3.3   The officer in charge of an investigation may delegate tasks to another investigator or to civilians employed by the police force, but he remains responsible for ensuring that these have been carried out and for accounting for any general policies followed in the investigation. In particular, it is an essential part of his duties to ensure that all material which may be relevant to an investigation is retained, and either made available to the disclosure officer or (in exceptional circumstances) revealed directly to the prosecutor.

3.4   In conducting an investigation, the investigator should pursue all reasonable lines of inquiry, whether these point towards or away from the suspect. What is reasonable in each case will depend on the particular circumstances.

3.5   If the officer in charge of an investigation believes that other persons may be in possession of material that may be relevant to the investigation, and if this has not been obtained under paragraph 3.4 above, he should ask the disclosure officer to inform them of the existence of the investigation and to invite them to retain the material in case they receive a request for its disclosure. The disclosure officer should inform the prosecutor that they may have such material. However, the officer in charge of an investigation is not required to make speculative enquiries of other persons: there must be some reason to believe that they may have relevant material. That reason may come from information provided to the police by the accused or from other inquiries made or from some other source.

3.6   If, during a criminal investigation, the officer in charge of an investigation or disclosure officer for any reason no longer has responsibility for the functions falling to him, either his supervisor or the police officer in charge of criminal investigations for the police force concerned must assign someone else to assume that responsibility. That person's identity must be recorded, as with those initially responsible for these functions in each investigation.

Recording of information

4.1   If material which may be relevant to the investigation consists of information which is not recorded in any form, the officer in charge of an investigation must ensure that it is recorded in a durable or retrievable form (whether in writing, on video or audio tape, or on computer disk).

4.2   Where it is not practicable to retain the initial record of information because it forms part of a larger record which is to be destroyed, its contents should be transferred as a true record to a durable and more easily-stored form before that happens.

4.3   Negative information is often relevant to an investigation. If it may be relevant it must be recorded. An example might be a number of people present in a particular place at a particular time who state that they saw nothing unusual.

4.4   Where information which may be relevant is obtained, it must be recorded at the time it is obtained or as soon as practicable after that time. This includes, for example, information obtained in house-to-house enquiries, although the requirement to record information promptly does not require an investigator to take a statement from a potential witness where it would not otherwise be taken.

Retention of material

(a)   Duty to retain material

5.1   The investigator must retain material obtained in a criminal investigation which may be relevant to the investigation. This includes not only material coming into the possession of the investigator (such as documents seized in the course of searching premises) but also material generated by him (such as interview records). Material may be photographed, or retained in the form of a copy rather than the original, if the original is perishable, or was supplied to the investigator rather than generated by him and is to be returned to its owner.

5.2   Where material has been seized in the exercise of the powers of seizure conferred by the Police and Criminal Evidence Act 1984, the duty to retain it under this code is subject to the provisions on the retention of seized material in section 22 of that Act.

5.3   If the officer in charge of an investigation becomes aware as a result of developments in the case that material previously examined but not retained (because it was not thought to be relevant) may now be relevant to the investigation, he should, wherever practicable, take steps to obtain it or ensure that it is retained for further inspection or for production in court if required.

5.4   The duty to retain material includes in particular the duty to retain material falling into the following categories, where it may be relevant to the investigation:

— crime reports (including crime report forms, relevant parts of incident report books or police officers' notebooks);

— custody records;

— records which are derived from tapes of telephone messages (for example, 999 calls) containing descriptions of an alleged offence or offender;

— final versions of witness statements (and draft versions where their content differs from the final version), including any exhibits mentioned (unless these have been returned to their owner on the understanding that they will be produced in court if required);

— interview records (written records, or audio or video tapes, of interviews with actual or potential witnesses or suspects);

— communications between the police and experts such as forensic scientists, reports of work carried out by experts, and schedules of scientific material prepared by the expert for the investigator, for the purposes of criminal proceedings;

— any material casting doubt on the reliability of a confession;

— any material casting doubt on the reliability of a witness;

— any other material which may fall within the test for primary prosecution disclosure in the Act.

5.5   The duty to retain material falling into these categories does not extend to items which are purely ancillary to such material and possess no independent significance (for example, duplicate copies of records or reports).

(b)   Length of time for which material is to be retained

5.6   All material which may be relevant to the investigation must be retained until a decision is taken whether to institute proceedings against a person for an offence.

5.7   If a criminal investigation results in proceedings being instituted, all material which may be relevant must be retained at least until the accused is acquitted or convicted or the prosecutor decides not to proceed with the case.

5.8   Where the accused is convicted, all material which may be relevant must be retained at least until:

— the convicted person is released from custody, or discharged from hospital, in cases where the court imposes a custodial sentence or a hospital order;

— six months from the date of conviction, in all other cases.

If the court imposes a custodial sentence or hospital order and the convicted person is released from custody or discharged from hospital earlier than six months from the date of conviction, all material which may be relevant must be retained at least until six months from the date of conviction.

5.9 If an appeal against conviction is in progress when the release or discharge occurs, or at the end of the period of six months specified in paragraph 5.8, all material which may be relevant must be retained until the appeal is determined. Similarly, if the Criminal Cases Review Commission is considering an application at that point in time, all material which may be relevant must be retained at least until the Commission decides not to refer the case to the Court of Appeal, or until the Court determines the appeal resulting from the reference by the Commission.

5.10 Material need not be retained by the police as required in paragraph 5.8 if it was seized and is to be returned to its owner.

Preparation of material for prosecutor

(a) Introduction

6.1 The officer in charge of the investigation, the disclosure officer or an investigator may seek advice from the prosecutor about whether any particular item of material may be relevant to the investigation.

6.2 Material which may be relevant to an investigation, which has been retained in accordance with this code, and which the disclosure officer believes will not form part of the prosecution case, must be listed on a schedule.

6.3 Material which the disclosure officer does not believe is sensitive must be listed on a schedule of non-sensitive material. The schedule must include a statement that the disclosure officer does not believe the material is sensitive.

6.4 Any material which is believed to be sensitive must be either listed on a schedule of sensitive material or, in exceptional circumstances, revealed to the prosecutor separately.

6.5 Paragraphs 6.6 to 6.11 below apply to both sensitive and non-sensitive material. Paragraphs 6.12 to 6.14 apply to sensitive material only.

(b) Circumstances in which a schedule is to be prepared

6.6 The disclosure officer must ensure that a schedule is prepared in the following circumstances:

— the accused is charged with an offence which is triable only on indictment;

— the accused is charged with an offence which is triable either way, and it is considered either that the case is likely to be tried on indictment or that the accused is likely to plead not guilty at a summary trial;

— the accused is charged with a summary offence, and it is considered that he is likely to plead not guilty.

6.7 In respect of either way and summary offences, a schedule may not be needed if a person has admitted the offence, or if a police officer witnessed the offence and that person has not denied it.

6.8 If it is believed that the accused is likely to plead guilty at a summary trial, it is not necessary to prepare a schedule in advance. If, contrary to this belief, the accused pleads not guilty at a summary trial, or the offence is to be tried on indictment, the disclosure officer must ensure that a schedule is prepared as soon as is reasonably practicable after that happens.

(c) Way in which material is to be listed on schedule

6.9 The disclosure officer should ensure that each item of material is listed separately on the schedule, and is numbered consecutively. The description of each item should make clear the nature of the item and should contain sufficient detail to enable the prosecutor to decide whether he needs to inspect the material before deciding whether or not it should be disclosed.

6.10 In some enquiries it may not be practicable to list each item of material separately. For example, there may be many items of a similar or repetitive nature. These may be listed in a block and described by quantity and generic title.

6.11 Even if some material is listed in a block, the disclosure officer must ensure that any items among that material which might meet the test for primary prosecution disclosure are listed and described individually.

(d) Treatment of sensitive material

6.12 Subject to paragraph 6.13 below, the disclosure officer must list on a sensitive schedule any material which he believes it is not in the public interest to disclose, and the reason for that belief. The schedule must include a statement that the disclosure officer believes the material is sensitive. Depending on the circumstances, examples of such material may include the following among others:

— material relating to national security;

— material received from the intelligence and security agencies;

— material relating to intelligence from foreign sources which reveals sensitive intelligence gathering methods;

— material given in confidence;

— material which relates to the use of a telephone system and which is supplied to an investigator for intelligence purposes only;

— material relating to the identity or activities of informants, or under-cover police officers, or other persons supplying information to the police who may be in danger if their identities are revealed;

— material revealing the location of any premises or other place used for police surveillance, or the identity of any person allowing a police officer to use them for surveillance;

— material revealing, either directly or indirectly, techniques and methods relied upon by a police officer in the course of a criminal investigation, for example covert surveillance techniques, or other methods of detecting crime;

— material whose disclosure might facilitate the commission of other offences or hinder the prevention and detection of crime;

— internal police communications such as management minutes;

— material upon the strength of which search warrants were obtained;

— material containing details of persons taking part in identification parades;

— material supplied to an investigator during a criminal investigation which has been generated by an official of a body concerned with the regulation or supervision of bodies corporate or of persons engaged in financial activities, or which has been generated by a person retained by such a body;

— material supplied to an investigator during a criminal investigation which relates to a child or young person and which has been generated by a local authority social services department, an Area Child Protection Committee or other party contacted by an investigator during the investigation.

6.13 In exceptional circumstances, where an investigator considers that material is so sensitive that its revelation to the prosecutor by means of an entry on the sensitive schedule is inappropriate, the existence of the material must be revealed to the prosecutor separately. This will apply where compromising the material would be likely to lead directly to the loss of life, or directly threaten national security.

6.14 In such circumstances, the responsibility for informing the prosecutor lies with the investigator who knows the detail of the sensitive material. The investigator should act as soon as is reasonably practicable after the file containing the prosecution case is sent to the prosecutor. The investigator must also ensure that the prosecutor is able to inspect the material so that he can assess whether it needs to be brought before a court for a ruling on disclosure.

Revelation of material to prosecutor

7.1 The disclosure officer must give the schedules to the prosecutor. Wherever practicable this should be at the same time as he gives him the file containing the material for the prosecution case (or as soon as is reasonably practicable after the decision on mode of trial or the plea, in cases to which paragraph 6.8 applies).

7.2 The disclosure officer should draw the attention of the prosecutor to any material an investigator has retained (whether or not listed on a schedule) which may fall within the test for primary prosecution disclosure in the Act, and should explain why he has come to that view.

7.3 At the same time as complying with the duties in paragraphs 7.1 and 7.2, the disclosure officer must give the prosecutor a copy of any material which falls into the following categories (unless such material has already been given to the prosecutor as part of the file containing the material for the prosecution case):

— records of the first description of a suspect given to the police by a potential witness, whether or not the description differs from that of the alleged offender;

— information provided by an accused person which indicates an explanation for the offence with which he has been charged;

— any material casting doubt on the reliability of a confession;

— any material casting doubt on the reliability of a witness;

— any other material which the investigator believes may fall within the test for primary prosecution disclosure in the Act.

7.4 If the prosecutor asks to inspect material which has not already been copied to him, the disclosure officer must allow him to inspect it. If the prosecutor asks for a copy of material which has not already been copied to him, the disclosure officer must give him a copy. However, this does not apply where the disclosure officer believes, having consulted the officer in charge of the investigation, that the material is too sensitive to be copied and can only be inspected.

7.5 If material consists of information which is recorded other than in writing, whether it should be given to the prosecutor in its original form as a whole, or by way of relevant extracts recorded in the same form, or in the form of a transcript, is a matter for agreement between the disclosure officer and the prosecutor.

Subsequent action by disclosure officer

8.1 At the time a schedule of non-sensitive material is prepared, the disclosure officer may not know exactly what material will form the case against the accused, and the prosecutor may not have given advice about the likely relevance of particular items of material. Once these matters have been determined, the disclosure officer must give the prosecutor, where necessary, an amended schedule listing any additional material:

— which may be relevant to the investigation,

— which does not form part of the case against the accused,

— which is not already listed on the schedule, and

— which he believes is not sensitive,

unless he is informed in writing by the prosecutor that the prosecutor intends to disclose the material to the defence.

8.2 After a defence statement has been given, the disclosure officer must look again at the material which has been retained and must draw the attention of the prosecutor to any material which might reasonably be expected to assist the defence disclosed by the accused; and he must reveal it to him in accordance with paragraphs 7.4 and 7.5 above.

8.3 Section 9 of the Act imposes a continuing duty on the prosecutor, for the duration of criminal proceedings against the accused, to disclose material which meets the tests for disclosure (subject to public interest considerations). To enable him to do this, any new material coming to light should be treated in the same way as the earlier material.

Certification by disclosure officer

9.1 The disclosure officer must certify to the prosecutor that to the best of his knowledge and belief, all material which has been retained and made available to him has been revealed to the prosecutor in accordance with this code. He must sign and date the certificate. It will be necessary to certify not only at the time when the schedule and accompanying material is submitted to the prosecutor, but also when material which has been retained is reconsidered after the accused has given a defence statement.

Disclosure of material to accused

10.1 If material has not already been copied to the prosecutor, and he requests its disclosure to the accused on the ground that

— it falls within the test for primary or secondary prosecution disclosure, or

— the court has ordered its disclosure after considering an application from the accused,

the disclosure officer must disclose it to the accused.

10.2 If material has been copied to the prosecutor, and it is to be disclosed, whether it is disclosed by the prosecutor or the disclosure officer is a matter for agreement between the two of them.

10.3   The disclosure officer must disclose material to the accused either by giving him a copy or by allowing him to inspect it. If the accused person asks for a copy of any material which he has been allowed to inspect, the disclosure officer must give it to him, unless in the opinion of the disclosure officer that is either not practicable (for example because the material consists of an object which cannot be copied, or because the volume of material is so great), or not desirable (for example because the material is a statement by a child witness in relation to a sexual offence).

10.4   If material which the accused has been allowed to inspect consists of information which is recorded other than in writing, whether it should be given to the accused in its original form or in the form of a transcript is a matter for the discretion of the disclosure officer. If the material is transcribed, the disclosure officer must ensure that the transcript is certified to the accused as a true record of the material which has been transcribed.

10.5   If a court concludes that it is in the public interest that an item of sensitive material must be disclosed to the accused, it will be necessary to disclose the material if the case is to proceed. This does not mean that sensitive documents must always be disclosed in their original form: for example, the court may agree that sensitive details still requiring protection should be blocked out, or that documents may be summarised, or that the prosecutor may make an admission about the substance of the material under section 10 of the Criminal Justice Act 1967.

INDEX